Encyclopedia
of Modern
BRITISH
ARMY
REGIMENTS

Encyclopedia of Modern BRITISH ARMY REGIMENTS

P.D. GRIFFIN

SUTTON PUBLISHING

First published in the United Kingdom in 2006 by
Sutton Publishing Limited · Phoenix Mill
Thrupp · Stroud · Gloucestershire · GL5 2BU

British Library Cataloguing in Publication Data
A catalogue record for this book is available from the British Library.

ISBN 0-7509-3929-X

Typeset in 10/13pt New Baskerville.
Typesetting and origination by
Sutton Publishing Limited.
Printed and bound in England by
J.H. Haynes & Co. Ltd, Sparkford.

CONTENTS

PREFACE

There is no such thing as the British Army, only a confederation of regiments, hopefully fighting on the same side, all preserving their individuality by being as different from one another as possible.

This observation from a journalist in the twentieth century is as true today as any time in the last 300 years. The enjoyable study of the different regiments that go to make up the British Army may be linked to that shared by collectors of stamps, coins, butterflies, etc. – a fascination with varieties. Regiments and their uniforms had a high profile in the first half of the twentieth century and I have fond memories of glistening soldiers lined up on toy-shop shelves in the grey 1950s, all gleaming red coats and white belts. In time toy soldiers gave way to model soldiers and war games on tables, but in the 1970s war games on fields, courtesy of forming historical re-enactment societies, took us to a new level of appreciation – the Sealed Knot's atmospheric re-creation of the Battle of Naseby drew armies and spectators approaching actual battle strength. Every period in history is represented by these admirable groups, which camp, cook and fight true to the ways of their chosen forefathers, and enthral crowds at home and abroad with their knowledge and skills.

A teenage craze for Napoleon's *Grande Armée* gradually drifted back to British regiments and their colourful forms shot through with stubborn inconsistencies. Regimental customs seemed to be an aspect that should not be overlooked in any study of this kind, but collecting them proved to be difficult. For practices that can only be seen behind the barrack wall I have had to rely on inside information, and thanks must go to all the regimental secretaries and curators whose correspondence over the past twenty-five years has been so necessary in compiling this book.

THE REGIMENT FAMILY

Definitions of the word 'regiment' rarely mention the qualities that give, and have given, an identity to the many soldiers whose own regiment was the only family they ever knew.

In an article written in 1989 by a secretary who had 'temped' for the army in Winchester, we are reassured of the idea of the regiment as a family:

> The walk across the parade ground, down to the drill square and round the dormitory block was always interesting. There might be a PT display, band practice or parade, and everywhere was scrupulously clean. After the unconsciously accepted litter and filth of everyday life (even in a cathedral city), it was a shock to the system, the order and cleanliness. In the office it was the same; streamlined, efficient, cost-effective, intelligent. . . . There was genuine comradeship between the men, regardless of rank or age or background; between officers and raw troopers probably away from home for the first time; between old comrades from both wars, their widows and children, the would-be officers hoping to join the Royal Hussars once they'd finished at Sandhurst. One and all were held warm and firm in the regimental embrace.

HOW THE REGIMENTS CAME

The earliest form of defence in the British Isles depended on villagers and townspeople, who could be called out from their work in times of emergency, but regulated bodies like the Saxon fyrd and the medieval *Posse comitatus* may be viewed as the seeds of a British army.

Two London volunteer corps of the sixteenth century, the Honourable Artillery Company (HAC) and the Inns of Court Regiment, managed to maintain a fairly continual existence through to the twentieth century, when they became a reliable source of officers for the army in the two world wars. The HAC was raised through a Charter of Incorporation granted by Henry VIII and remains today as a senior regiment of the Territorial Army, uniquely divided with its artillery and infantry sections. The Inns of Court Regiment was founded in 1584 to help protect London against Spanish invasion, and was embodied thereafter in times of emergency. In 1790 it was listed as the Bloomsbury and Inns of Court Volunteers, and in 1860 came through again as the 14th Middlesex (Inns of Court) Volunteer Rifle Corps.

The trained bands of Tudor England were made up of able-bodied men, the best known being the Tower Hamlets Militia, headed by the Constable of the Tower of London. From the trained bands came the county militia, companies of men pressed for readiness to be called up in the defence of their country. The Monmouthshire Militia, which can trace its history back to 1539, also survived the ups and downs of service in peace and war over the centuries and heads the Territorial Army list today.

The musters and drill exercises of the Militia lapsed around 1604 and were not revived again until 1648, at the height of the Civil War. This bitter conflict produced Cromwell's New Model Army, which is often regarded as the origin of the British Army, although Parliament's regiments were disbanded with the restoration of the monarchy in 1660. Two of them were re-engaged in the King's service, however, and live on today in the Guards.

Civil War re-enactment society in the dress of the New Model Army.

Two regiments first formed in Scotland under Charles I survived the rigours of seventeenth-century intrigues to be accepted into the army under James II: the Royal Scots and the Scots Guards.

Charles II was the first King of England to keep his regiments banded in peacetime, though he was obliged to class them as his Guards and Garrisons in order to appease a Parliament deeply suspicious of standing armies in the aftermath of the Civil War. His Guards have survived to the present day and their beginnings mark the birth of the army. When Charles took for his bride the daughter of the King of Portugal he acquired by dowry the Portuguese colonies of Tangier and Bombay. Protecting the North African port of Tangier gave the King an opportunity to raise a garrison from which the army gained its 1st Regiment of Dragoons and its 2nd of Foot.

Temporary regiments warranted for home defence in the Dutch Maritime Wars of the 1660s included marines and soldiers recalled from Dutch service. Marine regiments were formed in 1664, 1690, 1702 and 1739, and the permanent Royal Marines were founded under the Admiralty in 1755.

Professional soldiers who had sailed for the Low Countries to fight for the Dutch were required to undergo a test of loyalty during the Maritime Wars, and from those who elected to return to England at this time a regiment was made which was to become famous as The Buffs. A brigade that had gone to Dutch service in 1674 returned with William of Orange in 1688 to be secured as the 5th and 6th Regiments of the line.

Scotland in the seventeenth century was a troubled country plagued by lawless Highlanders and rebellious Covenanters – a strict religious sect, which harboured an armed force strong enough to worry the Scottish government. In 1678 Scotland's parliament raised a small army to keep

Re-enactment group in the guise of pikemen of the 1680s. Pikes were phased out of the army with the introduction of the ring bayonet around 1690.

order, from which emerged two regiments that were to gain a glorious future in the British Army as the Royal Scots Greys and the Royal Scots Fusiliers.

When James II succeeded his brother Charles to the throne in 1685 the small army he had inherited was enlarged by 200 per cent. Six regiments of horse, two of dragoons and nine of foot were raised in response to the Duke of Monmouth's Rebellion. The superior horse regiments were given precedence over all others that had been raised before them, with the exception of the Horse Guards, but they proved too costly to maintain and the senior regiments were reduced to the rank of dragoon guards in 1746.

By 1688 Parliament was at the end of its tether with King James and his pro-Catholic policies, and Whigs joined Tories to look abroad for a more enlightened monarch. James's Protestant daughter Mary and her husband William of Orange were duly invited to come over from Holland to take the crown of England. When William landed in Devon the army went over to his cause and more regiments were organised in the West Country. The deposed James created a following in Ireland and attempted to drive Protestant settlers from the country; the towns of Londonderry and Enniskillen were put under siege and regiments were hastily formed locally in their defence. Two of these continued in service under the title of Inniskilling, a name owed to the slip of a clerk's pen it is said. A sympathetic rising in Scotland during 1689 forced the government to commission regiments of foot to counter rebellions in the Highlands. William harnessed the strength of the

Covenanters in a regiment called the Cameronians after their martyred leader Richard Cameron, and in Edinburgh Leven's Regiment lived on to become the King's Own Scottish Borderers.

There followed a lull in recruitment until 1694, when many new regiments of foot were embodied for William's perpetual quarrels with France. A number of marching regiments formed in this year were stood down at the end of hostilities but three – the 28th to 30th of Foot – were re-formed for the new war of 1702. New regiments warranted by William in his last year of life were authorised by his successor Queen Anne and began life as marines.

When Anne died in 1714 the Protestant Elector of Hanover was invited to take the throne and Jacobites again rose up in Scotland. From the regiments formed to fight the rebellion, six were to gain a permanent footing in the army as the 9th to 14th Dragoons. The ebb and flow of campaign in Scotland stretched the old train of artillery to the extent that reorganisation was inevitable, and after 196 years of supervising the artillery and support arms, the Board of Ordnance relinquished its gunners and engineers to form their own separate bodies, each responsible for their own area of expertise.

When George II succeeded to the throne in 1727, Scotland was still an unsettled country and independent companies of Highlanders recruited from families loyal to the crown were hired to police the braes. Those patrolling to the north of Glasgow were known by their dark tartan as *Am Freiceadan Dubh* (the Black Watch), a name later adopted by the army's first Highland regiment to be enlisted after the Jacobite Rebellion of 1715. Lads for the Highland Regiment joined up in the belief that they were wanted for service in their own country and when they were ordered over the border in 1743 a hundred of them turned back, only to be hunted down and returned to London where the ringleaders were shot and the remainder transported. In the ensuing years some sixty Highland regiments were raised in times of war, and of these, seven line and nine fencible regiments were to mutiny against harsh conditions and broken promises.

Several marching regiments were raised with the outbreak of war in 1740, seven of which remained with the infantry. At this time regiments were identified by the name of their colonel but around 1751 a system of numbering according to seniority gave them a more permanent identity.

The 1750s found Britain and France locked in conflict around the world, and in Europe Frederick the Great was expanding Prussian territory into neighbouring countries. Existing regiments were brought up to war strength, more were commissioned, and, after the usual disbanding and renumbering at the end of the war, twenty-one new formations could be added to the army list: the 50th to 70th Regiments of Foot.

As the Seven Years War progressed, an experiment with light cavalry proved so successful that complete regiments of the kind were formed for service in the period 1759–60. All but three of the new light horse regiments were disbanded at the end of the war, but the concept thrived and eventually most of the heavy dragoon regiments were converted to a light role as hussars or lancers.

A Militia Bill passed during the Seven Years War to resurrect the old county militia regiments was implemented with a threat of invasion in 1759. It required a quota of able-bodied men to be chosen by lot in every county of the land, to be drilled in town and village every week from spring until autumn, ready to be called out when needed. The

Re-enactors in the dress of the Marlburian Wars 1703–12. The black felt hat of the last century was now turned up on three sides.

men proved quite willing when danger threatened but seldom looked to their duties after the end of the French wars.

The early part of the reign of George III was dominated by unrest in the colonies fought over in the Seven Years War. Riots and demonstrations in Massachusetts sparked a revolution that was to tie down the army for ten years and end in defeat. The surrender of a British column at Saratoga in 1777 stirred people at home to form volunteer units for local defence in case news from the colonies influenced French policy against England. In general English soldiers had little taste for fighting their own countrymen in America, but the Highland Scots had suffered great poverty after their defeat at Culloden in 1746 and gladly offered their services under arms for

the King's pay. The next twenty years saw the birth of the remaining Highland regiments of the British Army.

In 1787 intelligence was received that the Sultan of Mysore had made contact with French forces to converge on British interests in India, resulting in a hasty commissioning of four battalions to reinforce the Honourable East India Company's brigades in that region. These formations achieved status as the 74th to 77th Regiments of Foot.

The turbulent age of rebellion culminated in the French Revolution of 1789. The security of Britain was threatened and when the revolutionary government of France declared war in 1793 rumour spread that her citizen army was preparing to invade and a state of panic ensued. Parliament made an

Re-enactment group in the mid-eighteenth-century dress of a regiment of foot. The officer and 'battalion men' wear the tricorne of the period, whereas the tall grenadiers sport a cloth mitre cap to make them look even more imposing.

urgent survey of Britain's defences and found her Regular Army strung out across the world, the militia weak and inefficient, and most able-bodied men of poor birth more likely to collude with a revolutionary invader than repel him. Pitt the Younger took up the challenge and led his party to enlarge the militia and accept the offers of volunteers to serve under arms in the defence of their homeland. Permanent regiments of infantry raised in the period 1793–4 were placed as the 78th to 92nd of Foot.

The French Revolutionary War carried the army to Flanders, where great suffering in the winter of 1794 prompted the Duke of York to create a Corps of Waggoners to take

the necessary supplies to the army in the field. The corps served throughout the Napoleonic Wars and was reconstituted in Victorian times as the Army Service Corps. A similar want of mobility in the artillery at the time prompted the birth of the Royal Horse Artillery. When invasion threatened, men not already committed to the militia felt the need to volunteer for the many armed

Towards the end of the eighteenth century, lapels and cuffs had narrowed and the tricorne was flattening out to bicorne dimensions.

A member of the Napoleonic
Association in the infantry
uniform of 1800–12.

associations that were springing up around the country, and gentlemen of the middle classes and yeomen farmers got together to meet the aggressor with troops of volunteer cavalry. Most of these were put together to form regiments of Yeomanry Cavalry during the Napoleonic Wars, and the majority remained in service after the wars to provide an aid to the civil powers in the industrial, political and agricultural riots of the nineteenth century. In 1899 the new war in South Africa needed cavalry to cover the vast expanses, and brigades of yeomanry were formed to serve abroad for the first time.

The turn of the eighteenth century saw the emergence of a new elite among the infantry: riflemen dressed in green and armed with the short Baker rifle instead of the long, less accurate, musket of the redcoat regiments. These skirmishers proved their worth on the battlefield and inspired many volunteer units to emulate them.

In the long peace which followed the Battle of Waterloo, junior regiments of cavalry and infantry were disbanded and the militia served to exist in name only. Only the demands of the empire forced the formation of new regiments; these appeared in 1824 and ranked as the 94th to 99th Foot.

An act of 1852 called for the resurrection of the militia for the defence of the realm, this time manned by volunteers and not enlisted by lot. They were clothed as ever in the red coats of the regular infantry, though a trend towards green-coated riflemen was growing, and many more militia regiments than before were electing to take Light Infantry or Rifles titles.

Russian aggression in the east led to an Anglo-French coalition and the embarkation of an army to the Crimea in 1854. The rigours of the Crimean War so far from home highlighted deficiencies in transport, stores and supplies, policing and hospital services. Departments were formed in 1855 to meet these needs.

In 1857 Indian regiments serving alongside European regiments under the control of the Honourable East India Company (HEIC) mutinied, and the resulting campaign to restore order and discipline ended with India being taken under direct rule of the crown and the HEIC regiments transferred to the British Army. The cavalry took their post as the 19th, 20th and 21st Hussars and the infantry came in as the 100th to 109th Foot.

During 1859–60 the towns and counties of Britain were authorised by the Secretary of State for War to raise volunteer units to cover the new threat of French aggression, and a multitude of corps, largely infantry, emerged and flourished as rifle clubs in uniforms of grey or green. Unlike previous volunteer regiments, the rifle volunteers continued to train after the threat of war had passed and, in the 1880s, found themselves seconded to the regular county regiments as their volunteer battalions.

The year 1881 saw the first mass amalgamations of the regiments, when the Cardwell Reforms organised 109 regular infantry and 121 militia regiments into 69 district regiments. Around this time more support corps were created to take responsibility for physical training, nursing, veterinary care and pay in the army.

In 1908 all army volunteers were grouped under the heading of the Territorial Force. This covered yeomanry, volunteer battalions of regular infantry regiments and five independent regiments: the London, Hertfordshire, Cambridgeshire, Hereford-shire and the Monmouthshire. After the First World War, the 'Territorials', who had given so much in the conflict, were reorganised as the Territorial Army, but many units were then re-roled or disbanded.

The First World War brought forth new corps in the sciences of tank warfare, weaponry and signalling, but the old arts of war had taken a knock, and in 1921 eighteen regular cavalry regiments were reduced, and paired off as nine 'new' regiments. In the same period five Irish infantry regiments were disbanded with the birth of the Irish Free State.

During the 1920s and '30s most of the army's horse regiments were converted to armoured vehicles, and the Second World War saw the need for airborne regiments and more support corps. The Auxiliary Territorial Service enabled women to serve in trades hitherto reserved for men.

The reign of Elizabeth II will be remembered in the army as a time of great reductions in the armed forces. In the 1950s infantry regiments were organised into brigades, which were to act as a basis for amalgamations. This was visited on twenty-four regiments between 1958 and 1961. The Army Council's decision to make large regiments from the infantry brigades was implemented in 1964 with the Royal Anglians, but in 1968 two

Late Victorian infantry as
portrayed by the Die Hard
Company. The infantry pattern
helmet replaced the shako
in 1878.

old regiments, the Cameronians and the York
and Lancasters, were disbanded as the junior
regiments of their brigades.

In 1992 the government's Options for
Change scheme meant another wave of
amalgamations, which involved support
corps as well as regiments, and in 2004 the
Ministry of Defence asked for further cuts in
manpower to fund new technology and the
remaining small (single battalion)
regiments were 'drawn down' to be
restructured into larger but fewer infantry
regiments by 2007.

THE ORDER OF PRECEDENCE

The regiments and corps of the Regular
Army are listed in order of precedence
according to the army's old class system
where seniority does not always bring
priority:

1. **The Household Cavalry**, seniority over all
   other regiments given to the Horse
   Guards by a royal warrant of 1666.
2. **The Royal Horse Artillery**, formed in
   1793 but placed ahead of the cavalry in

9

A First World War re-enactment group in the universal khaki service dress issued in 1904. Full dress was suspended with mass enlistment in 1914.

the Queen's Regulations of 1873 because its parent regiment (see class 4) had priority over the infantry.

3. **The Royal Armoured Corps**, formed in 1939 with the inherited seniority of its cavalry regiments, which were given status second only to the Horse Guards in 1713. Dragoon Guards have precedence in the corps and regiments are listed by the seniority of their oldest antecedent.

4. **The Royal Regiment of Artillery**, promoted ahead of the foot regiments in 1756.

    The Corps of Royal Engineers, grouped with the RA for its parallel history.

The Royal Corps of Signals, placed under its parent corps, the Royal Engineers, although actually far more junior than this classification.

5. **The Foot Guards**, displaced from their rank next to the Horse Guards in 1713.

6. **Infantry regiments**, listed by the seniority of their oldest antecedents.

7. **Support corps** other than those in class 4 (listed in order of seniority).

8. **The Territorial Army** (regiments listed in the order of their affiliated regular regiments and corps).

THE REGIMENTS

THE HOUSEHOLD CAVALRY REGIMENT

This, the most senior of all British Army units, is a mix and match of two complementary regiments of Horse Guards that, since 1820, have served together as Household Cavalry, a term rooted in the royal household that they guard. The Life Guards were the first to have this exalted honour and have always headed the army list. The Blues and Royals are the product of the 1969 union of the Royal Horse Guards (nicknamed 'The Blues' from their distinctive coats) and the 1st Royal Dragoons ('The Royals'). All three regiments have London backgrounds and date back to the reign of Charles II.

The armoured squadrons based at Windsor fulfil the regiments' modern role, whereas the ceremonial mounted squadrons – the only true cavalry left in the army – operate their historic public duties from Hyde Park Barracks, home to the Life Guards since 1795.

DRESS DISTINCTIONS

The blue forage cap has the scarlet band of royal regiments and a Guards' pattern peak

Household Cavalry bands in mounted review order, Blues and Royals to the fore.

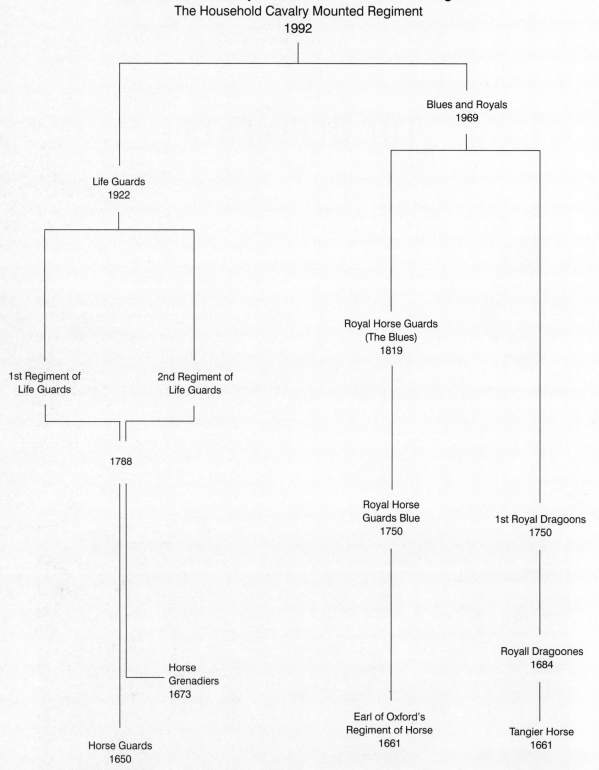

The Household Cavalry Armoured Reconnaissance Regiment
The Household Cavalry Mounted Regiment
1992

Blues and Royals
1969

Life Guards
1922

Royal Horse Guards
(The Blues)
1819

1st Regiment of
Life Guards

2nd Regiment of
Life Guards

1788

Royal Horse
Guards Blue
1750

1st Royal Dragoons
1750

Royall Dragoones
1684

Horse
Grenadiers
1673

Earl of Oxford's
Regiment of Horse
1661

Tangier Horse
1661

Horse Guards
1650

Troopers of the Life
Guards, 1997.

with gold braid according to rank: troopers
and musicians one row, lance corporal ranks
two rows, corporals of horse three rows,
squadron quartermaster corporals four rows
and corporal major five rows. The rank of
sergeant is not used in the Household Cavalry
because of the word's origin in 'servant' and
the Horse Guards' high-bred traditions. The
HC cap badge shows the sovereign's cypher
within a crowned Garter belt inscribed with
its motto *Honi soit qui mal y pense* (Shamed be
he who thinks evil of it).

On the khaki service dress cap a similar
badge is worn, which first appeared in 1914:
the cypher within a circle is inscribed with
the title of the regiment, customarily bright
in the Life Guards and bronzed in The
Blues and Royals.

Rank chevrons, uniquely made of gold wire
for HC No. 1 dress, are worn with a crown
above. This custom dates from 1815, when the
Prince Regent sent a box of small silver crowns
to the Horse Guards to show his appreciation
of their part in the great victory at Waterloo.

The HC Mounted Regiment and bands
are issued with traditional HC full dress.
The 1842 white metal helmet is fitted with a
white plume for the Life Guards, a black
plume for farriers of the Life Guards, and a
red plume for trumpeters of the Life
Guards and all members of The Blues and
Royals. The 1856 pattern tunic is scarlet
with blue facings for the Life Guards and
blue with scarlet facings for The Blues and
Royals, and farriers of the Life Guards.
Farriers historically wear a contrasting
uniform to the rest of their regiment. A buff
white cartouche belt is worn over the
shoulder with its red flask cord, a relic of
the eighteenth century when powder had to
be carried for the musket. Farriers wear an
axe belt in lieu of the cartouche belt and
carry a polished axe on parade to symbolise
their historic role in dispatching horses
wounded in battle. Commissioned and non-
commissioned officers have a system of gold
aiguillettes, which are worn from the
shoulder of the full dress tunic to indicate
rank, a HC custom from the reign of
George IV. The blue overalls are
regimentally marked – a wide scarlet stripe
in The Blues and Royals, a double scarlet
stripe with a central welt of the same colour
in the Life Guards (ex-2LG from 1832).

In Mounted Review Order, HC dress is shown in all its unique glory: white leather gauntlets and buckskin breeches with tall jackboots, all dating from 1812, and a polished silver nickel cuirass (from 1821) worn over the tunic. This heavy weight on large black horses inspired the nicknames 'Bangers' and 'Lumpers'. Musicians and trumpeters are privileged to wear the crimson and gold state coat in the presence of royalty, and the crimson state cloak in bad weather.

MUSIC

The Life Guards' quick march is a combination of *Milanollo* and *Men Of Harlech*. The latter (from the 2 LG) is also played in slow time with a march attributed to the pen of the Duchess of Kent and presented to the 1st Life Guards in 1820.

The Blues and Royals' quick march combines the Grand March from Verdi's *Aida* with *The Royals*. The march *Aida* was adopted by The Blues around 1874 but is often associated – through its Egyptian theme – with the moonlight charge of the Household Cavalry at Kassassin in 1882. The regimental slow march is an arrangement of those used in the Royal Horse Guards and the 1st Dragoons.

TRADITIONS

Waterloo Day (18 June) celebrates the stunning charges delivered by the Life Guards, The Blues and the Royal Dragoons in the battle. The Royals made off with the regimental eagle of the French 105th, and in 1898 a representation of it was cast as a collar badge for the regiment. In the 1914–18 war troopers made their own eagle badge to wear on the cap, but an imperial eagle standing on a tablet marked 105 did not officially become the cap badge of the Royal Dragoons until after the Second World War. Today the eagle badge is worn on the upper left sleeve of Blues and Royals' uniforms to represent the 1st Dragoons. Before 1914 it was the practice of the Kaiser Wilhelm, as Colonel-in-Chief of the 1st Royal Dragoons, to send a

A standard-bearer of the Life Guards flanked by an escort and a trumpeter in the crimson and gold state coat. Trumpeters traditionally ride greys, in contrast to the regiments' blacks.

Blues and Royals in Mounted Review Order at Hyde Park Barracks, with 'Green Goddess' fire engines visible. The man at left wears a corporal's aiguillette.

wreath for the regimental guidon at the Waterloo Day parade.

Colonels of the Household Cavalry fill the ancient appointments of Goldstick, and his deputy, Silverstick, the personal bodyguards to the sovereign. Lieutenant-colonels are addressed by their rank and warrant officers as 'Mister'. The junior subaltern in The Blues and Royals traditionally holds the old rank of cornet, which was officially dropped by other cavalry regiments in 1871.

The Blues and Royals' custom of saluting by hand even when bare headed, an act that could result in disciplinary action in any other regiment, originated in battle, most probably at Warburg in 1760. There The Blues' Colonel, the Marquis of Granby, is said to have lost both hat and wig in a wild cavalry charge before reporting to his commander-in-chief with a salute sans hat.

The warrant officers' and corporals' messes of the Life Guards have a tradition of hanging a 'brick' at Christmas time to symbolise the suspension of normal duties over the festive period. The custom dates back to 1888 when a forage master reportedly tossed a brick up onto the forage barn roof for much the same reason.

1ST THE QUEEN'S DRAGOON GUARDS

The 1st The Queen's Dragoon Guards (1QDG) were formed in 1959 from two armoured regiments that could trace a lineage back to 1685. The standing enjoyed by cavalry regiments raised under James II secured for them the highest position in the army, second only to the Household Cavalry.

The Queen's title was visited on both regiments but settled on the 2nd in 1727

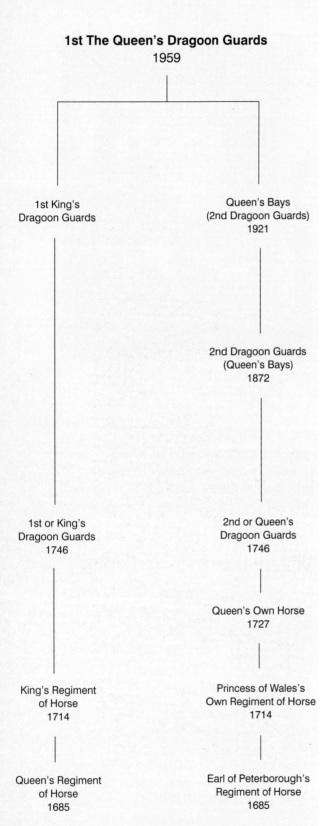

1st The Queen's Dragoon Guards
1959

1st King's
Dragoon Guards

Queen's Bays
(2nd Dragoon Guards)
1921

2nd Dragoon Guards
(Queen's Bays)
1872

1st or King's
Dragoon Guards
1746

2nd or Queen's
Dragoon Guards
1746

Queen's Own Horse
1727

King's Regiment
of Horse
1714

Princess of Wales's
Own Regiment of Horse
1714

Queen's Regiment
of Horse
1685

Earl of Peterborough's
Regiment of Horse
1685

when their titular head, the Princess of Wales (Caroline of Anspach), became Queen to George II. The Dragoon Guards title came twenty years later, when the three senior regiments of horse were relegated to dragoons with the suffix 'Guards' added to preserve dignity.

Bay mounts used by the 2nd from 1767 played such a prominent part in the regiment's image that it was called 'The Bays'. In 1872 the nickname was upgraded to official title and Queen's Bays was used alongside 2nd Dragoon Guards thereafter. The 1st Dragoon Guards were known by their initials KDG.

Regimental headquarters are at Maindy Barracks in Cardiff, recruiting takes place in Wales and the border counties, and the term 'Welsh Tankies' has been used to describe 1QDG.

DRESS DISTINCTIONS

The all-blue peaked cap is mounted with an Austrian eagle badge, items of KDG origin. The double-headed eagle, worn as a collar badge in the KDG from 1896, came from the arms of the Emperor Franz Josef of Austria, the Colonel-in-Chief of the regiment at the time. In 1915 the badge was put aside because of Austria's part in the First World War, but was taken on again in 1938.

The collar badge of the 1QDG is the word BAYS in Gothic script within a crowned wreath of bay leaves – formerly the badge of the Queen's Bays. Buttons are stamped with a Gothic Q over DG within the Garter on a crowned star.

Regimental full dress is heavy dragoon pattern: a brass helmet fitted with the scarlet plume of the KDG, a scarlet tunic with the blue facings of the KDG, and blue overalls with the white stripe worn by the Bays to complement their buff white facings adopted in 1855.

1QDG bandsmen at a cavalry memorial service in Hyde Park, *c.* 1990. Note the ex-officer of the Regimental Association, left, with his 'uniform' bowler and rolled umbrella.

Simkin's painting of a private man in the 2nd Dragoon Guards on a bay mount, *c.* 1806.

In barrack dress a regimental stable belt of royal blue may be worn.

MUSIC

The regimental slow march *Queen's Dragoon Guards* is accompanied by the quick march *Radetsky/Rusty Buckles*. Bandmaster Herr Schramm introduced Johann Strauss's *Radetsky March* to the KDG, probably because of its connection with the Austrian ruling family. 'Rusty Buckles' was a nickname for the Bays in the eighteenth century when the heavies spent long periods in Ireland. The new issue of horse brasses was missed and the regiment returned to England with irons rusted by decades of rainy conditions.

TRADITIONS

The regimental standard bears the cypher of Queen Caroline and the Bays' motto *Pro Rege et Patria* (For King and Country).

Waterloo/Gazala Day commemorates the regimental days of the KDG and the Bays together. At Waterloo surviving officers and sergeants of the 1st Dragoon Guards pooled their rations and dined together on the battlefield, a simple act of brotherhood the regiment turned into a tradition on Waterloo Day. Gazala Day honours the Bays' north African desert service, notably at the Cauldron and Knightsbridge, where they were in action with tanks for nineteen days continuously in the period 26 May–21 June 1942.

THE ROYAL SCOTS DRAGOON GUARDS

The Royal Scots Dragoon Guards (RSDG) were formed at Holyroodhouse in 1971 from two armoured regiments: the 3rd Carabiniers (Prince of Wales's Dragoon Guards) and the Royal Scots Greys. The 3rd Carabiniers were created in 1922 with the union of the 3rd Dragoon Guards and the Carabiniers (6th Dragoon Guards), both raised in 1685. The Greys, however, had a clear line of descent from 1681 when independent companies of Scottish dragoons, formed three years before to police the militant Covenanters, were made into a regiment.

The name Scots Greys initially came from Hodden grey coats worn by the Scotch Dragoons, but it later related to the grey horses that were procured for the regiment from 1690. It was in this year that the Queen Dowager's Horse gained their honour title at the Battle of the Boyne. William III dubbed the regiment King's Carbineers after the continental system of naming outstanding regiments from their arms, in this case the carbine.

The RSDG is Scotland's armoured regiment, with its headquarters at Edinburgh.

DRESS DISTINCTIONS

The band of the blue peaked cap is uniquely patterned with a yellow zigzag vandyke, the regimental mark of the Greys in the facing colour of the RSDG. Forage caps of the Scots Greys were bound with a vandyke from 1800, recorded in 1840 as being in gold for officers, white for other ranks and yellow for musicians.

The RSDG badge, an imperial eagle on crossed carbines, combines the Greys' Waterloo eagle (a replica of the regimental eagle of the French 45th taken in the battle) with carbines extracted from the badge of the 6th Dragoon Guards, adopted unofficially in 1826 with the Carabiniers' title. RSDG buttons carry this badge, though officers wear buttons with a thistle emblem.

The Prince of Wales's crest is worn today on the upper left sleeve to commemorate the 3rd Dragoon Guards, who bore the device from 1765 when they were honoured as the Prince of Wales's Dragoon Guards on the third birthday of the infant prince. Berets and pullovers are grey in this regiment, items of dress inherited from the Scots Greys. Stable belts are blue with adjacent stripes of grey/yellow/red.

A sergeant of the 3rd Dragoon Guards, *c.* 1905.

The Royal Scots Dragoon Guards
(Carabiniers and Greys)
1971

3rd Carabiniers (Prince
of Wales's Dragoon Guards)
1928

3rd/6th Dragoon Guards
1922

Royal Scots Greys
(2nd Dragoons)
1921

2nd Dragoons
(Royal Scots Greys)
1877

6th Dragoon Guards
(Carabiniers)
1826

6th Dragoon
Guards
1788

3rd or Prince of Wales's
Dragoon Guards
1765

2nd or Royal North
British Dragoons
1740

3rd Dragoon Guards
1747

3rd Irish Horse
1747

Royal North
British Dragoons
1707

King's Carbineers
1691

Royall Regiment of
Scotch Dragoones
1681

Earl of
Plymouth's Horse
1685

Lumley's Horse
1685

Musicians of the RSDG band, *c.* 1990. The bearskin has a crimson plume.

RSDG full dress, provided for drummers and honour guards mounted on greys, is reminiscent of the Scots Greys' uniform. The bearskin, with its Horse of Hanover emblem on the back, is worn with a white plume out of a brass grenade socket or a long crimson plume for trumpeters. It was Queen Anne who authorised the wearing of grenadier caps by the Greys in 1706,

following their defeat of three French grenadier regiments at the Battle of Ramillies. The caps evolved to bearskins around 1788, a thistle badge within the circle of St Andrew on the front plate and the Hanover Horse on the back a distinction dropped by the officers around 1800. The bearskins developed full and tall after the Napoleonic Wars, with the long crimson

Sullivan's painting of the 2nd or Royal North British Dragoons at Waterloo, with bearskins and grey mounts, Sgt Ewart taking the French eagle.

plume across the top for musicians from 1830. A white bearskin, assigned to the kettle drummer between 1887 and 1897, and again from 1937, was thought to have been a gift from the Czar of Russia, Colonel-in-Chief of the Scots Greys until his death in 1917.

The scarlet dragoon tunic bears the yellow facings of the 3rd Dragoon Guards ('The Old Canaries'). The blue overalls are regimentally distinguished by a double stripe, a distinction of the 6th Dragoon Guards, in the yellow facing colour of the RSDG. This abnormality dates from 1851, when the 6th were ordered to India as a regiment of light dragoons. Their heavy

dragoon brass helmets were retained but the red jackets were swapped for the braided blue tunics of the light cavalry, and trousers were re-tailored with a light cavalry double stripe in white, the facing colour of the regiment. This hybrid uniform characterised the Carabiniers as much as bearskins did the Greys.

Pipers wear traditional Scottish garb, the feathered bonnet distinguished by the regimental zigzag band. Their kilt and plaid are made of Royal Stuart tartan, a privilege granted to the Greys in 1946 when pipers from disbanding regiments were taken into the regiment.

MUSIC

The regimental slow march *Garb Of Old Gaul* was once that of the Greys, the quick march *3DGs* came from the 3rd Dragoon Guards (composed by Bandmaster Brophy in 1879) and *Men of Harlech* from the same regiment relates to the Prince of Wales's tradition. Popular Scottish marches are also played and pipers officially march along to *My Home* in slow time and *Highland Laddie* in quick time.

In the officers' mess the band traditionally plays *God Bless the Prince of Wales* (3DG) and *The Imperial Russian Anthem* in honour of Czar Nicholas II, a custom of the Scots Greys.

TRADITIONS

Anniversaries celebrated in the RSDG are the regimental birthday (2 July), Waterloo Day (18 June) and Nunshigum Day (13 April), the regimental day of the 3rd Carabiniers, which commemorates the struggle for the Nunshigum Ridge in Burma in 1944. On this day 'B' Squadron is led out on parade by its sergeant major and without officers in memory of a critical stage in the battle when the tank commanders had been picked off by Japanese snipers and Sgt Maj Craddock rallied the squadron to attack the enemy entrenched along the ridge.

In the officers' mess the loyal toast is taken seated, a custom that was practised in both the Greys and the 3DG. The Greys' tradition is reckoned to date back to George III, who often dined with the regiment and may not have been able to rise for the toast.

The RSDG also inherited from the Greys their unique privilege of flying the Scottish royal standard over regimental headquarters and the Queen's personal pipe banner, carried by the pipe major in her presence and on her birthday.

THE ROYAL DRAGOON GUARDS

The Royal Dragoon Guards (RDG) were created in 1992 from two armoured regiments formed seventy years previously out of four heavy cavalry regiments that were raised in the troubled days of James II. Regimental headquarters are at York.

The 4th/7th Royal Dragoon Guards emerged from the union of the 4th (Royal Irish) Dragoon Guards and the 7th (Princess Royal's) Dragoon Guards, which were commissioned as a regiment by William III after giving aid to Princess Anne in her flight from London in 1688.

The Royal Dragoon Guards desert training with Omani forces. *(MoD)*

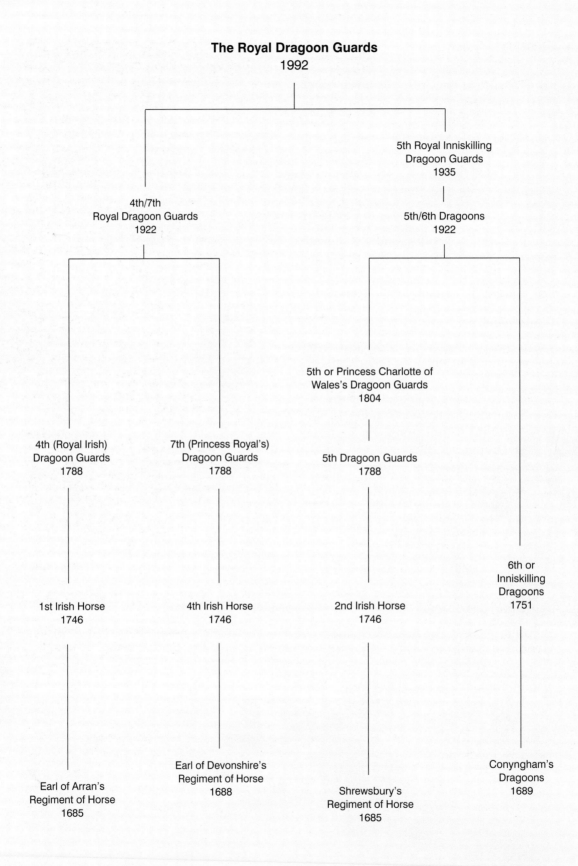

The Royal Dragoon Guards
1992

5th Royal Inniskilling
Dragoon Guards
1935

4th/7th
Royal Dragoon Guards
1922

5th/6th Dragoons
1922

5th or Princess Charlotte of
Wales's Dragoon Guards
1804

4th (Royal Irish)
Dragoon Guards
1788

7th (Princess Royal's)
Dragoon Guards
1788

5th Dragoon Guards
1788

6th or
Inniskilling
Dragoons
1751

1st Irish Horse
1746

4th Irish Horse
1746

2nd Irish Horse
1746

Earl of Devonshire's
Regiment of Horse
1688

Conyngham's
Dragoons
1689

Earl of Arran's
Regiment of Horse
1685

Shrewsbury's
Regiment of Horse
1685

Standard-bearer and escort of the 7th Dragoon Guards, brass helmets fitted with a black/white plume, black collars mounted with the Earl of Ligonier's crest.

RDG, 1998, the RQMS at left with the Salamanca Staff. *(Grenadier Publishing)*

The 5th Royal Inniskilling Dragoon Guards were the result of the 1922 linking of the 5th Dragoon Guards, one of six horse regiments raised in 1685, with the 6th Inniskilling Dragoons ('The Skins') formed in 1689 from the Protestant defenders of Enniskillen, fighting against the Catholic supporters of the deposed James.

DRESS DISTINCTIONS

The blue peaked cap and star badge are 4/7RDG in origin. The Star of the Order of St Patrick was authorised to the 4th (Royal Irish) Dragoon Guards in 1838 when they were in London for the coronation of Queen Victoria. From 1904 their star badge bore the Roman numerals MDCCLXXXIII, being the year in which the order was instituted (1783), and the motto *Quis separabit* (Who shall separate us?). The 4th/7th used this star for their cap badge, but with its centre shamrock

design substituted by the cross from the Order of the Garter superimposed with the coronet of the Princess Royal from the insignia of the 7th Dragoon Guards.

In adopting this badge the RDG changed its inscription to ROYAL DRAGOON GUARDS MCMXCII, being their date of formation (1992), and replaced the central coronet with the castle of Enniskillen with St George's flag flying (the badge of the Inniskillings and collar badge of the 5RIDG).

Senior NCOs wear a Horse of Hanover badge with their ranking, a custom of the 5th Dragoon Guards who gained the emblem in 1804 with their Princess Charlotte of Wales's title and the motto *Vestigia nulla retrorsum* (No going backward).

Service dress is noticeable for its use of green trousers (the modern mark of Irish ancestry) and the D-Day sleeve flash. This diamond shape flash was issued in 1944 and retained by the 4th/7th to commemorate their 'First and Last' reputation, acquired after the *Daily Telegraph* reported the regiment's tanks were first onto and last off the Normandy beaches. This echoes the First World War, when the 4th Dragoon Guards reputedly made the first kill of the war (at Casteau on 22 August 1914) and the 7th Dragoon Guards the last (at Lessines on 11 November 1918). No. 1 dress 'blues' are worn with green trousers or green overalls fashioned with a primrose-yellow stripe, a distinction of the 5RIDG, green being the facing colour of the 5th and yellow the facing colour of the Inniskillings.

Full dress and mess jackets are scarlet with blue facings.

MUSIC

The regimental quick march *Fare Ye Well Inniskilling* was adopted by 5RIDG in 1952 to replace The Skins' *Sprig o'Shillelagh* and the 5th Dragoon Guards' *Soldiers Chorus*. It was written by Bandmaster Adams, based on the old ballad *The Inniskilling Dragoon*.

The regimental slow march is the same as that arranged for the 4th/7th: the opening refrain of *The Blue Horse March*, named after the eighteenth-century nickname of the 4th Dragoon Guards from their blue facings, leading into *The Black Horse March* of the 7th, similarly named after their facing colour. The eighteenth century was a colourful time for the 7th, who were also called 'The Virgin Mary's Bodyguard' after a remark attributed to men of the Royal Horse Guards, contemptuous of the high number of Catholics in the Black Horse at the time of the War of the Austrian Succession.

Before taking the loyal toast in the officers' mess the Belgian national anthem would be played to honour King Leopold III, who had succeeded his father as Colonel-in-Chief of the 5RIDG in 1937. This ritual had come down from the 5th Dragoon Guards, who used to play the anthem for King Albert I, Colonel-in-Chief of the 5th from 1915.

TRADITIONS

St Patrick's Day (17 March) is observed as a regimental holiday, when breakfast is served by the officers and NCOs, with 'gunfire' tea and shamrock. Irish stew is the norm for lunch, with a sports afternoon for dessert. On the Sunday closest to 17 March the regiment remembers the bravery of Capt Oates of the Inniskilling Dragoons, who sacrificed himself on Scott's 1912 Antarctic expedition in order to give his comrades a better chance of survival. Oates Sunday was observed by the 5RIDG.

Another custom of the regiment, revived by Maj Gen Evans in 1930, is the French drum major's mace. It is paraded by a warrant officer on Salamanca Day (22 July) with its inscription, 'This trophy was taken in the charge by the 5th Dragoon Guards at the Battle of Salamanca, 22nd July, 1812, in which, among others, the 66th French Regiment was annihilated. Major General Ponsonby begs leave to present it to the 5th Dragoon Guards to be carried by the Trumpet Major on all occasions of review as a memory of That Glorious Day.'

The Dettingen Day celebrations of the 4th/7th are perpetuated on a weekend near to 27 June with a regimental revue and families' day. At the Battle of Dettingen in 1743, Ligonier's Regiment of Horse (later the 7th Dragoon Guards) got cut off from the main body and had to plough their way back through the enemy to their own lines. Cornet Richardson suffered thirty-seven sword cuts and bullet wounds in his defence of Ligonier's standard. Earl Ligonier developed his regiment to a high level of efficiency between 1720 and 1749, and in 1899 his crest and motto were adopted by the 7th as their badge.

Greetings are sent to regiments that participated with the 4th, 5th and 6th in the Charge of the Heavy Brigade at Balaklava in 1854.

Queen's Own Hussars on a freedom march in Birmingham on the tercentenary of the regiment in 1985.

THE QUEEN'S ROYAL HUSSARS

The Queen's Royal Hussars (QRH) were formed in 1993 from two armoured regiments created in 1958 – the Queen's Own Hussars (QOH) and the Queen's Royal Irish Hussars (QRIH) – amalgamations of four hussar regiments which had evolved from dragoons raised in the turbulent days of the seventeenth century: the 3rd (King's Own), 4th (Queen's Own), 7th (Queen's Own) and the 8th (King's Royal Irish). The Queen's title was first conferred on the 7th Dragoons in 1727 with the accession of George II. The Royal title came from the 8th Light Dragoons in 1777. Regimental headquarters are at the Regent's Park Barracks in London.

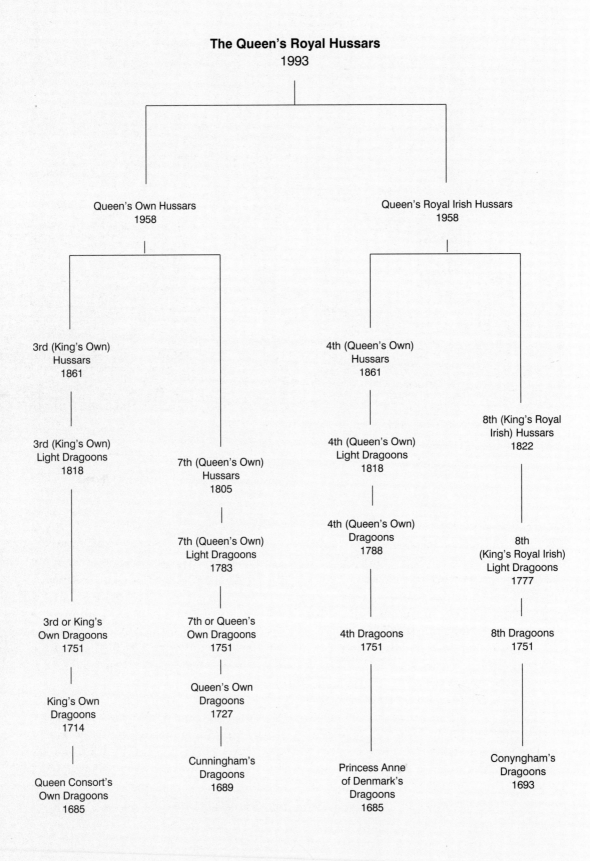

The Queen's Royal Hussars
1993

Queen's Own Hussars
1958

Queen's Royal Irish Hussars
1958

3rd (King's Own)
Hussars
1861

4th (Queen's Own)
Hussars
1861

8th (King's Royal
Irish) Hussars
1822

3rd (King's Own)
Light Dragoons
1818

7th (Queen's Own)
Hussars
1805

4th (Queen's Own)
Light Dragoons
1818

7th (Queen's Own)
Light Dragoons
1783

4th (Queen's Own)
Dragoons
1788

8th
(King's Royal Irish)
Light Dragoons
1777

3rd or King's
Own Dragoons
1751

7th or Queen's
Own Dragoons
1751

4th Dragoons
1751

8th Dragoons
1751

King's Own
Dragoons
1714

Queen's Own
Dragoons
1727

Queen Consort's
Own Dragoons
1685

Cunningham's
Dragoons
1689

Princess Anne
of Denmark's
Dragoons
1685

Conyngham's
Dragoons
1693

8th Hussars at Bognor, 5 June 1944, prior to leaving for their D-Day dispersal area; some of the officers are wearing the green and gold 'tent hat'. *(Bill Bellamy)*

DRESS DISTINCTIONS

The scarlet peaked cap, a light cavalry custom, was common to both the QOH and the QRIH. The cap badge is made up of the 7th Hussars' Queen's cypher with the royal crest and Irish harp of the 8th superimposed, and a title scroll beneath.

The galloping horse collar badge was inherited from the 3rd Hussars by way of the QOH, both of which used it as their cap badge. This Horse of Hanover was authorised to the 3rd Dragoons with their King's title in 1714, when George I of Hanover came to the throne.

The scarlet and silver sleeve badge also came from the QOH. This, the Maid of Warsaw, was awarded to the 7th Hussars by the commander of the 2nd Polish Corps in the Second World War to commemorate the bravery of the regiment when supporting the Poles in the Italian campaign of 1944–5.

Items of QRIH dress perpetuated in the QRH are the green 'tent' hat adopted by the 8th Hussars officers in 1909, green berets and pullovers, and the double chevron worn by lance corporals (8th Hussars).

No. 1 dress 'blues' are light cavalry pattern, regimentally distinguished by the scarlet collar allowed for the 3rd Hussars' uniform in 1861. The Victorian hussar uniform did not have coloured facings, but the 3rd and 13th were permitted to wear collars of their respective facing colours.

Full dress is basic hussar pattern with the distinctions of the senior 3rd Regiment: a Garter blue busby bag and scarlet collar. The busby plume, however, is white and scarlet as worn in the 7th and 8th Hussars.

Irish pipers introduced into the QRIH in 1987 wore a curious green hussar-corded 'doublet' with the traditional Irish saffron kilt and cloak. A plain green doublet replaced the corded type soon after, and pipers and drummers were to be seen in a green *caubeen* adorned with the regimental white/scarlet hackle.

MUSIC

The regimental quick march combines Von Suppe's *Light Cavalry* of the QOH with *St Patrick's Day* of the QRIH.

The slow marches of the antecedent regiments together form the regimental slow march: *The 3rd Hussars Slow March*, which includes *General Bland's Inspection March* composed in 1745 (probably by his daughter) in honour of the regiment's conduct at Dettingen; *Litany of Loretto*, based on thirteenth-century Italian plainsong and adopted by the 4th Hussars in 1890; *Garb of Old Gaul*, marking the Scottish origins of the 7th Hussars; and *March of the Scottish Archers* from the 8th Hussars.

The regimental trot *Encore* and the canter gallop *Bonnie Dundee* are inherited from the QOH.

TRADITIONS

The regimental motto, *Mente et manu* (With mind and hand), which comes from QRIH, has graced the badge of the 4th Hussars since 1906. The regimental journal *The Crossbelts* is named after the journal of the QRIH, inspired by an old nickname of the 8th. At the Battle of Almenara in 1710, Pepper's Dragoons (later the 8th) overthrew a body of Spanish horse and marked the victory by wearing the Spaniards' sword belts across their own pouch belts in the manner prescribed only for regiments of horse. The custom was maintained for half a century, so the 8th Dragoons achieved some notoriety in the army as 'The Crossbelt Dragoons'.

Battle honour days celebrated in the QRH are Dettingen (27 June), Balaklava (25 October) and Alamein (2 November). Balaklava Day commemorates the 4th and 8th in the Charge of the Light Brigade, and Alamein Day when the 3rd, 4th and 8th Hussars fought in tanks on the Western Desert in 1942. The 3rd Hussars kept 23 October as Alamein Day in memory of their near annihilation when fighting

The QRH pipe major plays in Challenger tanks for arming, Bosnia 1996. *(MoD)*

alongside the 2nd New Zealand Division. The fern leaf emblem of the NZ Division was permitted to be carried by the 3rd on their tanks, as the QRH do today.

At the Battle of Dettingen in 1743, the 3rd Dragoons won great approbation for their repeated charges on the French cavalry, which they penetrated to capture four sets of kettledrums. The King commanded that silver drums taken in the battle were to be paraded on a drum horse with a serjeant drummer and it became a tradition in the regiment for the drummer employed on this duty to wear the silver collar presented by Lady Fitzroy in 1772. The Dettingen drums were destroyed in a fire in 1855 and solid silver replacements procured at the officers' expense were engraved with the battle honours of the regiment and paraded without banners. In the officers' mess of the 3rd Hussars the junior subaltern was expected to wear the drummer's silver collar to dinner. The QRH maintain the drum horse tradition with a mounted drummer in full dress, complete with silver collar.

The Churchill Cup, awarded every year to the best gunnery troop, takes its name from Sir Winston Churchill, who served with the 4th Hussars.

THE 9TH/12TH ROYAL LANCERS

The 9th/12th Royal Lancers (9/12RL) were formed in 1960 by the union of two armoured regiments that had survived the cavalry cuts of 1921. Both were raised in the troubled year of 1715 as part of the response to the rebellion in Scotland. In 1816 they were among the first to be equipped as lancers, a class of cavalry modelled on Napoleon's *Lanciers* in the recent wars. Regimental headquarters are at Leicester.

The 12th Light Dragoons re-enactment group in the dress of the 1812–15 period, perfect in every detail except for the horse's undocked tail.

Bandsmen of the 9th/12th RL in their new 'Victorian' lancer caps, 1980s.

The 9th/12th Royal Lancers
(Prince of Wales's)
1960

```
                    |
        ┌───────────┴───────────┐
        |                       |
  9th (Queen's Royal)           |
     Lancers                    |
       1830                     |
        |                       |
        |                       |
   9th Lancers          12th (Prince of Wales's
      1816                Royal) Lancers
        |                      1816
        |                       |
        |                       |
9th Light Dragoons              |
      1783                      |
        |              12th or Prince of Wales's
        |                 Light Dragoons
        |                      1768
        |                       |
   9th Dragoons          12th Dragoons
      1751                    1751
        |                       |
        |                       |
 Wynne's Dragoons        Bowles' Dragoons
      1715                    1715
```

DRESS DISTINCTIONS

The scarlet peaked cap, with blue piping and quarter welts peculiar to lance regiments, is a legacy of the 12th. Side hats are blue (9th Lancers) for officers and scarlet (12th Lancers) for other ranks. The cap badge combines a crown and the Prince of Wales's crest on crossed lances, with a scroll below marked IX–XII.

The Prince of Wales's feathers, displayed by the 12th since 1768, are now seen on the NCOs' ranking and on back pouches. Buttons show the AR cypher of Queen Adelaide, reversed and interlaced, on crossed lances with a crown above. The cypher was borne by the 9th from 1830, when William IV inspected the regiment and conferred on it the Queen's title.

Lanyards and stable belts are yellow (facing colour of the 12th Light Dragoons) and scarlet (facing colour of both regiments after their conversion to lancers).

No. 1 dress cavalry pattern has a scarlet collar for officers and a scarlet gorget patch for other ranks. Full dress is lancer pattern with scarlet facings and 9th Lancers' pattern cap (blue top with a black and white plume). Musicians wear the traditional bandsmen's scarlet plume.

MUSIC

The regimental quick march, *God Bless the Prince of Wales*, is fairly common in regiments with a connection to the title. The slow march is in two parts: *Men of Harlech* from the 9th and *Coburg* from the 12th. Other marches in the regiment's repertoire are *The Soldiers' Chorus*, *The Irish Washerwoman*, *Norma*, *St Cecilia*, *Quand Madelon*, *Pupchen* (once played for reveille on May Day) and *Low Backed Car*.

The tradition of playing hymns in the evening came from the 12th Lancers, who had three theories for the custom: the wish of the Pope on a visit to Civita Vecchia by

Caton Woodville's painting of the 9th Lancers at Mons in 1914.

officers of the 12th in 1795; an officer's wife who once presented instruments to the regimental band with a request for *The Vesper Hymn* to be played every night; and – the soldiers' favourite – by order of the Duke of Wellington as a 104-year penance for the 'Supple Twelfth', whose Peninsular War record was reportedly blighted by a raid on a nunnery where 104 bottles of wine had been liberated. In the event, *Sicilian Vespers*, *The Russian Hymn* and *Spanish Chant* were played by the regimental band every

An enthusiast of the 10th Dragoons (*see* The King's Royal Hussars) in the regiment's attire of the 1750s.

evening and on dinner nights in the mess until 1939, and again after the war, but on a less frequent basis.

TRADITIONS

Mons/Moy Day marks the last mounted charges with the lance, made by C Squadron, 12th Lancers on 28 August and B Squadron, 9th Lancers on 7 September 1914 against German dragoons.

The regimental journal, *The Delhi Spearman*, was named after a reputation gained by the 9th Lancers during the Indian Mutiny – 'The Delhi Spearmen'.

THE KING'S ROYAL HUSSARS

The King's Royal Hussars (KRH) were formed in 1992 from two armoured regiments, the Royal Hussars (a 1969 amalgamation of the 10th and 11th Hussars, which were originally raised for the Jacobite Rebellion of 1715) and the 14th/20th Hussars (a 1922 amalgamation of which the 14th also dated back to 1715).

The King's part of the title dates from 1830, when William IV bestowed his title on the 14th Light Dragoons after inspecting them. The Royal part of the title goes back to 1811, when the Prince Regent honoured the 10th Hussars with it as a public acknowledgement of their valour in the Peninsular War. Of the four antecedents, only the 20th did not boast an extra title, and were known as 'Nobody's Own'.

KRH headquarters are in Preston (14/20KH) and Winchester (RH).

DRESS DISTINCTIONS

The regiment's unique crimson peaked cap was inherited from the Royal Hussars, a legacy of the 11th. Its black Prussian eagle ('The Burnt Budgie' in modern army parlance), with its crown, orb, sceptre and FR cypher in gold, was the badge of the 14/20KH. Officers wear the eagle in gilt on a cherry patch for beret and side hat. The emblem was permitted for the 14th Light Dragoons in 1798, after they had provided an escort for Princess Frederika of Prussia en route to her wedding with the Duke of York. The 14th Hussars wore the eagle until 1915, when it was withdrawn because of its Germanic connotations until 1931. The badge was blackened for officers of the 14/20 in the 1950s and for other ranks in 1961.

The Prince of Wales's crest, the badge of the RH and the 10th before them, is now worn on the collars of KRH uniforms. It represents an

KRH warrant officer in mess kit, with its crimson lapels and overalls. Note the small Gurkha badge at the top of his sleeve. *(Grenadier Publishing)*

episode in the history of the 10th Hussars when the Prince Regent favoured them with his patronage. The tradition continued with Prince Edward (Colonel-in-Chief of the 10th

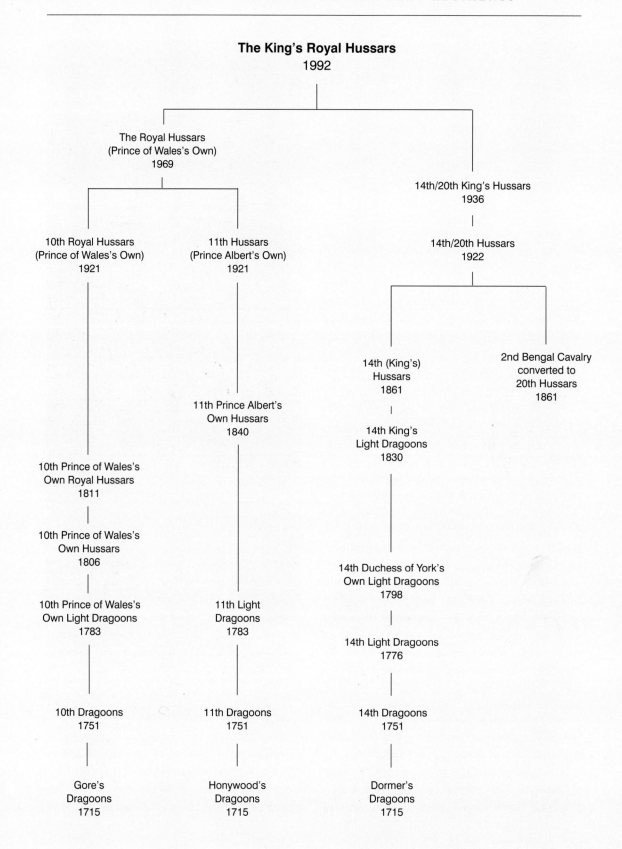

The King's Royal Hussars
1992

The Royal Hussars
(Prince of Wales's Own)
1969

14th/20th King's Hussars
1936

10th Royal Hussars
(Prince of Wales's Own)
1921

11th Hussars
(Prince Albert's Own)
1921

14th/20th Hussars
1922

14th (King's)
Hussars
1861

2nd Bengal Cavalry
converted to
20th Hussars
1861

11th Prince Albert's
Own Hussars
1840

14th King's
Light Dragoons
1830

10th Prince of Wales's
Own Royal Hussars
1811

10th Prince of Wales's
Own Hussars
1806

14th Duchess of York's
Own Light Dragoons
1798

10th Prince of Wales's
Own Light Dragoons
1783

11th Light
Dragoons
1783

14th Light Dragoons
1776

10th Dragoons
1751

11th Dragoons
1751

14th Dragoons
1751

Gore's
Dragoons
1715

Honywood's
Dragoons
1715

Dormer's
Dragoons
1715

in 1863) and his eldest son, the Duke of Clarence, who was gazetted into the regiment and served until his death in 1892. When the Prince Regent became King the most expensive uniforms in the army belonged to the 'Shiny Tenth', whose officers could boast ornamental chains on their pouch belts and cowrie shells on their bridles.

A small silver badge of crossed kukris is worn on the upper sleeve, a custom of the 14/20 which commemorated a Second World War bond with the 6th Gurkha Rifles.

Trousers and overalls worn in No. 1 dress 'blues', No. 2 dress and mess dress are crimson in this regiment, another part of the unique apparel of the RH first worn in the new hussar dress of the 11th designed by Prince Albert in 1840. Lord Cardigan, who had joined the 11th Light Dragoons in 1819, arranged for his regiment to escort Prince Albert on his arrival in England for his marriage to Queen Victoria, and thereby enhanced its status to Prince Albert's Own Regiment of Hussars in the same year. The regiment's famous nickname, 'Cherrypickers', related not to the cherry pantaloons, though, but to an incident in the Peninsular War when a foraging patrol was surprised by enemy dragoons in an orchard.

In working dress the KRH are conspicuous by their cherry/brown berets, another rare distinction of the RH, once the province of the 11th Hussars. When the 11th were mechanised in 1928, berets requested for use in tanks were refused and the quartermaster's wife responded by making a batch out of brown cloth hemmed with a cherry red band.

Full dress is hussar pattern with the distinctive crimson busby bag and overalls worn in the RH and 11th Hussars.

MUSIC

The regimental quick march, *The King's Royal Hussars*, heads a list of traditional titles. *Coburg*, from the 11th Hussars, evokes a family name of Prince Albert and is played in slow

King's Royal Hussars corporals in green coveralls and the regimental brown beret, 1995.

time. *The Eagle*, formerly the slow march of the 14/20, is now used for the general salute.

The 11th Hussars' quick march, *Moses in Egypt*, celebrated the services of C Squadron in the Egyptian campaign of 1801, which gave the regiment its Sphinx battle honour, a rarity in cavalry circles. For this contribution to regimental honours C Squadron has always enjoyed senior squadron status in the regiment.

The march, *Royal Sussex*, long played unofficially in the 14th, was authorised in 1961 after permission was sought from the colonel of the Royal Sussex Regiment. The march had spread from the one regiment to

A corporal of the 14th Hussars in the mounted review order of 1880–1900.

the other in 1798, when the band of the 35th (Royal Sussex) Regiment stepped in to cover for the band of the 14th Light Dragoons, who were found unfit to play for their regiment after time spent in a Kent tavern.

Other marches in the regiment's repertoire are *Up Light Loo* (regimental trot 14/20), *Light of Foot* (quick march, RH, until 1976), *Merry Month of May* and *God Bless the Prince of Wales*.

The band of the Royal Hussars would play the regimental hymns of 'The Don't Dance Tenth' on Tuesdays and Thursdays when in barracks. These were introduced to the 10th by Lt-Col Baker in 1866, to be played between first and last post: *Thy Will Be Done*, *As Pants the Hart* and Trent's *Chant No. 1*.

TRADITIONS

On guest nights in the officers' mess a toasting cup called 'The Emperor' is used in the tradition of the 14/20, and the 14th Hussars before them. This silver travelling chamber pot was taken by men of the 14th Light Dragoons from the coach

of Joseph Bonaparte in the French Army's rout at the Battle of Vittoria in 1813. Subalterns of the 'Emperor's Chambermaids' were not required to drain 'The Emperor' of its liquor after 1929, but officers drank from it for the loyal toast and, after 1969, a special toast to their Colonel-in-Chief, Princess Anne.

The regiment's affiliation with the Royal Gurkha Rifles originated with the 14/20H in 1942. In 1945 they came together with the 6th Gurkha Rifles again for the push through Italy and attacked a German Panzer division at Medicina. The KRH keep 16 April as Medicina Day in the way of the 14/20.

Other important regimental anniversaries are Ramnuggur Day (22 November), commemorating 'The Ramnuggur Boys' of the 14th and their death or glory charge against the Sikh cavalry in 1848; Ramadi Day (28 September), traditionally celebrated in the corporals' mess of the 14th Hussars in honour of their action against the Turks in 1916; El Alamein Day (23 October); and Balaklava Day (25 October), when the 11th Hussars charged with the Light Brigade in 1854.

The custom of sounding the Last Post at 2150 hr, instead of the regulation 2200, began with the 11th Hussars. It was their way of honouring their famous leader, Lord Cardigan, who died at this hour.

THE LIGHT DRAGOONS

Unlike other armoured reconnaissance regiments created in the 'Options for Change' mergers of 1992, the Light Dragoons (LD) opted to change from the obvious hussar titles of their recent history and reached further back, to a time when their antecedents were light dragoons. The original four were linked up in 1922 as the 13th/18th Hussars and the 15th/19th Hussars.

In No. 1s for the Guidon Parade, Germany, 1995. *(Light Dragoons)*

The Light Dragoons' headquarters are at Newcastle upon Tyne, the former home of 15/19H – 'The Geordie Hussars'. The 13/18H were 'Yorkys' and the LD still recruit in Yorkshire and the north-east. Diana, Princess of Wales, was the first Colonel-in-Chief of the regiment, and in 2003 King Abdullah II of Jordan was appointed to the post.

DRESS DISTINCTIONS

The scarlet peaked cap (15/19H) is mounted with the Maltese Cross which distinguished shakos of the light dragoon regiments from 1832, a bold departure from normal badging practice. The cross is superimposed with the lion and crown (15H) above a wreathed circle encompassing the monogram LD and inscribed with the mottoes *Viret in aeturnum* (Forever green – 13H) and *Merebimur* (Worthy of our deeds – 15H). The badge is mounted on a scarlet backing, a 15/19H custom that is noticeable on the blue beret.

The 13/18H were recognisable by their unique white caps (with blue band), which inspired nicknames like 'The Milkmen' and 'The Sailors'.

Except for a buff white collar (the uniform distinction of the 13th), No. 1 dress 'blues' are 15/19H pattern: scarlet cap, box

chainmail shoulders, the lion and crown NCOs' sleeve badge (15LD by royal permission, 1801) and light cavalry double yellow stripe on trousers/overalls. The white collar is adorned by gold Austrian lace for officers and a badge for other ranks. The Austrian lace commemorates a charge at Villers-en-Cauchies in which the 15th Light Dragoons scattered six French battalions to save the Emperor of Austria from defeat. The collar badge is composed of the lion and crown crest of the 15/19H on the Z-shape scroll that formed the backbone of the badge of the 13/18H.

18th Hussars with a 'captured' French eagle during a Napoleonic encounter, 2004.

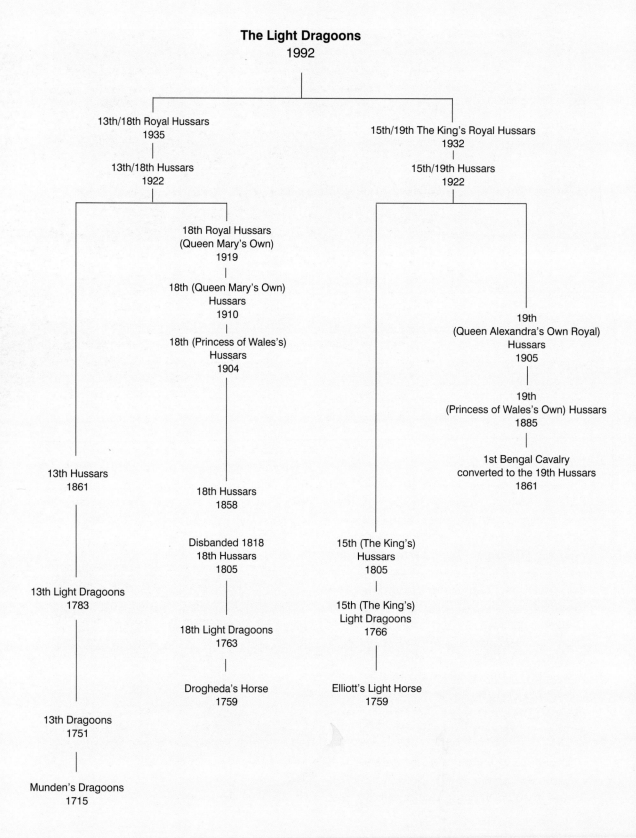

The Light Dragoons
1992

13th/18th Royal Hussars
1935

15th/19th The King's Royal Hussars
1932

13th/18th Hussars
1922

15th/19th Hussars
1922

18th Royal Hussars
(Queen Mary's Own)
1919

18th (Queen Mary's Own)
Hussars
1910

18th (Princess of Wales's)
Hussars
1904

19th
(Queen Alexandra's Own Royal)
Hussars
1905

19th
(Princess of Wales's Own) Hussars
1885

13th Hussars
1861

18th Hussars
1858

1st Bengal Cavalry
converted to the 19th Hussars
1861

Disbanded 1818
18th Hussars
1805

15th (The King's)
Hussars
1805

13th Light Dragoons
1783

15th (The King's)
Light Dragoons
1766

18th Light Dragoons
1763

Drogheda's Horse
1759

Elliott's Light Horse
1759

13th Dragoons
1751

Munden's Dragoons
1715

Bandsmen of the 13th/18th Royal Hussars in the 1980s. The white facings originated with the 13th Hussars.

The blue mess dress features a buff white waistcoat in addition to the buff white collar.

Cross belt pouches are mounted with a silver elephant and its battle honour 'Assaye'. These honours, given for service in India at the start of the 19th century, were won by the 19th Light Dragoons (1781–1821) and authorised to the 19th Hussars in 1874.

In service and combat dress a large blue/white South Africa flash is worn on the sleeve, a custom of the 13/18H. Its name comes from the helmet patch used to identify the 13th Hussars in the Boer War.

MUSIC

The regimental quick march, *Balaklava*, originated as a ballad sung after the Crimean War and was adopted by the 13th Hussars to mark their part in the battle. The slow march, *Denmark*, comes from the 19th Hussars, whose Colonel-in-Chief, Queen Alexandra, was of Danish extraction.

Other marches are *Elliott's Light Horse*, *The Bold King's Hussar*, *Sahagun Song* and *Haste To The Wedding* (15/19H). *A Life on the Ocean Wave* was played by the 13/18H before their quick march to mark the crossing to Normandy in 1944, where they went ashore in amphibious tanks.

TRADITIONS

Sahagun Day (21 December) marks the 15th Hussars' surprise attack on the snow-covered garrison in Spain in 1808. The story of how Lord Paget led them by the light of the moon used to be retold in a ballad sung by the band on this day.

Balaklava Day (25 October) remembers the exploits of the 13th Light Dragoons on the front rank of the Charge of the Light Brigade in the Crimea in 1854.

Assaye Day (23 September) was celebrated in the 15/19H for the first time in 1924. It remembered the old 19th Light Dragoons at the bloody Battle of Assaye, the culmination of the First Mahratta War in 1803.

Esla Day (31 May) was first observed by the 15/19H in 1928. It involved the King's Own Yorkshire Light Infantry, whose officers were honorary guests of the 15/19H mess. The two regiments would meet to compete in sport on the anniversary of the crossing of the Esla river in the Peninsular War for a painting that depicts men of the 51st Foot braving the current by clutching

Band of the 16th/5th Queen's Royal Lancers in their scarlet tunics, *c.* 1989.

at the stirrups of the 15th Hussars. The LD maintain the custom whenever possible.

Normandy Day (6 June) was kept by the 13/18H for their part in the D-Day Landings of 1944. After the breakout from the coast the regiment was instrumental in clearing the Mont Pincon and enabled the pursuit of the Germans back to the Rhine.

Lajj Day (5 March) commemorated the last mounted charge made by the 13th Hussars. Its recipients were a Turkish rearguard in the advance to Baghdad in 1917.

THE QUEEN'S ROYAL LANCERS

The Queen's Royal Lancers (QRL) were established in 1993 by the union of the 16th/5th Lancers ('The Vulgar Fraction') and the 17th/21st Lancers, both products of the 1922 mergers. The 5th (Royal Irish) Lancers were successors to the 5th (Royal Irish) Dragoons formed in the Siege of Enniskillen, honoured in Marlborough's wars, but disbanded in 1799 after insurgents had infiltrated its ranks during the Irish Rebellion of the previous year.

The Queen's Royal title came from the 16/5L, Queen's bestowed on the 16th Light Dragoons in 1766 for excellent service in Portugal. The Royal part was conferred on the 5th in 1704 for its part in the Battle of Blenheim. When the two were linked together in 1922 the 16th were given precedence in the new title because of the 5th Lancers' break in lineage, and therefore loss of seniority in the cavalry.

QRL headquarters are at the 17th/21st Lancers' Prince William of Gloucester Barracks near Grantham. The regimental museum is situated in nearby Belvoir Castle, once home to John Manners, who raised the 21st Light Dragoons in 1760.

17th Lancers re-enactment group in the review order of 1880–1900.

DRESS DISTINCTIONS

The scarlet peaked cap, with its blue band and quarter welts (representing the four corners of the lancers' full dress cap), is 16/5 colouring. The cap badge is referred to as a motto – the skull and crossbones with the OR GLORY scroll of the 17th. It was first adopted for Hale's Light Horse as a *memento mori*, relating to the death of Gen Wolfe at Quebec in 1759. Col Hale was the officer entrusted with bringing the battle's dispatches back to the King, for which he was commissioned to raise his own regiment of light horse. Before long this became the 17th, the only cavalry unit in the Wolfe Society. The motto stands out among army badges and caused the 17th to be called 'The Death or Glory Boys'. Their nickname 'Tots' came in after the South African War of 1899–1902, from the Boer word for death's head – *Totenkopf.* Modern names for wearers of the motto range from 'The Boneheads' to 'Blackbeard's Mob'.

The collar badge is the same as that worn in the 16/5L from 1954, a C cypher within a Garter belt juxtaposed with a circle inscribed *Quis separabit* (Who shall separate us?) and containing an Irish harp and a crown, all on crossed lances. The C cypher belonged to Queen Charlotte, wife of George III and Queen of the 16th's title.

Except for the scarlet cap, No. 1 dress 'blues' are 17/21 in appearance: a double white stripe on the trousers/overalls and white gorget patches on the collar. Col Hale got the 17th into white facings from the outset to echo the facings of his former regiment, the 47th of Foot.

The scarlet mess jacket, an unusual colour for lancers to wear, dates back to 1832 when William IV attempted to have the whole army in red. The edict was rescinded in 1840 but the 16th Lancers were away in India and either missed or ignored the directive. When their tour of duty came to an end in 1846 Col Vandaleur asked permission of the Queen for his regiment to continue in scarlet and the 16th were known as 'The Scarlet Lancers' thereafter.

MUSIC

The regimental quick march, *Stable Jacket,* harks back to horse days, the slow march, *Omdurman,* to the battle where the 21st Lancers made their reputation in 1898.

Other marches in the QRL repertoire are *The White Lancer* and Wagner's *Rienzi* from the 17/21, and *Queen Charlotte* and *Scarlet and Green* from the 16/5. The Spanish National Anthem, *Marcha Real,* was played in honour of King Alphonso XIII, Colonel-in-Chief of the 16th Lancers from 1905 and of the 16th/5th until his death in 1941. During one memorable visit to the regiment the King arrived with his Sam Browne belt fastened with the cross-strap on back to front, and in order not to embarrass His Majesty all officers on parade were hastily instructed to change theirs to match. Ever since that occasion the officers have maintained the idiosyncrasy as a regimental custom.

TRADITIONS

The chief battle anniversaries are Blenheim (13 August), when the 5th remembered the prowess of their forebears in the 1704 conflict; Balaklava Day (25 October) for the 17th, the only lance regiment in the Charge of the Light Brigade; Khartoum Day (2 September), commemorating the battle of the 2nd Sudan War where the 21st fell upon a hidden horde of Dervishes, a much publicised episode at the time which resulted in their achieving the title 'The Empress of India's'.

Aliwal Day (28 January) celebrates the magnificent charge of the 16th Lancers on the Sikh artillery at the Battle of Aliwal on the Sutlej river in 1846, the culmination of the First Sikh War. After the battle lance pennons of the 16th were so encrusted with dried blood that they developed a 'concertina' effect, a symbol of the fighting the regiment exploited afterwards by crimping its pennons to simulate the effect. The QRL continue this custom and the Aliwal tradition of the 16th, who also held the reputation of having been the first to charge with the lance (at Bhurtpore in 1825) and the last (at Mons in 1918).

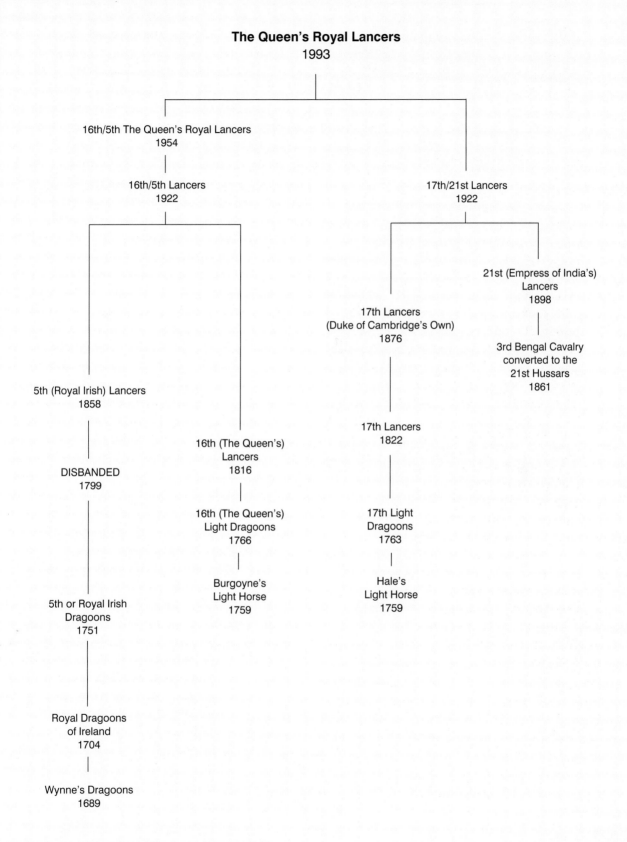

The Queen's Royal Lancers
1993

16th/5th The Queen's Royal Lancers
1954

16th/5th Lancers
1922

17th/21st Lancers
1922

21st (Empress of India's)
Lancers
1898

17th Lancers
(Duke of Cambridge's Own)
1876

3rd Bengal Cavalry
converted to the
21st Hussars
1861

5th (Royal Irish) Lancers
1858

16th (The Queen's)
Lancers
1816

17th Lancers
1822

DISBANDED
1799

16th (The Queen's)
Light Dragoons
1766

17th Light
Dragoons
1763

Burgoyne's
Light Horse
1759

Hale's
Light Horse
1759

5th or Royal Irish
Dragoons
1751

Royal Dragoons
of Ireland
1704

Wynne's Dragoons
1689

THE ROYAL TANK REGIMENT

The Royal Tank Regiment (RTR) was born in the middle of the First World War as the heavy section of the Machine Gun Corps. The section specialised in armoured cars fitted with machine guns; these developed into tanks, and in the following year, 1917, the unit became the Tank Corps. In 1923 the corps received its royal title and, in 1939, on the formation of the Royal Armoured Corps, it became the Royal Tank Regiment. Headquarters are at Bovington Camp in Dorset.

DRESS DISTINCTIONS

The black beret, worn in all orders of dress, is the mark of the regiment. It was pioneered by the Royal Tank Corps in 1924 as the most convenient form of headgear for wearing in tanks, black to disguise oil stains. Other units were not permitted the beret at first, and when they were, colours other than black had to be worn. The regimental badge, a prototype tank on a crowned wreath with the motto *Fear naught*, was adopted in 1923.

The white tank badge worn on the upper left sleeve dates back to the First World War, when personnel volunteered to the Tank Corps could be united with a single badge.

Regimental work coveralls, jumpers, gloves, shoes and belts are all black, hence the nickname 'The Blacks on Tracks'. The stable belt is in regimental colours taken from Gen Elles's flag flown at Cambrai in 1917: brown, red and green, said to represent the regiment's struggles in the First World War, 'from the mud, through the blood to the green fields beyond'. A beret hackle of these colours is worn by regimental bandsmen on ceremonial occasions.

'Tankie' in the black beret and coveralls, his saffron cravat giving his regiment as 2 RTR.
(Grenadier Publishing)

The Mark V arrived at the front in 1918 and was used in action at Hamel and Moreuil.

The tank regiments within the RTR have always been distinguishable by their own coloured markings, on shoulder flashes at first, then lanyards and now cravats too.

MUSIC

The quick march, *My Boy Willie*, was adopted in 1922, an adaptation of the old Worcestershire folk song *Billy Boy*. The name connection was to the early tanks code-named Big Willie and Little Willie, after the Kaiser Wilhelm and his son. After the Second World War the air *Cadet Roussel*, from the Cambrai region of France, was added to the march to lend it more variety.

The regimental slow march, *The Royal Tank Regiment*, opens with the old Tank Corps call.

The various regiments of the RTR have a march additional to the above. *Lippe Detmold* recalls the German town where 1RTR was stationed from 1946 to 1954; *Saffron* was inspired by the lanyards of the 2RTR; *On the Quarterdeck* celebrates the victory of 3RTR over the Royal Navy in the Portsmouth Whaler Sailing Championship in 1948; *Blue Flash*, the regimental distinction of 4RTR; *on Ilkla Moor/Lincolnshire Poacher* for 5RTR; and *Waltzing Matilda*, the unofficial march of 7RTR, chosen because of the Matilda tanks used by the 7th between 1940 and 1942.

TRADITIONS

Regimental Battle Honours Day is held on 20 November, the anniversary of the first day of the Battle of Cambrai in 1917. It was at Cambrai the Mark IV tank was first used against the Germans en masse. The employment of the tank was instrumental in bringing the 1914–18 war to an end.

The ash plant stick carried by officers of the regiment today was first used in the First World War for testing the ground to take the weight of tanks.

A 105mm light gun, *c.* 1978.

THE ROYAL REGIMENT OF ARTILLERY

Under the Stuarts the army was supported by the Board of Ordnance, whose practice it was to hire civilians with their own teams to pull its guns in times of war. After the Jacobite Rebellion of 1715, when the service broke down en route to the campaign in Scotland, the board recommended the formation of two regular companies of soldier gunners, which proved to be the basis of a regiment formed in 1722.

Space at the Arsenal barracks became inadequate for the growing regiment however, and extensive new buildings were erected on high ground above Woolwich town towards the end of the eighteenth century, to include a magnificent officers' mess, the first of its kind in the army.

The concept of fast-moving 'horse gunners', complete with their own teams and drivers, was realised in 1793 to improve the mobility of the arm in battle. The Royal Horse Artillery, regarded, then as now, as a *Corps d'elite* within the RA, was soon to prove its worth on the battlefields of Europe, and became famous as 'The Galloping Gunners'.

The regiment expanded throughout the Victorian era and reached a peak in the First World War. In the Second World War a quarter of all serving soldiers were gunners, and today the army's largest regiment provides 80 per cent of its firepower. Each of the Royal Artillery's fifteen regiments specialises in one of its sophisticated weapons: the self-propelled gun, the light gun, rocket launchers and air defence missiles. One regiment is responsible for unmanned air vehicles and another for surveillance and target acquisition.

In 2006, after 300 years in Woolwich, the RA moved its headquarters and principal messes to Larkhill, home of the Royal School of Artillery on Salisbury Plain.

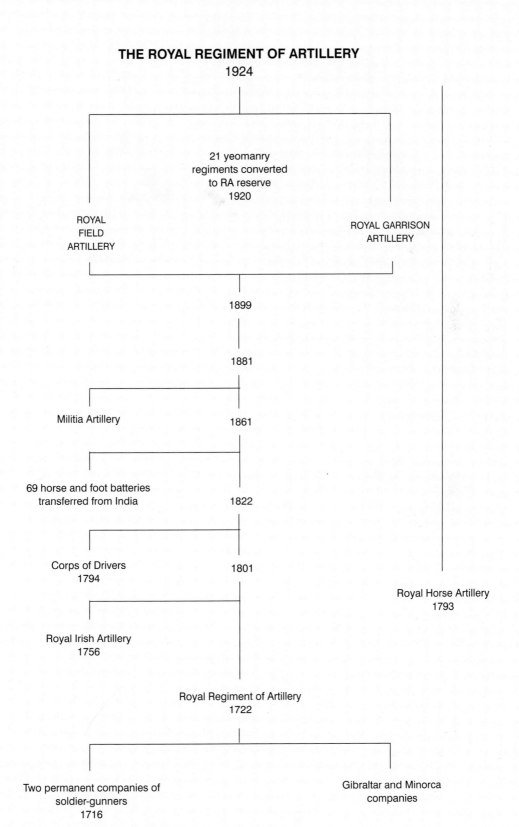

THE ROYAL REGIMENT OF ARTILLERY
1924

21 yeomanry
regiments converted
to RA reserve
1920

ROYAL
FIELD
ARTILLERY

ROYAL GARRISON
ARTILLERY

1899

1881

Militia Artillery

1861

69 horse and foot batteries
transferred from India

1822

Corps of Drivers
1794

1801

Royal Horse Artillery
1793

Royal Irish Artillery
1756

Royal Regiment of Artillery
1722

Two permanent companies of
soldier-gunners
1716

Gibraltar and Minorca
companies

RA captain in No. 1 dress. His cap lines mark him out as belonging to an RHA regiment.

DRESS DISTINCTIONS

The universal blue peaked cap bears the scarlet band of a royal regiment and the familiar gun badge. This 1902 design sites a cannon between two scrolls, the upper inscribed *Ubique* (Everywhere) and the lower scroll *Quo fas et gloria ducunt* (Whither right and glory lead). Cannons have been part of the regiment's insignia since the eighteenth century, originating with the three cannons on the shield of the Board of Ordnance. Senior NCOs wear the gun without motto scrolls as a sleeve badge. Trade badges are also worn on the sleeve.

The collar badge (a grenade with *Ubique* scroll), dates back to 1832 and, in the case of this regiment, represents an early mortar shell. NCOs and gunners of the Royal Horse Artillery wear its own badge on the collar – the sovereign's cypher within an oval Garter belt above a title scroll.

No. 1 dress 'blues' show the regimental broad scarlet stripe on the trousers. RHA personnel wear half-ball buttons and gold or yellow cap lines around the neck, relics of their old full dress. Only the ceremonial King's Troop now wear RHA full dress.

RA full dress, issued to the regimental band, displays the regimental busby (with its scarlet bag and frontal plume) and the blue tunic with scarlet facings. The fur busby, confirmed for RA full dress in 1928, was first used in the regiment between 1857 and 1878 to complement its grenade badge.

Stable belts are red with a blue band in the centre divided by a yellow stripe. RHA have a light blue belt with a yellow stripe in the middle.

MUSIC

The regimental quick march, *British Grenadiers*, relates to the grenade badge. It was authorised to the regiment in 1882 and was adapted a hundred years later to include Alford's *Voice of the Guns*. The RA slow march, adopted in 1836, is *The Duchess of Kent's March*. The regimental trot past is *The Keel Row*, the gallop past, *Bonnie Dundee*.

Guest nights in the officers' mess have been marked by Kipling's *Screw Guns* sung to *The Eton Boating Song*.

TRADITIONS

Royal Artillery Day (26 May) celebrates the formation of the first independent companies of 1716. The date of 11 November marks the birth of the Royal Horse Artillery in 1793.

Bandmaster and trombonist of the South Notts Hussars TA Band in 2001. The uniform evolved by 1880. The SNH was one of twenty-one yeomanry regiments converted to the RA in 1920. It was first moved to RHA in 1938.

St Barbara's Day is celebrated at Woolwich (and in some batteries and RA Association branches) on the Sunday closest to 4 December, with a church parade or old comrades' social. St Barbara, the patron saint of artillerymen everywhere, is said to have been avenged by a bolt of lightning, which is represented by a zigzag pattern on the regimental tie. She was invoked to grant safety in thunderstorms, and latterly the thunder of guns. The day is seen as an appropriate time to exchange greetings with artillery regiments of allied armies.

The prestigious spring and autumn dinners held at the main mess provide an opportunity to entertain guests. In the 1980s the autumn dinner was renamed Alamein Dinner in honour of the batteries which served in the desert victory of 1942. The regiment's annual Ceremony of Remembrance takes place at the Royal Artillery Memorial at Hyde Park Corner.

Individual battery anniversaries have adapted to recent amalgamations within the RA, but the better-known should be mentioned. At first light on 1 September, L (Nery) Battery would parade to fire a single round from a First World War gun in homage to Capt Bradbury, BSM Dorrell and Sgt Nelson, who bravely kept their gun firing when all others had been silenced at Nery, in the German offensive of 1914. Drivers' Day (5 May), celebrated by I Battery RHA, remembers the desperate gallop to save the guns at Fuentes d'Onor in 1811. Battle Axe Day was the province of 74 Battery, who held a parade on which the tallest gunner carried a French pioneer's axe taken in battle on the island of Martinique in 1809. Officers of O Battery ('The Rocket Troop') RHA made a special toast to the King of Sweden, Commander-in-Chief of the Allies at the Battle of Leipzig in 1813, where O Battery represented the British Army.

Hauling an 18-pounder field gun through the summer mud of Flanders, 1917. *(IWM)*

Joan Wanklyn's painting of RA trains in the Low Countries, 1740. *(RA Institute)*

Around the time of the formation of the regiment the head of the Artillery held the rank of captain general, a title later replaced by colonel-in-chief. In 1951 King George VI wished to revert to the old rank and it was duly reinstated for this appointment, which is traditionally held by the reigning monarch. In the officers' mess the loyal toast is made to 'The Queen, our Captain General'.

The Master Gunner, St James's Park, head of the RA in all regimental matters, is the channel of communication between the regiment and the captain general. This appointment was instituted in 1678 as Master Gunner of Whitehall and St James's Park, responsible for the artillery defence of the palaces of Whitehall and Westminster. The Director Royal Artillery is the professional head of the regiment. At the other end of

the scale the rank of bombardier (for corporal) was sanctioned in 1920 and gunner (in place of private) in 1933.

Colours are not carried in the RA, but its guns and guided weapons are accorded the same compliments as standards and guidons in the cavalry, and colours in the infantry.

Since 1880 the Royal Horse Artillery has been synonymous with royal gun salutes in Hyde Park. After the Second World War the King wished for the old ceremonials to continue and the RHA Riding Troop was formed. It moved to the old cavalry barracks at St John's Wood, was supplied with RHA full dress uniform and trained in the traditional duties of the saluting battery. In 1947 the King visited the barracks and altered its title to read King's Troop, a troop that went on to thrill the public with daring

A gun team of the King's Troop RHA behind the scenes at a show in the 1990s. Gunners are seen in three orders of dress.

displays of horsemanship. Over the years the troop has been gradually integrated with high-profile duties normally associated with the Guards, and on the Queen's Birthday Parade it proudly takes its rightful place of honour (when on parade with its guns) before the Household Cavalry.

THE CORPS OF ROYAL ENGINEERS

In 1716 a corps of engineer officers was detached from the Board of Ordnance to oversee civilian tradesmen in the building of military works. The first permanent body of military tradesmen was formed on Gibraltar in 1772, though the Governor thought their reliability questionable and made a request for skilled men from the line regiments to replace them. These soldier-tradesmen proved themselves in the great siege of 1779–83 and led to the formation of the blue-coated Royal Military Artificers in 1787, the same year in which their officers were honoured as the Corps of Royal Engineers (CRE).

After years of siege operations in the Peninsular War the artificers were renamed the Royal Sappers and Miners to reflect their work in digging saps (trenches) and tunnels. The Rock of Gibraltar is a labyrinth of caves and tunnels dug out for defensive measures through the centuries.

Musicians of the RE Band waiting to go onto a bandstand, *c.* 1990.

In 1856 the Royal Sappers and Miners were joined with their Royal Engineers officers in the CRE as one corps and a depot was established at Chatham. It now numbers around 9000 'sappers' in ten regular regiments (including an Explosive Ordnance Regiment and a parachute squadron), nine TA regiments, two training regiments and a Topographic Survey Squadron.

DRESS DISTINCTIONS

The blue peaked cap is distinguished by scarlet piping around the crown and the top of the band. The cap badge is the sovereign's cypher within a crowned Garter and laurel wreath. Like the gunners of the Royal Artillery, sappers wear on the collar a grenade badge with *Ubique* scroll, conferred in 1832 to show that they serve all over the world. Sergeants wear the grenade alone as a sleeve badge in addition to the various trade badges.

The corps stable belt is dark red with two blue stripes.

RE full dress is issued to musicians. It combines a busby (with a white plume out of a grenade socket on the left and a blue bag on the right), scarlet tunic (blue facings and yellow piping) and blue overalls with the broad scarlet stripe adopted in 1832. Busbies were first embraced after the 1856 amalgamation, a right that came with the grenade badge.

MUSIC

In 1870 the German folk melody, *Path across the Hills*, and the march, *Wings*, composed by 'Dolores' (Ellen Dickinson, the daughter of an artillery brigadier) were arranged by Bandmaster Newstead as the corps march. *British Grenadiers* was substituted by order of

THE CORPS OF ROYAL ENGINEERS

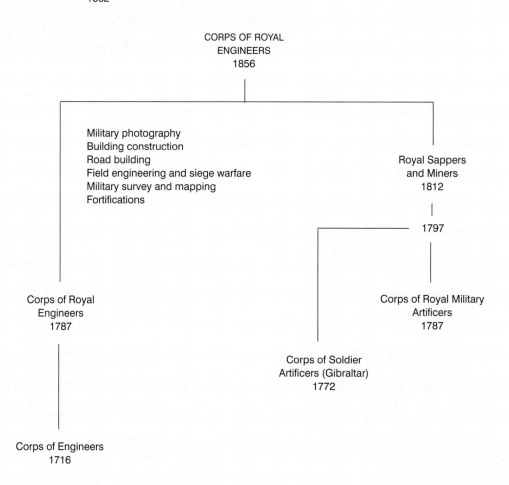

Airfield construction
Assault and armoured engineers
Parachute squadrons
Water supply engineers
Mine clearance
Tunnelling
Electrical and mechanical engineering
Aviation (Royal Flying Corps formed in 1912)
Searchlight operation
Bridge building
Railway construction and operation
Post and telegraph services
Transportation
Military ballooning
Submarine mining and diving

Hon. East India
Company engineers
absorbed into CRE ——————— 1862

CORPS OF ROYAL
ENGINEERS
1856

Military photography
Building construction
Road building
Field engineering and siege warfare
Military survey and mapping
Fortifications

Royal Sappers
and Miners
1812

1797

Corps of Royal
Engineers
1787

Corps of Royal Military
Artificers
1787

Corps of Soldier
Artificers (Gibraltar)
1772

Corps of Engineers
1716

A sapper directing one of the Corps of Royal Engineers' versatile tractors. *(MoD)*

the Duke of Cambridge as being more correct for a grenade-badged corps but Lord Kitchener intervened to restore *Wings* in 1902. *British Grenadiers* is now recognised as the second corps march.

Members of the RE mess would be familiar with the singing of 'Hurrah for the CRE', the song of the sappers in South Africa. The rank of sapper in the RE equates with private in other corps.

TRADITIONS

RE responsibilities developed over the years to give engineering support to keep the army moving (armoured vehicles for breaching obstacles, earth moving, road building, bridging and mine detection); counter-mobility (impeding enemy movement with obstacles, minefields and demolition); defence (building, water supply, concealment and deception) and airfield construction and repair.

Officers new to the RE had to be 'gauged' through a heavy drinks cabinet as an initiation to the mess. Aspirant subalterns would be stripped of scarlet mess jacket, waistcoat and spurs, fed between the shelves of the 'gauge' and beaten with rolled newspapers until ejected back to their fellow subalterns.

THE ROYAL CORPS OF SIGNALS

The Corps of Signals was formed in 1920 out of the Royal Engineers' Signal Service, which had evolved over sixty-six years from cable telegraph, through Morse, flag and lamp signalling to heliographs, telephone, wireless and even pigeon post. It was the

Signaller with radio equipment installed in the back of a Land Rover.

Duke of Wellington who first organised a system of dispatch riders during the Peninsular War. The Morse code and electric telegraph, invented in 1837, were used in the Crimea and perfected in the colonial wars that followed. During the First World War the RE Signal Service grew to 70,000 men, so necessary had the science of signalling become to modern warfare.

In the defence cuts of the 1990s the corps was reduced to ten signal regiments, an electronic warfare regiment and five independent signal squadrons, some 8,000 personnel in all. The Satellite Communications Regiment and the Tactical Communications Regiments employ a large range of equipment to provide essential information to commanders in the field and operations centres around the globe via voice, data and IT systems.

Corps headquarters were located at Catterick until 1967, when they were moved to the School of Signals at Blandford Forum in Dorset, the headquarters of the Telegraph Troop in 1872.

DRESS DISTINCTIONS

The blue peaked cap is worn with the corps badge, the figure of Mercury (the winged messenger) holding a *caduceus*, poised on a globe, with the corps motto *Certa cito* (Swift and sure) below, and a crown above. Mercury was the brainchild of Maj Beresford of the Telegraph Battalion RE in 1884.

Yeomanry regiments transferred to the corps in 1920 as its TA element were allowed to keep their own badges and some other items of uniform.

No. 1 dress 'blues' are plain except for the broad scarlet RE stripe on the trousers and the black belt worn by the Signals with this order of dress.

In combat/barrack dress signallers may be identified by their age-old sleeve flash, which is diagonally divided white/blue, and the corps stable belt, which is banded light blue and green with a blue dividing stripe to represent communications over sky, land and sea respectively.

The corps band is issued with full dress, which is RE pattern, except that the busby has a scarlet bag and plume, the scarlet tunic a simple cuff design, and spurs are worn. Dress spurs testify to the cavalry origins of the corps and the mounted sections that operated in the field with cable carts before mechanisation in the 1930s.

MUSIC

The corps quick march, adopted in 1926, is an arrangement of the old folk tunes *Begone Dull Care* and *Are You Not from Newcastle?* The slow march *HRH The Princess Royal* was adopted in 1936 in honour of Princess Mary, Colonel-in-Chief of the RCS until her death in 1965.

The famous White Helmets motorcycle display team demonstrating the skills of Royal Signals' dispatch riders, developed over a century of service. *(MoD)*

TRADITIONS

After the formation of the corps in 1920 its private soldiers were given the rank of signaller. Their trades evolved from mounted linesmen and drivers, and motorcycle dispatch riders, to radio operators, systems/installation technicians, area systems operators, specialist electronic warfare operators and electricians. The Yeoman of Signals plans and supervises the deployed communications structure.

TA squadrons are rich in the customs of the volunteer regiments converted to signals units at various times during the twentieth century. Elements of 37 Signal Regiment adhere to their own version of the loyal toast.

THE GRENADIER GUARDS

The first companies of the regiment were formed at Bruges in 1656 from loyal supporters of Charles II in exile. When he came to the throne in 1660 Charles commissioned a new regiment for his personal protection at home and in 1664 he brought the two together in a body soon to become the 1st Regiment of Foote Guards.

In 1815 the 1st Guards were instrumental in defeating Napoleon's Guards at Waterloo, and

Grenadier Guards, 1952; the officer's black armband was worn for the late King. Note the regimental white plumes.

were honoured by the Prince Regent in the same year as the 1st or Grenadier Regiment of Foot Guards to mark their repulse of the *Grenadiers de la Garde* in the battle.

DRESS DISTINCTIONS

The Guards' blue cap has a scarlet band and the grenade badge adopted with the Grenadier title in 1815. In the same year all members of the regiment were issued with a bearskin cap fitted with a white side plume, another sign of the Grenadier (since 1768) and the start of the bearskin custom in the Guards. The white plume is said to represent the puff of white smoke that used to come out of early grenades when primed.

The royal cypher, adopted with the Garter belt when Queen Victoria was crowned in 1838, appeared on pouches, belt plates and officers' pagris before it replaced the grenade on shoulder straps in 1920. It takes the form of the reigning monarch's initials (VR, GR or ER), reversed and interlaced. A royal cypher of this kind has appeared on the buttons of Grenadier Guards' uniforms since 1855.

MUSIC

The march, *Scipio*, was presented to the 1st Guards by Handel prior to its first performance in 1726, eighty years before the adoption of a second slow march, *The Duke of York*, who was the Colonel-in-Chief of the regiment at the time.

The quick marches, *British Grenadiers* and *The Grenadiers' March*, long played for Grenadier companies of the army, were adopted with the change of title in 1815.

The regimental band was first formed in 1665.

TRADITIONS

Waterloo Day (18 June) has been celebrated every year since 1816, principally because of the battle's importance to the regiment's identity. It was a custom of the Grenadier Guards to march 'at attention' when passing the Duke of Wellington's house at Hyde Park Corner.

Inkerman Day (5 November) was commemorated in the 3rd Battalion to

A GG drummer in the role of stretcher-bearer at the Queen's Birthday Parade in 2005. Drummers of the Foot Guards still wear the elaborate royal pattern lace (white with blue fleur-de-lys) of the eighteenth century.

honour 'The Sandbags', the 100 Grenadiers who won the imagination of the army with their dogged defence of the Sandbag Battery at Inkerman in 1854.

The senior company of the regiment has the extra duty of being the sovereign's own guard, an honour instituted by Charles II. It requisitions the tallest guardsmen for the Guards of Honour at coronations, state occasions and funerals. The company commander has always been known as *Captain of the King's* (or *Queen's*) *Company* irrespective of his true rank. A special standard carried in the presence of the monarch is regarded as a personal gift and is buried with the sovereign, a tradition begun in 1910.

THE COLDSTREAM GUARDS

The Coldstream was formed in 1650 as Monck's Regiment, with companies drawn from Heselrigge's at Newcastle and Fenwick's at Berwick.

In 1660 George Monck marched his regiment from the Scottish border town of Coldstream to London in order to restore law and order that had suffered after the death of Cromwell. Londoners knew them by their town of origin – 'The Coldstreamers'. Early in 1661 the regiment was paraded on Tower Hill and formally disbanded as a parliamentarian

Coldstream in guard order, 1912. Note the regimental spacing of the tunic buttons and the lance sergeant's regimental cap.

2nd or Coldstream Guards re-enactment society in the dress of the 1770s, when the regiment served in the American War of Independence.

regiment, but promptly re-engaged in the service of Charles II as the Lord General's Regiment of Foote Guards, though it continued for many years after purged of royalists. Even today it is the only one of the seven Guards regiments whose colonel has no royal title. After the death of Monck in 1670 the regiment's nickname was invoked and they were officially given as the 2nd or Coldstream Regiment of Foote Guards.

Armed with the knowledge that the 1st Foot Guards had actually been raised after them, the Coldstream never really accepted their 2nd Guards status, and in 1783 a group of officers formed the *Nulli Secundus* Club to highlight the fact that they were 'second to none'. By 1817 the 2nd Guards title was dropped and the terms Coldstream, Coldstreamers, 'Coleys' (but never 'Coldstreams'), were used thereafter.

DRESS DISTINCTIONS

The Guards' blue peaked cap has been regimentalised with a white band and welt since the 1860s. Its badge is the Star of the Order of the Garter, bestowed on the regiment by William III in 1696. The officers' 'cap star' is in the old elongated form with the cross of St George in red.

Buttons are worn in pairs in this regiment to conform with the Foot Guards' code of seniority first displayed on the red coat around 1770, when the Coldstream was still listed as the 2nd Guards.

Full dress is Foot Guards' pattern, the bearskin with a scarlet plume on the right side to contrast with those of the Grenadiers. A Tudor rose emblem, first worn on the bearskin adopted in 1832, was later transferred to shoulder straps on the scarlet tunic. The senior NCOs' colour badge, worn on the right sleeve, shows the elongated star and the sphinx campaign honour.

MUSIC

The quick march *Milanollo*, authorised to the Coldstream in 1882, is named after two violinist sisters who toured Europe in the 1840s. The slow march, *Figaro*, was adopted in 1805 from Mozart's opera of the same name.

The Band of the Coldstream Guards dates from about 1770.

TRADITIONS

Coldstream customs stem from early service. St George's Day celebrates the Garter Star badge with its cross of St George; recruiting is done in the areas through which Monck's Regiment marched on their way to London in 1660 – the north-east and the Midlands, and in Brigade Order it is said the Coldstream preferred not to parade second to the Grenadier Guards but opted for the other places of honour, left of the line or rear on the march.

THE SCOTS GUARDS

A 'Scotch Regiment of foote Guards' was raised on a commission of Charles I in 1642, but after the defeat of his son at the Battle of Worcester in 1651, it was dispersed by Cromwell and not rebuilt again for another nine years.

The first companies of Scotch Guards, raised in 1660 to guard the castles at Edinburgh and Dumbarton, were accepted onto the English establishment by James II in 1686, subordinate to the 1st and 2nd Guards. In spite of efforts made by Queen Anne to get the Scots' long history recognised in the hierarchy of the Foot

Guards they were finally placed as the 3rd Guards in 1713, the 'kiddies' of the brigade.

In 1831 bearskins were issued and the regiment was forced to adopt the title Scots Fusilier Guards as a reason to wear them, but in 1877 the name was simplified to the Scots Guards (SG).

DRESS DISTINCTIONS

The Guards' blue peaked cap is distinguished with a red, white and blue diced band and a red welt around the crown. Officers have a gold welt. The cap badge is the Star of the Order of the Thistle.

Full dress is Foot Guards' pattern, the bearskin with no plume, originally a statement on the regiment's standing in the Foot Guards (junior of the three and therefore centre of the line, not a flank regiment like the other two). The scarlet tunic has a white thistle collar badge and buttons set in groups of three, in accordance with the Foot Guards seniority custom. The senior NCOs' colour badge depicts the star badge and the sphinx awarded to the regiment in 1802 for its part in the Egyptian campaign of the previous year.

SG pipers were issued with the feathered Highland bonnet in 1928 to level them up to the bearskins of the regiment. Otherwise

SG lieutenant (with cased colour) and the escorts to the colour at Waterloo for the 150th anniversary of the battle. Guards cap peaks were less severe in 1965.

Pipers and drummers of the Scots Guards at Wellington Barracks, *c.* 1992.

their dress has not changed since Queen Victoria's day: a blue doublet with castellated wings, a kilt and plaid of Royal Stuart tartan, white hair sporran with three long black tails, and hose of red and green marl.

MUSIC

Regimental marches are the familiar *Highland Laddie*, which dates back to the seventeenth century, and *The Garb of Old Gaul* (1770) in slow time:

In the Garb of Old Gaul, with the fire of Old Rome,
From the heath-covered mountains of Scotia we come . . .

Musicians employed by the regiment in the early eighteenth century were replaced by a full band about 1816.

TRADITIONS

The principal day of celebration, St Andrew's (30 November), is celebrated in traditional manner wherever the regiment is stationed, with the piping in of the haggis. In the officers' mess the Picquet Officer leads the way in to dinner and there acts as mess president.

THE IRISH GUARDS

The regiment was created in 1900 on the wishes of Queen Victoria to mark the bravery of her Irish soldiers in the Boer War. It was known then as 'Bob's Own' after their colonel, Lord Roberts.

DRESS DISTINCTIONS

The Guards' blue cap, regimentally enhanced by a green band and welt, is badged with the Star of the Order of St Patrick.

Full dress is Foot Guards' pattern, the bearskin with a plume of St Patrick's blue on its right side, the scarlet tunic with a white shamrock collar badge. Buttons are stamped with a harp and crown, and worn in groups of four.

Pipers are dressed in traditional Irish green caubeen (with the blue hackle), green doublet, saffron kilt and green socks.

MUSIC

The regimental quick march is the popular *St Patrick's Day*, the slow march *Let Erin Remember*. Other airs of Irish extraction, some from the disbanded Irish regiments, are now played as company marches.

Irish Guardsmen in 2000: lance sergeant drummer (standing, left), colour sergeant (centre) and pipe major (standing, right). *(Grenadier Publishing)*

TRADITIONS

On St Patrick's Day (17 March) shamrock is distributed to all members of the regiment, a custom requested by Queen Victoria to commemorate its service in the South African war. The presentation ceremony was instituted by Queen Alexandra in 1901 and continued after her death in 1925 by Princess Mary. Queen Elizabeth The Queen Mother presented the shamrock every year from 1968 until her death in 2003.

'The Micks' have paraded an Irish wolfhound mascot since 1902. The dogs are traditionally named after ancient Irish chieftains.

THE WELSH GUARDS

The regiment was formed by royal warrant in 1915, with 'Taffs' hurriedly drawn from other units to enable it to parade on St David's Day. The early nickname 'The Foreign Legion' was inspired by these Welshmen with their various cap badges.

DRESS DISTINCTIONS

The Guards' blue cap has a black figured braid band and leek badge.

Full dress is Foot Guards' pattern, the bearskin with a white/green/white plume on the left side, the scarlet tunic with a white leek collar badge. The Welsh Guards rank fifth in the Foot Guards and wear their buttons grouped in fives to show this. On the buttons are a crown and leek encompassed by a scroll inscribed *Cymru Am Byth* (Wales for ever). The senior NCOs' colour badge (right sleeve) has the Welsh dragon and motto.

MUSIC

The regimental quick march, *The Rising of the Lark*, is an arrangement of an eighteenth-century Welsh song, probably from the pen of the harpist David Owen. *Men of Harlech* and *Men of Glamorgan* are played in slow time.

TRADITIONS

On St David's Day (1 March) leeks are presented by a member of the royal family. In 1969 Princess Anne made her first solo engagement doing this.

The senior company of the regiment is called the Prince of Wales's Company and its old nickname 'The Jam Boys' tells of the austere time after the Second World War when it made an application for extra jam rations to compensate for the taller guardsmen in its ranks.

THE ROYAL REGIMENT OF SCOTLAND

This 'super regiment' was blueprinted in the 'Future Army Structures' of 2004 to accommodate the six famous-name Scottish infantry regiments. It was the most controversial of the planned mergers of that year and the motto *Nemo me impune lacessit* (Let no one provoke me with impunity), which was displayed by three of the condemned regiments, spoke for the mood of the Scottish people in 2004.

Highland regiments had been formed in times of war from 1689 but the Jacobite uprisings in the north of Scotland guaranteed that none achieved permanence until well into the next century. Foot regiments raised in the Lowlands and employed against the Jacobites were given a place in the army and stood among the senior regiments of infantry. The Royal

Men of the 7th (Service) Battalion Seaforth Highlanders returning from the front at the Somme, July 1916.

Scots were born in 1633 under a warrant of the Privy Council for service with the French Army, and on their return to Charles II gained seniority of the infantry. The Royal Scots Fusiliers came out of the troubles of 1678, when the Earl of Mar founded a regiment to police the lawless clans and the Presbyterian Covenanters, a sect persecuted by the Stuarts. When that dynasty came to an abrupt dip in 1688 the Covenanters found themselves on the right side of the law and readily pledged their martial arm, called the Cameronians, to the new King's cause to put down the Jacobites. A new regiment, quickly mustered in Edinburgh to help the King's forces in Scotland, later evolved to become the King's Own Scottish Borderers (KOSB).

Of the sixty-one Highland regiments raised between 1689 and 1803 only eleven secured a permanent position in the army. The first of these eleven was assembled at Aberfeldy in 1739 from independent companies of Highland watch that had been set up fourteen years before. It was known as the 'Black Watch' because of the dark government tartan worn by the lads of these companies. Other famous Highland regiments, the Seaforth, Gordon, Cameron and the Argyll and Sutherland, were enlisted later on in the century as a direct response to the colonial and French wars. The Highland Light Infantry, deprived of its Highland dress in 1809, was often categorised with the Lowlanders, and eventually merged with a Lowland regiment.

Bandsmen of the Royal Highland Fusiliers in No. 1 dress, *c.* 1988.

Historic regimental headquarters are located all over Scotland and the Borders:

Royal Scots (Royal Regiment)	Edinburgh
Royal Scots Fusiliers	Ayr
King's Own Scottish Borderers	Berwick-upon-Tweed
Cameronians (Scottish Rifles)	Lanark
Black Watch (Royal Highland Regiment)	Perth
Highland Light Infantry	Glasgow
Seaforth Highlanders	Fort George
Gordon Highlanders	Aberdeen
Queen's Own Cameron Highlanders	Inverness
Argyll and Sutherland Highlanders	Stirling

DRESS DISTINCTIONS

Scottish infantry uniforms have long been seen as the most distinctive and glamorous in the army. Highland regiments acquired the feathered bonnet, kilt and hose of their native north lands, though many of them lost the garb in 1809 for a want of Highland recruits. These last looked little different from their English counterparts until after the Crimean War, when a Highland 'doublet' with double Inverness flaps was issued to the Highland regiments. Full Highland attire was acquired by 1881, when the Lowland regiments were provided with doublet and trews. Regimental tartans went on to individualise the uniforms and the Royal Stuart tartan was permitted for

Member of the Napoleonic Association in the garb of the 42nd Royal Highland Regiment at a 'living history' show in the 1990s.

Black Watch sword dancers waiting to enter an arena at a showground in the 1990s.

pipers of the KOSB, Black Watch and Royal Scots as a mark of royal favour.

When full dress gave way to khaki service dress in 1914 the Scottish infantryman was recognisable by his soft headwear: the glengarry (introduced in 1840) and the flat balmoral bonnet (or tam-o'-shanter), which replaced the glengarry for the trenches in 1915. After the First World War glengarries and bonnets were interchangeable for most orders of dress.

Royal Regiment of Scotland (RRS) glengarries and tam-o'-shanters are worn with the large regimental badge on a square patch of Government tartan. The blue glengarry has the red, white and blue squared dicing that was worn by half of the antecedent

regiments. Tall black cocks' feathers, worn in the Royal Scots and the KOSB since 1902, are pinned onto the glengarry for ceremonials. The khaki tam-o'-shanters are distinguished by battalion hackles pinned behind the badge – Cameronians' black in the 1st, Royal Scots Fusiliers' white in the 2nd, Black Watch red in the 3rd, Camerons' blue in the 4th and green in the 5th. The green hackle is based on the Sutherland tartan of the A&S Highlanders. The short blue cut feather hackle was awarded to the Cameron Highlanders in 1940 to mark their stand in being the last to wear the kilt on active service. Companies of the 6th and 7th (TA) battalions wear the hackle of their local regular battalion.

The Royal Regiment of Scotland
2006

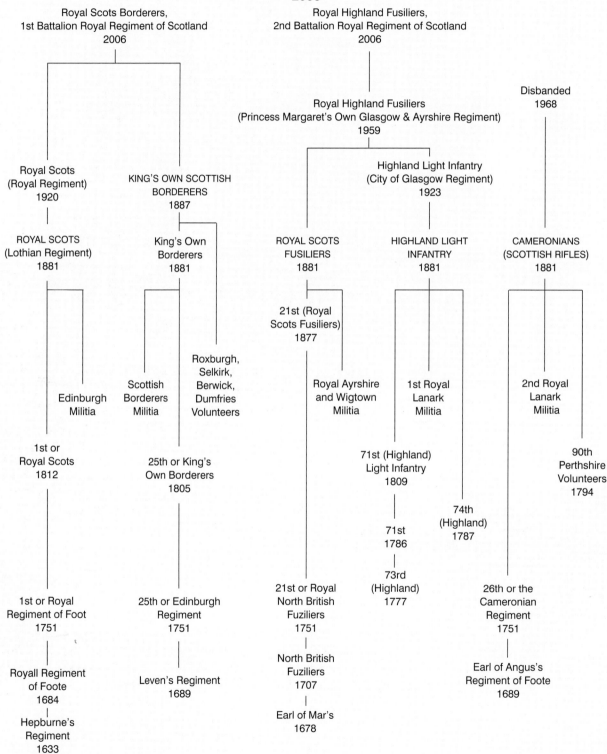

Royal Scots Borderers,
1st Battalion Royal Regiment of Scotland
2006

Royal Highland Fusiliers,
2nd Battalion Royal Regiment of Scotland
2006

Disbanded
1968

Royal Highland Fusiliers
(Princess Margaret's Own Glasgow & Ayrshire Regiment)
1959

Royal Scots
(Royal Regiment)
1920

KING'S OWN SCOTTISH
BORDERERS
1887

Highland Light Infantry
(City of Glasgow Regiment)
1923

ROYAL SCOTS
(Lothian Regiment)
1881

King's Own
Borderers
1881

ROYAL SCOTS
FUSILIERS
1881

HIGHLAND LIGHT
INFANTRY
1881

CAMERONIANS
(SCOTTISH RIFLES)
1881

21st (Royal
Scots Fusiliers)
1877

Roxburgh,
Selkirk,
Berwick,
Dumfries
Volunteers

Scottish
Borderers
Militia

Edinburgh
Militia

Royal Ayrshire
and Wigtown
Militia

1st Royal
Lanark
Militia

2nd Royal
Lanark
Militia

71st (Highland)
Light Infantry
1809

74th
(Highland)
1787

90th
Perthshire
Volunteers
1794

1st or
Royal Scots
1812

25th or King's
Own Borderers
1805

71st
1786

73rd
(Highland)
1777

21st or Royal
North British
Fuziliers
1751

26th or the
Cameronian
Regiment
1751

1st or Royal
Regiment of Foot
1751

25th or Edinburgh
Regiment
1751

North British
Fuziliers
1707

Royall Regiment
of Foote
1684

Leven's Regiment
1689

Earl of Mar's
1678

Earl of Angus's
Regiment of Foote
1689

Hepburne's
Regiment
1633

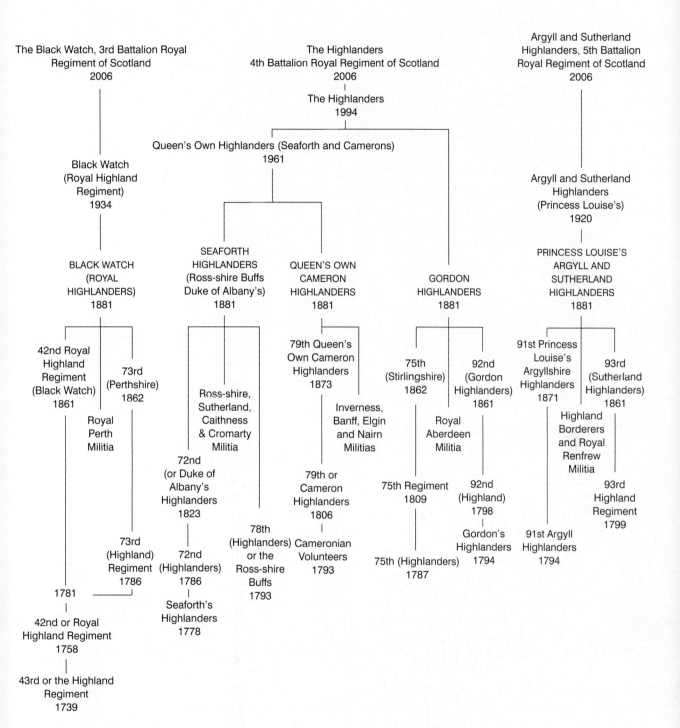

The Black Watch, 3rd Battalion Royal
Regiment of Scotland
2006

The Highlanders
4th Battalion Royal Regiment of Scotland
2006

Argyll and Sutherland
Highlanders, 5th Battalion
Royal Regiment of Scotland
2006

The Highlanders
1994

Queen's Own Highlanders (Seaforth and Camerons)
1961

Black Watch
(Royal Highland
Regiment)
1934

Argyll and Sutherland
Highlanders
(Princess Louise's)
1920

BLACK WATCH
(ROYAL
HIGHLANDERS)
1881

SEAFORTH
HIGHLANDERS
(Ross-shire Buffs
Duke of Albany's)
1881

QUEEN'S OWN
CAMERON
HIGHLANDERS
1881

GORDON
HIGHLANDERS
1881

PRINCESS LOUISE'S
ARGYLL AND
SUTHERLAND
HIGHLANDERS
1881

42nd Royal
Highland
Regiment
(Black Watch)
1861

73rd
(Perthshire)
1862

Royal
Perth
Militia

Ross-shire,
Sutherland,
Caithness
& Cromarty
Militia

79th Queen's
Own Cameron
Highlanders
1873

Inverness,
Banff, Elgin
and Nairn
Militias

75th
(Stirlingshire)
1862

92nd
(Gordon
Highlanders)
1861

Royal
Aberdeen
Militia

91st Princess
Louise's
Argyllshire
Highlanders
1871

93rd
(Sutherland
Highlanders)
1861

Highland
Borderers
and Royal
Renfrew
Militia

72nd
(or Duke of
Albany's
Highlanders
1823

79th or
Cameron
Highlanders
1806

75th Regiment
1809

92nd
(Highland)
1798

93rd
Highland
Regiment
1799

73rd
(Highland)
Regiment
1786

72nd
(Highlanders)
1786

78th
(Highlanders)
or the
Ross-shire
Buffs
1793

Cameronian
Volunteers
1793

75th (Highlanders)
1787

Gordon's
Highlanders
1794

91st Argyll
Highlanders
1794

1781

Seaforth's
Highlanders
1778

42nd or Royal
Highland Regiment
1758

43rd or the Highland
Regiment
1739

Pipers of the Queen's Own Highlanders, *c.* 1988. Their dress was based on that worn by pipers of the Cameron Highlanders.

The regimental badge combines the heraldic Scottish lion rampant, the Cross of St Andrew and the Scottish crown with the motto of the royal Scottish regiments. Another motto, the Seaforths' *Cuidich n' Righ* (Help to the King) – a reference to feudal times and Alexander III – is earmarked to accompany the thistle emblem as the regiment's collar badge. The old regimental badges are borne by the pipers and the corps of drums.

The Archer green doublet, developed in the latter half of the twentieth century for Scottish No. 1 dress, and blue patrols for senior ranks are retained. The scarlet mess jacket has royal blue facings. In shirt sleeve order officers and senior NCOs wear the light grey shirts of the Royal Highland Fusiliers and Argylls.

All orders of dress (except Combats) may be worn with the kilt or trews, which are of Government tartan – the sombre sett first worn and made famous by the Black Watch. Other regiments built on the tartan by adding colourful lines to create regimental

tartans. Pipers still wear the 'music tartans' of their regiments – Royal Stuart in the 1st and 3rd battalions, red Erskine (RSF) in the 2nd and Cameron Erracht in the 4th.

The kilt is worn with a white goat's hair sporran with twin black tassels by officers, senior NCOs and pipers, and a brown leather purse by other ranks. Hose is red and black, as worn in the Black Watch and Gordon Highlanders, and the white spats are fastened with black buttons, a custom of the Gordons that honours the death of Sir John Moore at Corunna in 1809.

MUSIC

The most popular traditional marches among Scottish regiments are *Highland Laddie*, played in quick time, and *In the Garb of Old Gaul*, the slow march of a few regiments but none more fittingly than the Royal Scots, whose first forty years of existence were spent in the service of France. Their quick march, *Dumbarton's Drums*, is reckoned to be the army's oldest, having been recorded in the 1667 diary of Samuel Pepys: 'After meeting with the corps in Rochester, here in the streets I did hear the Scotch March by the drums before the soldiers, which is very odde.' In the presence of royalty, Donizetti's *Daughter of the Regiment* is played in memory of Queen Victoria, whose father was colonel of the 1st Regiment of Foot when she was born. *Princess Mary's March* may be played on the pipes after the loyal toast in the mess, a traditional tribute to the Colonel-in-Chief of the Royal Scots from 1918 to 1965.

The regimental quick march of the Royal Highland Fusiliers is a combination of the Royal Scots Fusiliers' *British Grenadiers* and the Highland Light Infantry's cheeky *Whistle o'er the Lave'ot* (Whistle over the bits you leave out). The hymn, *Abide with Me*, was always played after last post on Sundays in the RSF.

The quick march, *All the Blue Bonnets Are over the Border* was chosen by the Black Watch, the original wearers of the headgear in the eighteenth century, and the

Borderers. It was immortalised for the KOSB in 1915 after Piper Laidlaw recklessly played the tune on the parapet of his trench in order to encourage his battalion through a gas attack at Loos. Their slow march included *The Standard on the Braes of Mar*. The pipes and drums of the Black Watch traditionally play *My Home* and *Highland Cradle Song*; they used to play a *Crimean Long Reveille* on the 15th of every month.

The Highlanders march to the *Pibroch o' Donuil Dhu*, as played in both the Camerons and the Seaforths, and *The Cock o' the North* from the Gordons. Like Piper Laidlaw at Loos, the Highlanders have two examples of a similar devotion to duty. Piper Findlater of the Gordon Highlanders, shot through both ankles in the battle for Dargai (1896), continued to play his comrades on up the heights with lively pibrochs. At Waterloo Piper McKay of the 79th Cameron Highlanders left the comparative safety of his battalion square to march around its perimeter with *Cogadh no Sith* (Peace or War).

Musicians of the Lowland Band (formed in 1994) deploying to the Gulf in support of 33 Field Hospital Regiment. *(MoD)*

Minden Day in the King's Own Scottish Borderers, 1970s. A private of the Royal Army Pay Corps assists in the presentation of red roses for the glengarries.

Bandmaster Ricketts of the 2nd Argyll and Sutherland Highlanders composed *The Thin Red Line* in 1908, inspired by the famous nickname of his battalion earned in the Crimean War. It was given official status in 1960, displacing *The Campbells Are Coming* as the regimental quick march, around the time that *The Skye Boat Song* was arranged as a slow march for the pipes and drums. The custom of playing *Rule Britannia* in the Argyll and Sutherland Highlanders' mess is attributed to a nineteenth-century shipwreck that involved a wing of the regiment.

The Cameronians had *Within a Mile of Edinburgh Toun* (1st Battalion) and *The Gathering of the Grahams* (2nd Battalion). Thomas Graham founded the 90th Perthshire Volunteers after French Revolutionaries had desecrated the body of his dead wife.

TRADITIONS

Formation Day (28 March) marks not only the birth of the RRS in 2006, but also that of Scotland's oldest regiment the Royal Scots, raised as Hepburne's Regiment in 1633. Sir John Hepburne, an officer of Scottish mercenaries appointed colonel in the service

of Louis XIV, is regarded as the father of the regiment. This antecedence is a point of pride; the nickname 'Pontius Pilate's Bodyguard' is said to derive from an argument with a French regiment over the question of seniority. The French claimed descent from soldiers who had stood watch over the tomb of Christ, but the Scots retorted that they would not have succumbed to sleep if they had been on that watch.

KOSB customs are remembered on three days of the year. Minden Day (1 August) sees the distribution of red roses for the glengarries in the tradition of 'Minden regiments' that gathered roses from the fields in the 1759 battle. St Andrew's Day (30 November) is celebrated with officers and sergeants competing in a light-hearted tournament that culminates with Atholl brose drunk from a quaich. Burns' Night (25 January) is marked with a sergeants' mess supper, which has a special significance for the KOSB since the poet once joined one of their antecedent regiments, the Dumfries Volunteers.

The Royal Highland Fusiliers' Assaye/ Inkerman Day commemorates battle anniversaries of the HLI and the RSF respectively. At the Battle of Assaye in 1803 the 74th (Highland) Regiment won Wellesley's admiration and an honorary colour. Colours were presented to both the 74th and the 78th regiments by the Indian government in recognition of their outstanding conduct in the battle. The prized Assaye colour used to be trooped by a quartermaster in the 2nd Battalion HLI on Assaye Day in memory of Quartermaster Grant, the senior survivor of the 74th, who led the remnant from the field. It was replaced by the City of Glasgow in 1931 and the original, which was damaged by fire in 1918, was laid up. A 1936 replacement modelled on the original has an elephant on a white field emblazoned with ASSAYE, LXXIV and SERINGAPATAM. The buff honorary colour of the 78th was replaced by the 2nd Seaforth Highlanders in 1899, but eventually laid up in Fort George. The Queen's Own Highlanders kept 23 September as Assaye Day to mark the honour. Inkerman Day (5 November) honoured the part played by the 21st Fusiliers in this Crimean battle of 1854. On a foggy day remembered for its see-saw actions of confused skirmishing, the 21st fought a static position at a stone breastwork called the Barrier. In spite of several Russian attempts to force the position the 21st doggedly held on and provided an anchor for soldiers separated from their companies.

Officers and soldiers of the 72nd High-landers, originally drawn from the same clan, messed together on special days, such as St Andrew's and Hogmanay. The Seaforth Highlanders celebrated the New Year by booting out the oldest-serving soldier at midnight and welcoming in the youngest.

Red Hackle Day (4 June) celebrates the time in 1795 when the 42nd Royal Highlanders made a halt at Royston on their way home from Flanders to mark the King's birthday. On the parade each man was given a red feather plume for his bonnet in recognition of gallantry in recent campaigns. The plume was ratified by an army order of 1822 and has been a proud distinction of the Black Watch ever since.

The famous painting of *The Thin Red Line* of 93rd (Sutherland) Highlanders repulsing Russian cavalry at Balaklava in 1854.

Band of the Queen's Regiment, *c.* 1990, now part of The Princess of Wales's Royal Regiment.

Balaklava Day (25 October) commemorates the 'thin red line' of the 93rd (Sutherland) Highlanders, who stood between the Crimean port of Balaklava and a horde of 3,000 Russian cavalry in 1854. It was William Russell of *The Times* who coined the sobriquet for the battalion – a strand of hope in a seemingly hopeless situation. The 93rd faced the overwhelming odds with Sir Colin Campbell's exhortation that 'each man must die where he stands', but as the cavalry lumbered over the plain the Highlanders sent a disciplined volley into its midst and halted the assault.

Regimental pet mascots were popular from the reign of George III, with some Highland regiments adopting a stag. Today the Argylls' Shetland pony is the only example in the regiment. Its name *Cruachan* came from the old war cry of the Clan Campbell; Duncan Campbell of Lochnell was the first colonel of the 91st High-landers. The first Shetland pony was presented to the 1st Argylls in 1929 by Princess Louise, Duchess of Argyll.

Cameronians Day (12 May) com-memorates the regiment that began life in the religious sect known as the Covenanters and joined the army of William III on condition that it would be allowed to keep chaplains of its own persuasion. On 12 May (Founders' Day) a conventicle would be held in the open and picquets posted around the service to symbolise life under the Stuarts, when the Covenanters were persecuted. Rifles were always carried on church parades when suitable racks were available and the march to and from church would be made in silence. Drinking the loyal toast was against the Presbyterian code, so Cameronian officers devised a method of passing a glass round the table without pausing to drink from it.

THE PRINCESS OF WALES'S ROYAL REGIMENT

The Princess of Wales's Royal Regiment (PWRR) was formed in 1992 by the merger of the Queen's Regiment (the 1966 host to the four regiments of the Home Counties Brigade) and the Royal Hampshire Regiment. The PWRR title was inspired by Diana, Princess of Wales, Colonel-in-Chief of the Royal Hampshires from 1985 and of the PWRR until her untimely death in 1997. By coincidence the old Queen's Regiment (1661–1959) went under the same PWRR title between 1715 and 1727.

The old Queen's and the Buffs (so called from their flesh-coloured facings) date back to the reign of Charles II, making the PWRR the senior English regiment in the infantry. The

Diana, Princess of Wales, with the Royal Hampshires. The different cap badges are regimental officers' pattern (front row), other ranks (centre) and Army Physical Training Corps (right).

PWRR private in No. 2 dress, 1995. Bronzed buttons are a regimental custom inherited from officers of the Royal Hampshire Regiment. The bronzed badge is pinned to a black/yellow/black patch, the colours of the Hampshires now used on the PWRR stable belt too. (Grenadier Publishing)

old Queen's were raised for the garrison of Tangier, part of Catherine of Braganza's dowry to Charles II in 1661; the Buffs, who claimed descent from the London trained bands that went to fight for the Dutch in 1572, were accepted by Charles when Holland repatriated mercenaries loyal to England as the two countries came to war in 1665.

Headquarters are at Howe Barracks in Canterbury, the old depot of the Buffs.

DRESS DISTINCTIONS

The blue peaked cap has the scarlet band of a royal regiment and the badge of the 1966 Queen's Regiment modified to accept the Hampshire rose. It has four parts: the Prince of Wales's crest, conferred on the 77th Regiment in 1810 (an appropriate ingredient for the PWRR); the Garter belt confirmed to

The Princess of Wales's Royal Regiment
1992

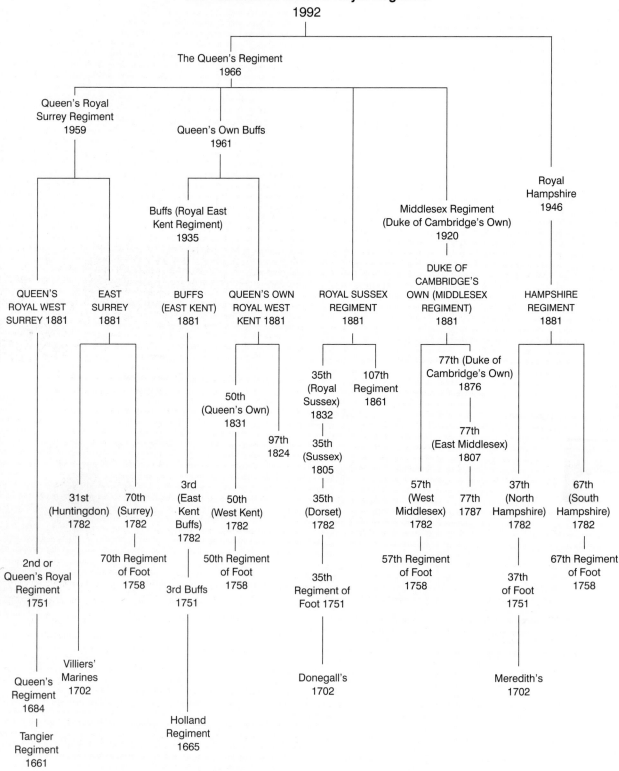

The Queen's Regiment
1966

Queen's Royal
Surrey Regiment
1959

Queen's Own Buffs
1961

Royal
Hampshire
1946

Buffs (Royal East
Kent Regiment)
1935

Middlesex Regiment
(Duke of Cambridge's Own)
1920

DUKE OF
CAMBRIDGE'S
OWN (MIDDLESEX
REGIMENT)
1881

QUEEN'S
ROYAL WEST
SURREY 1881

EAST
SURREY
1881

BUFFS
(EAST KENT)
1881

QUEEN'S OWN
ROYAL WEST
KENT 1881

ROYAL SUSSEX
REGIMENT
1881

HAMPSHIRE
REGIMENT
1881

77th (Duke of
Cambridge's Own)
1876

35th
(Royal
Sussex)
1832

107th
Regiment
1861

50th
(Queen's Own)
1831

77th
(East Middlesex)
1807

97th
1824

35th
(Sussex)
1805

57th
(West
Middlesex)
1782

77th
1787

37th
(North
Hampshire)
1782

67th
(South
Hampshire)
1782

31st
(Huntingdon)
1782

70th
(Surrey)
1782

3rd
(East
Kent
Buffs)
1782

50th
(West Kent)
1782

35th
(Dorset)
1782

70th Regiment
of Foot
1758

50th Regiment
of Foot
1758

57th Regiment
of Foot
1758

67th Regiment
of Foot
1758

2nd or
Queen's Royal
Regiment
1751

3rd Buffs
1751

35th
Regiment of
Foot 1751

37th
of Foot
1751

Queen's
Regiment
1684

Villiers'
Marines
1702

Donegall's
1702

Meredith's
1702

Tangier
Regiment
1661

Holland
Regiment
1665

the 35th (Royal Sussex) in 1879 through its connection with the 4th Duke of Richmond KG; a dragon from the arms of the City of London and Elizabeth I, conferred on the Buffs by Queen Anne as a symbol of their antecedence in that place and time; and the Tudor rose of the Hampshire Militia, conferred on the trained bands of Hampshire by Henry V to mark the support given him at Agincourt in 1415, which was adopted by the Hampshire Regiment.

The collar badge, designed for the Queen's Regiment in 1967, embodies the Garter Star (backed by an upright plume) of the Royal Sussex Regiment with the rearing Horse of Kent at its centre. The Roussillon plume represents hat plumes of the French Roussillon Regiment taken by Otway's Regiment (the 35th) as a symbol of victory at the Battle of Quebec in 1759. The White Horse of Kent, with its motto *Invicta* (Unconquered), is the county emblem once worn by the Kent Militia and adopted by the Queen's Own Royal West Kent Regiment for its cap badge.

Buttons of the regiment, which also date from 1967, are impressed with the lamb and star badge of the Queen's Royal Surreys. The paschal lamb is a religious symbol probably adopted by the Old Tangier Regiment in its fight against the Moors of north Africa. The ironic nickname 'Kirke's Lambs' got attached to the regiment after its bloody handling of Monmouth's supporters in 1685. When the regiment became the 2nd of Foot, the lamb was displayed with one or other of the mottoes conferred on the Queen's after their heroic defence of Tongres in 1703: *Pristinoe virtutis memor* (Mindful of former glory) and *Vel exuviae triumphant* (Even the remnant triumph).

Dress jackets and tunics are distinguished by a black square patch on the upper left sleeve bearing a royal tiger in gold. The tiger, which formed part of the badge of the Hampshire Regiment from 1881, was awarded to the 67th in 1826 with the word

The Buffs' 1st Volunteer Battalion camp, *c.* 1904, green rifles uniform (centre) and khaki service dress (outer). *(Military Historical Society)*

'India' for twenty-one years of service in that country between 1805 and 1826. In this period the battalion marched from 'Bengal to Bombay subduing riots, investing fortresses, fighting in hills and jungle, and endured monsoons and disease'.

MUSIC

The regimental quick march, *The Farmer's Boy/Soldiers of the Queen*, brings together two popular Victorian songs, neither of which had been officially adopted by an army regiment before 1966, when the new Queen's Regiment took the music hall ballad, *Soldiers of the Queen*, as its jaunty quick march. *The Farmer's Boy*, a favourite among Wessex regiments, was often played unofficially in the Hampshires, like in the 4th Battalion's *Trooping the Swede* ceremony to honour 'The

Seventeenth-century re-enactment group in the dress of the 1680s, when the Old Tangier Regiment returned to London and their new title, Queen's.

Swedebashers' who flocked to the colours in 1914 but never returned. The march was officially adopted by the PWRR on formation.

The regimental slow march, *Minden Rose*, refers to the rose traditionally worn on Minden Day and was written in 1990.

Former regimental marches played on appropriate occasions are *Braganza*, *Scipio* and *We'll Gang Nae Mair to Yon Toun* (West Surreys); *The Buffs* and *Men of Kent* (Queen's Own Buffs); *A Southerly Wind and a Cloudy Sky*, *A Life on the Ocean Wave*, *Lass o' Gowrie* and *Lord Charles Montague's Huntingdonshire March* (East Surreys); *Royal Sussex*, *Roussillon*, *Lass of Richmond Hill* and *Sussex by the Sea* (Royal Sussex Regiment); *The Hampshire* (formerly *The Highland Piper*), *A Hundred Pipers* and *Bonnets of Blue* (West Kents); and *Sir Manley Power*, *Paddy's Resource* and *The Caledonian* (Middlesex).

The march *Old Queen's* was banned from being played in public by Queen Victoria because of its distorted version of the national anthem, and was confined to the

officers' mess of the West Surreys thereafter. In the officers' mess of the Buffs it was the custom for the Danish national anthem to be played as a toast was made to 'The King of Denmark'. The connection between the regiment and the Danish royal family began in 1689 when it was made Prince George of Denmark's Regiment of Foot. King Frederick IX of Denmark became Colonel-in-Chief of the Buffs in 1947, as had King Christian X in 1912 and Frederick VIII in 1906. Many Danes fought in the ranks of the Buffs during the Second World War.

TRADITIONS

Albuhera Day (16 May) commemorates the bravery of the 3rd, 31st and 57th regiments in the Peninsular battle of 1811. The Buffs and the Middlesex Regiment observed the anniversary with a service of remembrance for the appalling losses sustained in the battle. Lt Latham of the Buffs was left for dead after defending his King's Colour but lived to achieve fame as a hero both in and out of his regiment. The Middlesex always ended the day with their Die Hard Ceremony, at which a toast was made to the 'Immortal Memory' of the 'Die-hard' 57th, severely mauled in a deadly firefight with the French. Their nickname came from the dying exhortation of Col Inglis to 'Die hard, 57th, die hard!'

Minden Day (1 August) celebrates the infantry victory over the French cavalry in Germany 1759. Before the taking of Villers Bocage on Minden Day in 1944 the Hampshires stopped to pick roses from a field to wear on their steel helmets in the tradition started by the 37th at Minden.

The Glorious First of June celebrates the great naval victory off the coast of Ireland in 1794, in which detachments of the 2nd or Queen's Royal Regiment were aboard five ships of Lord Howe's fleet. The 1st Battalion's mess mallet was made from timbers off the *Queen Charlotte*. A naval crown awarded to the Queen's Royal West Surreys for its part in the battle was shown on regimental buttons and now flies on the PWRR regimental colour.

Salerno Day (9 September), formerly observed by the West Surreys in respect of their TA battalions landing on Sicily in 1943, is perpetuated to include the brigade of Hampshire battalions also present. This date was chosen for the formation of the PWRR.

The East Surreys observed 23 April as Ypres Day, in memory of their 1st and 2nd Battalions on the Western Front in 1915, and 27 June as Dettingen Day, notable for the passing of the Dettingen Cup around the mess table. On 10 February (Sobraon Day) the 1st Battalion colours would be handed over to the care of the sergeants in memory of Sgt McCabe of the 31st and the gallantry he displayed at the Battle of Sobraon – the final defeat of the Sikh army on the banks of the Sutlej in 1846. Officers dining in the mess were required to take their salt from a special cellar with a concealed fragment of the regimental colour carried by the 31st at Sobraon. When salt was taken the fragment was revealed and the officer reminded of his responsibilities, a custom perpetuated by the Queen's Regiment from 1966. In the 2nd Battalion a toast to 'The British Battalion' was made in honour of the composite unit made up of the remnants of the 1st Leicesters and the 2nd East Surreys in Malaya in 1941.

The Die Hard Company, an award-winning display team that depicts the Middlesex Regiment in the 1880s.

The Royal Sussex observed Quebec Day (13 September) in memory of Otway's Regiment in Wolfe's last victory. The Royal Hampshires' connection with Gen Wolfe began in 1758, when he became colonel of the 67th. Although he spent most of the year on campaign in Canada, Wolfe found time to visit his regiment twice at its camp near Salisbury before returning to Canada for the last time. Their membership of the Wolfe Society has been inherited by the PWRR.

The Hampshires kept Gallipoli Day (25 April) to commemorate the landings at Helles and Suvla Bay from the HMT *River Clyde* by the 2nd Battalion in 1915. The 1st Battalion gained the reputation of 'stonewallers' during the war for their tenacity in trench warfare.

The West Kents kept Corunna Day (16 January) in memory of Charles Napier and Charles Stanhope, who together led the 50th in clearing the village of Elvina during the Battle of Corunna in 1809. It became a part of the officers' mess ritual on this day to make a toast to 'The Corunna Majors', neither of whom managed to escape from Spain with the army. Sevastopol Day (8 September) was observed to mark the services of the 50th and 97th Regiments in the Crimean siege of 1855.

The East Surreys were raised as a regiment of marines and cultivated an affiliation with the Royal Marines, adopting their march in 1942. The 50th Regiment served with the fleet in 1778 and took up the custom of piping in to dinner where *Rule Britannia* would be played, a tradition continued in the West Kents.

In the 1st Royal Sussex the loyal toast was taken seated (naval fashion) and responded to by each officer in turn, a custom perpetuated after the amalgamation of 1966, which went back to the regiment's earliest days in northern Ireland, when Donegall's men spent long periods shut up on ships. In 1702 officers of Donegall's Regiment were ordered to repeat the toast individually so that each man's allegiance to the crown could be tested. When Queen Juliana of the Netherlands was appointed Colonel-in-Chief of the Royal Sussex in 1953, she allowed the mess to toast her health seated, in accordance with regimental custom. The Freedom of the City of Belfast was conferred on the Sussex in 1961. Officers of the 2nd Battalion, without the benefit of this history, would stand for the loyal toast in the normal manner.

A large sea-green colour kept permanently in the protection of the officers' mess was handed down from the Queen's Royal West Surreys. The Queen's carried a colour with the cypher of Catherine of Braganza in the belief that it was a gift from the Queen, but it was extra to the regulation pair of colours after 1750 and was ordered not to be carried in the ranks again. Colours of this regiment have always carried the Queen's cypher.

THE DUKE OF LANCASTER'S REGIMENT

The Duke of Lancaster's Regiment (DLR) title was created in 2006 for the unification of three infantry regiments of north-west England.

The King's Own Royal Border Regiment (KORBR) was formed in 1959 by the union of the King's Own, which was raised for the ailing garrison of Tangier in 1680, and the Border Regiment, whose title was created in 1881 for the merger of the 34th (Cumberland) Regiment and the 55th (Westmorland). KORBR headquarters in Carlisle Castle was the home of the Border Regiment, and the 34th Regiment since 1703.

The King's Regiment, formed in 1958, brought together the city regiments of Liverpool and Manchester. In the Cardwell Reforms of the 1870s certain regiments

The Duke of Lancaster's Regiment (King's, Lancashire and Border)
2006

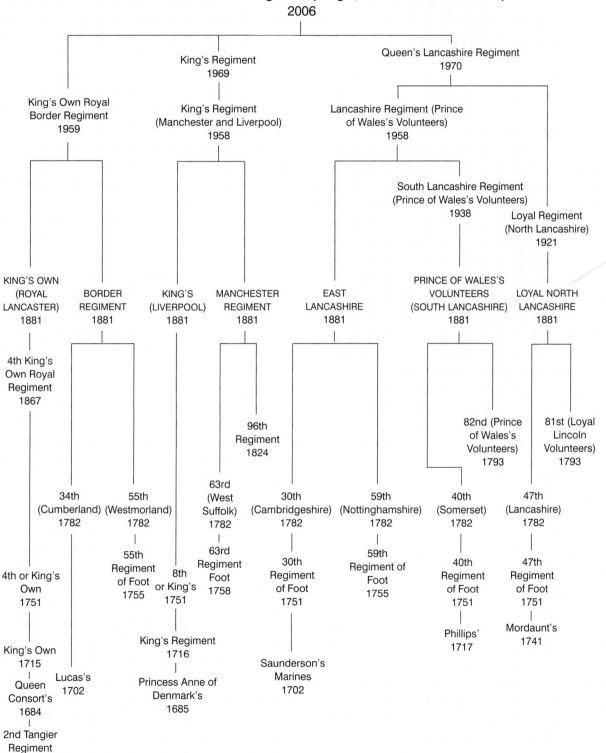

King's Regiment
1969

Queen's Lancashire Regiment
1970

King's Own Royal
Border Regiment
1959

King's Regiment
(Manchester and Liverpool)
1958

Lancashire Regiment (Prince
of Wales's Volunteers)
1958

South Lancashire Regiment
(Prince of Wales's Volunteers)
1938

Loyal Regiment
(North Lancashire)
1921

KING'S OWN
(ROYAL
LANCASTER)
1881

BORDER
REGIMENT
1881

KING'S
(LIVERPOOL)
1881

MANCHESTER
REGIMENT
1881

EAST
LANCASHIRE
1881

PRINCE OF WALES'S
VOLUNTEERS
(SOUTH LANCASHIRE)
1881

LOYAL NORTH
LANCASHIRE
1881

4th King's
Own Royal
Regiment
1867

96th
Regiment
1824

82nd (Prince
of Wales's
Volunteers)
1793

81st (Loyal
Lincoln
Volunteers)
1793

63rd
(West
Suffolk)
1782

34th
(Cumberland)
1782

55th
(Westmorland)
1782

30th
(Cambridgeshire)
1782

59th
(Nottinghamshire)
1782

40th
(Somerset)
1782

47th
(Lancashire)
1782

55th
Regiment
of Foot
1755

63rd
Regiment
Foot
1758

30th
Regiment
of Foot
1751

59th
Regiment of
Foot
1755

40th
Regiment
of Foot
1751

47th
Regiment
of Foot
1751

4th or King's
Own
1751

8th
or King's
1751

Phillips'
1717

Mordaunt's
1741

King's Own
1715

Lucas's
1702

King's Regiment
1716

Saunderson's
Marines
1702

Queen
Consort's
1684

Princess Anne of
Denmark's
1685

2nd Tangier
Regiment
1680

A subaltern of the King's Regiment dressed for public duties in London, 1994. His green colour belt shows the regiment's fleur-de-lys badge, the arms of the City of Manchester and the arms of the City of Liverpool (lower). *(Grenadier Publishing)*

Loyal Regiment (North Lancashires) and the product of the 1958 merger of the East and South Lancashire Regiments: simply named the Lancashire Regiment. The Queen's title is not traditional in any of these regiments; it was inspired by the Colonel-in-Chief of the regiment, and of the Loyals since 1953, HM Queen Elizabeth II. QLR headquarters and regimental museum at Fulwood Barracks in Preston was the location of the regimental depot of the Loyals from 1873.

DRESS DISTINCTIONS

The blue peaked cap with scarlet band was common to all three regiments. The DLR cap badge combines the red rose and crown of the QLR with the wreath of the KORBR and the motto of the King's Regiment. The Lancaster rose was worn in one form or another by most Lancashire regiments through their 1881 links with the Royal Lancashire Militia. The laurel wreath was awarded to the 34th Regiment after the disastrous Battle of Fontenoy in 1745 to mark its gallantry in saving the army with a disciplined rearguard action. It distinguished badges and buttons of the 34th (Cumberland) until 1881, and badges of the Border Regiment after that date. The motto *Nec aspera terrent* (Nor shall difficulties deter us) came from the Hanover badge conferred on the King's Regiment in 1716 in recognition of its loyalty during the recent Jacobite Rebellion and its heavy losses at Dunblane. When worn on the khaki beret the DLR badge is pinned to a red diamond-shape patch formerly worn by the KORBR. The QLR badge (except officers) was worn on a primrose yellow diamond, the facing colour of the old 30th taken up again by the 1st East Lancashires during the First World War with a yellow diamond helmet flash.

The Lion of England collar badge came from the uniforms of the KORBR, and originally the King's Own Lancasters. It was bestowed on the Queen's (later the King's

were located to the industrial north to draw recruits from the growing populations of the mill towns. Of those sent to Lancashire the 8th King's (raised in Derbyshire in 1685 and honoured as the Princess Anne of Denmark's) became the mainstay of the Liverpool Regiment, and the 63rd and 96th the Manchester Regiment.

The Queen's Lancashire Regiment (QLR) represents the three former county regiments of Lancashire, basically the East, South and the North Lancashires. It was formed in 1970 by the amalgamation of the

The band and drums of the King's Own Royal Border Regiment on Arroyo Day, with five members dressed as drummers of the 34th (Cumberland) Regiment of 1811.

Own) by William III for the regiment's support when he landed at Torbay for the throne of England. The lion appeared on the regimental colour in 1751, on belt plates from 1774, officers' caps from 1834, collars from 1874 and on other ranks' caps from 1896.

DLR buttons are graced with the badge of the King's Regiment – a fleur-de-lys with a rearing horse on its centre. The fleur-de-lys was adopted by the 63rd Regiment after taking the French West Indian island of Guadaloupe in 1759. By wearing this French emblem, the shape of which closely resembled a mosquito indigenous to the Caribbean, the 63rd proudly became known as 'The Bloodsuckers'. The Manchesters used the badge to replace their Arms of the City of Manchester in 1923, not least because the latter had been unflatteringly likened to a tram conductor's badge. The Horse of Hanover, which stands on the fleur-de-lys today, was part of the Hanover emblem allowed to the King's in 1716. Men of the

King's Liverpool wore the horse prancing on a scroll labelled 'The Kings' in old English script.

The glider badge worn at the top of the right sleeve was awarded to the Border Regiment and the South Staffords in 1950 for their air landing at the invasion of Sicily in 1943. It was the army's first major assault by gliders, remembered for the many that fell into the sea and the soldiers who drowned.

Regimental badges that will appear on the regimental colour in addition to the above are the sphinx and the China dragon. The sphinx on a tablet inscribed EGYPT was granted to the 8th, 30th, 40th and the Queen's Germans for their part in the 1801 campaign to drive Napoleon from Egypt. The Queen's Germans were ranked as the 96th Regiment before disbanding in 1818. A new 96th, formed at Salford Barracks in 1824, was allowed to bear the honours of the former 96th in 1874 and took their sphinx as its collar badge, a distinction passed on to the Manchester Regiment in 1881. The East and South Lancashire Regiments had the sphinx incorporated into their cap badges. The dragon with CHINA superscribed, a campaign honour awarded to the 55th Regiment for its part in the Opium War of 1841, was shown on buttons in the KORBR. The smaller buttons of the officers' caps and mess waistcoats were embossed with the Bath Star to commemorate the fact that the first three colonels of the 34th held rank in the Order of the Bath.

Stable belts and lanyards are maroon as in the QLR.

The Corps of Drums of the three regiments currently parade in infantry full dress with differences. The King's drummers are the most conventionally dressed, their scarlet tunics with the deep green facings of the 63rd returned to the Manchesters in 1937. Queen's drummers have blue facings and inverted sleeve

chevrons not seen on infantry drummers since the Crimean War, an idiosyncrasy of the 1958 Lancashire Regiment. KORBR drummers are the most conspicuous in full dress because of the white marine helmets issued to the regimental band and drums in 1970 to highlight an episode in the history of the regiment. The King's Own served as marines in the Mediterranean between 1703 and 1710, and the 34th served with the fleet on a few occasions between 1708 and 1740.

MUSIC
L'Attaque/The Red Rose, the QLR quick march, is made up of the East Lancashires' quick march *L'Attaque* (learned from the French by the 30th in the Crimea) and *Red, Red Rose*, adopted by the Loyals in 1885 to complement the Lancashire rose in their badge.

Long Live Elizabeth, the QLR slow march, from Edward German's *Merrie England*, was adopted on the formation of the regiment

Drummers of the Queen's Lancashires in 2000, their scarlet tunics archaically distinguished by sleeve chevrons. *(Grenadier Publishing)*

Roger Fenton's photograph of men from the 30th Regiment in the Crimea. It shows (from the left) a private of a battalion company, a sergeant of the Light Company, a captain in undress and a sergeant major. *(National Army Museum)*

in 1970 to honour its Colonel-in-Chief, Elizabeth II.

John Peel/Corn Riggs, the KORBR quick march, combines the famous Cumbrian hunting song *D'ye Ken John Peel* (as adapted for the Border Regiment) and *Corn Riggs Are Bonny*, a Scottish air from the time of the formation of the King's Own in 1680. The march opens with a few bars of the *34eme Regiment March*, a parody of the French regiment captured in the Peninsular War by the 34th (Cumberland) Regiment.

Trelawney, the KORBR slow march (ex-King's Own), tells of the sad fate of Bishop Trelawney, brother of the regiment's colonel in 1685, who was imprisoned on the orders of James II for upholding the Protestant faith in the face of the King's Roman Catholic policies. A similar incident occurred in the Princess Anne of Denmark's Regiment, where six captains were brought to trial for refusing to accept Catholics into their companies.

The Kingsman, the regimental march of the King's, contains the Liverpools' *Here's to*

a Maiden of Bashful Fifteen (from incidental music composed by Thomas Linley in 1777) and *The Manchester*, an adaptation of the popular Neapolitan songs *La Luisella* and *Fenesta Vascia*. The rank of kingsman in the King's (and now the DLR) and volunteer in the Prince of Wales's Volunteers, both introduced around the time of the Second World War, are rare examples in the infantry of alternative forms of the rank of private.

Lord Ferrers' March, the King's regimental slow march, combines the Liverpools' *English Rose* with an arrangement from the opera *Merrie England* and *Farewell Manchester*, which was based on Felton's *Gavotte*, a piece written for harpsichord in 1728. Lord Ferrers of Chartley was given command of the King's Regiment when it was first raised, in 1685.

The King's Are Coming Up the Hill, the regimental song of the King's Regiment, dates from 1958.

God Bless the Prince of Wales, the march of the South Lancashire Regiment, is played at the end of band programmes in the QLR mess in

The last survivors of the 1st Manchesters at Caesar's Camp during the siege of Ladysmith in 1900. *(Trustees of the King's Regiment Collection)*

the tradition of the 1st East Lancashires, whose custom it was to have the march played on guest nights after 1871, when the Prince of Wales had suffered an illness.

Somerset Poacher, a traditional English air used by the 40th (2nd Somersetshire) Regiment, and the 1st South Lancashires after 1881, is played on Waterloo Day when the battalion has formed a battle square.

Lancashire Witches was adopted by the 2nd South Lancashire Regiment. It became the regimental slow march in 1931.

Lancashire Lad, an old folk tune played in the 59th, was given its Lancashire title when the 59th became 2nd Battalion of the East Lancashire Regiment in 1881. *The Lancashire Lad* was the name given to the QLR's regimental journal.

Lincolnshire Poacher was adopted by the 81st Regiment in 1820, when it carried a Lincoln title.

Mountain Rose was adopted by the 47th Regiment and played long after 1885, when the march was officially superseded by *The Red Rose*. The regiment also marched to *Quebec* and *The 47th*.

Zakhmi Dil is an old Pathan tune collected by the 2nd Liverpools on the India/Afghanistan border, probably after the First World War. It was the custom for this 'Wounded Heart' to be played on guest nights in the mess in memory of days on the North-West Frontier.

Rawtenstall Annual Fair is a bawdy traditional county song and QLR march.

The Young May Moon, a traditional air and march of the Manchester Regiment, is played in quick and slow time.

The Border Regiment Slow March, adopted in 1950 but never published, unites the *Chinese Airs*, arranged by Maj Geary when the 1st and 2nd Battalions were at Shanghai in 1927, with *The Horn of the Hunter* and *Soldier Will You Marry Me?* When playing in the officers' mess the band of the Border Regiment would always render the regiment's Spanish and Chinese airs with *Rule Britannia*. The KORBR further honoured its marine history by including *A Life on the Ocean Wave* in its repertoire.

The Prince was written for the Prince of Wales's Volunteers at the time of the 1930 Tidworth Tattoo.

TRADITIONS

Regimental days vary in importance and observance, and are therefore listed by date order.

Kimberley Day (15 February), marked by the Loyals' Regimental Association in Preston every year, commemorates the battle honour 'Defence of Kimberley', which took place in 1899. The townspeople expressed their gratitude with great silver centrepieces for both the officers' and the sergeants' messes.

Ladysmith Day (27 February) celebrates the relief of the long siege in 1900.

In Warrington the South Lancashire Regiment Association relive their 1st Battalion's sweep of the Boer trenches at the bayonet, and in the King's a sergeants' mess ball celebrates the end of the trials of the Manchester and Liverpool battalions that were caught up in the siege. Ladysmith is the principal day of the King's, as it was the Manchesters.

Italy Day (16 March) remembers the 2nd Liverpools and 9th Manchesters in the Italian campaign of 1944.

Francilly-Selency Day (2 April) commemorates the 2nd Manchesters' capture of a battery of German 77mm guns in 1917.

Ahmed Khel Day (19 April) is the 2nd East Lancashires' commemoration of its fierce battle of 1880 in the Second Afghan War.

St George's Day (23 April), celebrated in the KORBR by the wearing of a red rose in the cap, was first observed by the King's Own in 1908 to mark its connection with Lancaster.

Burma Day (15 May) remembers the Chindits of the Liverpool and the Manchester regiments in their hot battles with the Japanese around the Kohima Ridge in 1944.

Guadaloupe Day (10 June), the Manchesters' celebration of the capture of the island in 1759, was perpetuated with a corporals' mess dinner in the King's Regiment.

Hooge Day (16 June) was kept by the 4th Battalion South Lancashire Regiment to commemorate the battle of 1915.

Waterloo Day (18 June) is observed in the way of the South Lancashire Regiment, now to honour the services of the 30th and 40th Regiments in the great victory of 1815. A wreath of laurel leaves is fixed to the top of the colours and the companies on parade are ordered to form a hollow square, as their forebears did on the field of battle to repel Napoleon's cavalry charges. The junior subaltern then reads out the Waterloo Citation, after which laurel leaves are given out for the cap.

Somme Day (1 July) is remembered in Liverpool and by the East Lancashire Regiment Association in a church service

The 47th Regiment re-enactment group in the uniform worn at the Battle of Bunker Hill in 1775.

The QLR laurel leaf worn on Waterloo Day.
(Grenadier Publishing)

for the huge losses sustained on the first day of the great battle in 1916.

Maida Day (4 July) is the annual celebration of the 81st (and the 2nd Loyal North Lancashire Regiment) of the victory over Napoleon's army in southern Italy in 1806. After the battle Lt-Col Kempt dined on tortoise, the shell of which was later mounted in silver as a snuffbox and presented to the officers' mess.

Blenheim Day (13 August) is marked by the King's as the first on its list of battle honours. It commemorates the part played by the Queen's (later King's) Regiment in Marlborough's epic victory of 1704.

Quebec Day (13 September) is the QLR trooping the colour parade, during which the band plays *The 47th Regiment Slow March*

and *Quebec* in quick time in honour of the regiment called 'Wolfe's Own'. Membership of the Wolfe Society comes by right of the 40th Regiment (at Louisburg in 1758), the 47th Regiment (at Quebec in 1759) and the 4th or King's Own, in which James Wolfe served his captaincy in 1744.

Delhi Day (14 September) commemorates the struggle to storm Delhi and its defences in the Indian Mutiny of 1857. The King's lost fifty men before reaching the first breach.

Arroyo Day (28 October), celebrated by the KORBR in the manner made famous by the Border Regiment, features a parade on which drummers troop captured French drums to *La Marseillaise* in the yellow jackets of the 34th Regiment drummers circa 1811. In this battle of the Peninsular War the 34th overran its opposite number in the French Army and marked the coup by wearing the French soldiers' red and white pom-poms in their own shakos. In 1845, however, Queen Victoria ordered the regiment to conform to dress regulations and substituted the loss of distinction with the battle honour 'Arroyo dos Molinos'.

Inkerman Day (5 November) is observed in the tradition of the Manchester Regiment. The colours are marched to the guardroom for the day and returned without officers in memory of the officers of the 63rd who were killed in battle on this day in 1854.

Maharajpore Day (29 December), the battle anniversary of the 40th Regiment, marked its engagement with the Marathas in the Gwalior campaign of 1843.

On Tarifa Day (31 December) the 1st Loyals used to hold a sergeants' mess ball in celebration of the 47th Regiment's repulse of a strong French assault on the small British garrison of this walled Spanish town in 1811.

Drums taken from the enemy in battle are regarded as legitimate trophies. Like the Arroyo drums of the KORBR, the 30th used to parade its Waterloo Drum and the 40th its Maharajpore Drum. The Magdala Drum of the King's Own, taken in the Abyssinian campaign of 1868 and split into three parts for the three regiments present, is now in the care of the 1st Battalion officers' mess.

Mess customs proliferate in the Lancashire and Border group. The loyal toast, traditionally taken seated in naval manner by the KORBR, is proposed with the sovereign's local title 'The Duke of Lancaster' added. This custom was initiated by King Edward VII after inspecting the 4th and 5th Battalions of the East Lancashire Regiment in 1909. It was restricted to toasts made within the county until Queen Elizabeth directed that it should be included on all occasions wherever Lancastrians are gathered.

Mess silver is placed according to custom: an equestrian statuette of Queen Elizabeth II, purchased by officers of the Loyal Regiment in 1958, is traditionally set before the commanding officer, who uses a silver goblet acquired by the 1st Loyals during their time in China in 1924–5. The President of the Mess Committee has a goblet decorated with hunting scenes and a silver fox (Loyal Regiment, 1928) placed before the junior subaltern. The Subaltern's Cup (47th Regiment), which stands before the senior subaltern, is a vehicle for a drinking ritual when promotion to captain takes effect. In the 1st Battalion officers' mess, Lt Maguire's beaker is placed in front of the commanding officer as a reminder of the brave actions of an officer of the 4th or King's Own in the Peninsular War.

The regiment's Black Pudding Club meets informally for lunch at Preston once a month to appreciate the North Country delicacy.

THE ROYAL REGIMENT OF FUSILIERS

The Royal Regiment of Fusiliers (RRF) was formed in 1968 by the amalgamation of the four English infantry regiments that achieved a fusilier title at various times in the three centuries of their existence.

The first was created as a regiment of 'fuzileers' in 1685, each man armed with a

1st Volunteer Battalion Lancashire Fusiliers at Conway, 1990. *(LF Regiment Museum)*

Fusiliers back in the trenches for the re-burial of Pte Henry Wilkinson of the 2nd Lancashire Fusiliers, killed on 10 November 1914. *(MoD)*

fuzil instead of a musket to guard the artillery ordnance stored in the Tower of London. Muskets of the time had a burning match and therefore could not be carried in the vicinity of gunpowder stores. The regiment was officially connected to the City of London in 1881 and gained the Freedom of the City in 1924.

The regiments that shared a common history in the force sent to fight for Holland in 1674, and subsequently returned to England with William of Orange in 1688, were assigned to more northerly areas in 1782: the 5th (Northumberland) was given the fusilier title in 1835 and the Royal Warwickshire (RWF) as late as 1963.

The 20th Regiment anticipated the fusilier title in 1813 when attached to the Fusilier Brigade on campaign and was accepted by it as 'The Young Fusiliers'. They became officially transformed as the Lancashire Fusiliers (LF) in 1881.

RRF headquarters and museum are in the Tower of London.

DRESS DISTINCTIONS

All ranks wear a beret with grenade badge and regimental hackle, a feature of fusilier regiments from 1946. Officers swapped caps for berets after amalgamation. The various grenade badges worn by the old fusilier regiments were adapted for the RRF, which took the Royal Fusiliers' grenade and replaced its Tudor Rose with St George and Dragon (Royal Northumberland Fusiliers (RNF)), enveloped by the Minden Wreath (LF). The red over white feather hackle comes from the RNF. It originated in the white plumes plucked from French hats by the 'Old Fifth' after the battle for St Lucia in 1778 and worn as a mark of victory until 1829, when white plumes became standard wear in the infantry. The 5th then changed to red and white

The drummer's colour with roses on St George's Day, 1990. *(Brian L. Davis)*

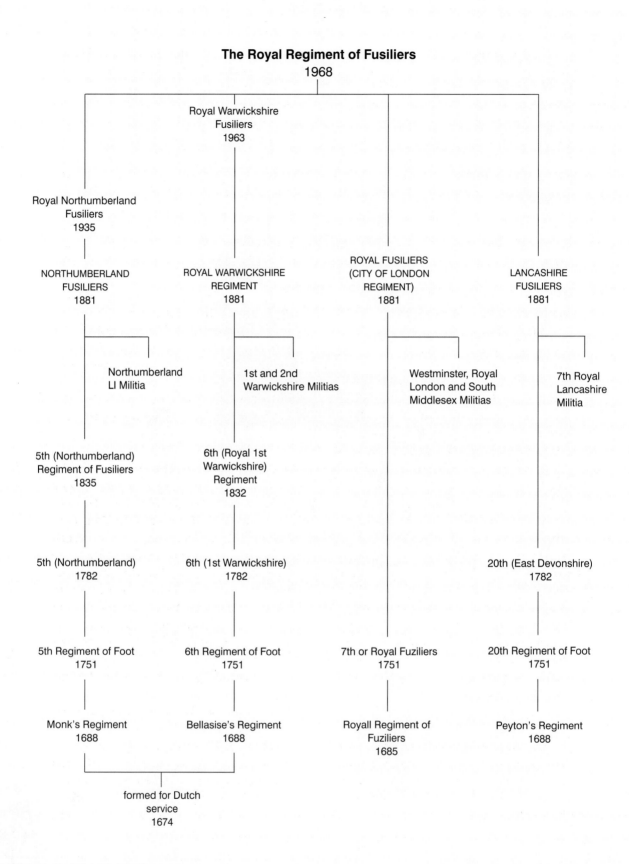

The Royal Regiment of Fusiliers
1968

Royal Warwickshire
Fusiliers
1963

Royal Northumberland
Fusiliers
1935

NORTHUMBERLAND
FUSILIERS
1881

ROYAL WARWICKSHIRE
REGIMENT
1881

ROYAL FUSILIERS
(CITY OF LONDON
REGIMENT)
1881

LANCASHIRE
FUSILIERS
1881

Northumberland
LI Militia

1st and 2nd
Warwickshire Militias

Westminster, Royal
London and South
Middlesex Militias

7th Royal
Lancashire
Militia

5th (Northumberland)
Regiment of Fusiliers
1835

6th (Royal 1st
Warwickshire)
Regiment
1832

5th (Northumberland)
1782

6th (1st Warwickshire)
1782

20th (East Devonshire)
1782

5th Regiment of Foot
1751

6th Regiment of Foot
1751

7th or Royal Fuziliers
1751

20th Regiment of Foot
1751

Monk's Regiment
1688

Bellasise's Regiment
1688

Royall Regiment of
Fuziliers
1685

Peyton's Regiment
1688

formed for Dutch
service
1674

plumes to conform to the colours of St George, and when raccoon-skin caps were ordered to fusilier regiments in 1868 only the 5th Northumberland Fusiliers were permitted to wear them with a plume attached.

In 1900 the Royal Fusiliers were allowed the use of their old white plume and the Lancashire Fusiliers a plume of yellow (former facing colour) to honour their losses at the Battle of Spion Kop. The Royal Warwicks adopted a blue over deep yellow hackle in 1963, yellow to represent the facings colour of the 6th Regiment before 1832 and blue for the facings after that year.

RRF buttons are graced with an antelope within a crowned Garter belt, a design previously found on uniforms of the Royal Warwickshire Regiment. The ancient badge of an antelope 'gorged with a ducal coronet and a rope flexed over its back' was first borne by the 6th Regiment, though the reason has yet to be established. The animal appeared among the royal badges of Henry VI, but it has also been attributed to an antelope found on a Moorish flag taken by the regiment in battle at Saragossa in 1710.

No. 1 dress 'blues' are defined by the beret and hackle, and a broad scarlet stripe on the trousers. This peculiarity of the Royal Fusiliers links the RRF with the dress of the Royal Artillery and thereby commemorates its origin as a guard for the train of artillery.

Musicians dedicated to the Northumbrian pipes, a custom of the Royal Northumberland Fusiliers, wear a black and white check 'Shepherd's tartan' over their uniform. Pipers are schooled in the ancient instrument by the TA battalion in Northumberland.

MUSIC

The regimental quick march, *British Grenadiers*, was ordered to all regiments badged with a grenade in 1835. The fusiliers' connection with the grenade badge came from their fur (grenadier) caps. Marches traditionally played after *British Grenadiers* are *Blaydon Races* (RNF), *Fighting with the 7th Royal Fusiliers* (a popular music-hall ballad used by the RF) and *Minden March*, an arrangement of the old hymn *Lammas Day* adopted by the LF in commemoration of the Battle of Minden, which was fought on Lammas Day in 1759. *Warwickshire Lads* was adapted from a song score written in 1769 for Shakespeare celebrations at Stratford.

The official RRF slow marches are *Rule Britannia* and *De Normandie*. The former ('Britannia rule the waves') was considered appropriate in the RNF and RF to recount seagoing expeditions of the 5th and the 7th Regiments in the eighteenth century. Other slow marches of the regiment are played when appropriate: *St George* in Northumberland, *MacBean's* (written by a lieutenant of that name in 1782) in Warwickshire and *The Lancashire Fusiliers' Slow March*, an adaptation of *The Minden Waltzes*.

TRADITIONS

The Colonel-in-Chief of the regiment, the Duke of Kent, upholds a tradition going back to 1789, when Prince Edward, later Duke of Kent, was appointed colonel of the 7th Royal Fusiliers. The regiment's privileged connections with the royal family were established by William IV, who sometimes dined with the 7th and bade its officers to dispense with the usual protocol that surrounds the drinking of the loyal toast.

The regimental mascot, an Indian blackbuck antelope, is kept in the care of two handlers and paraded at the head of the regiment. Wild antelopes of this variety were kept by the Royal Warwickshires from 1871, when the regiment first adopted one in India to complement its antelope badge.

St George's Day (23 April) is celebrated true to the ritual previously associated with the Royal Northumberland Fusiliers, with red and white roses fitted to badges, drums and

The antelope mascot between kneeling handlers in RRF full dress. *(MoD)*

honour 'Wilhelmstahl'. This resolved the regiment's transgression in carrying French standards captured at Wilhelmstahl in 1762 against regulations. Bearskins issued with the regiment's fusilier achievement similarly satisfied its self-imposed right to grenadier caps brought from the battlefield and worn by the 5th to publicise its capture of the *Grenadiers de France.*

Albuhera Day (16 May) honours the two battalions of the 7th Fusiliers which withstood shot and shell in the 1811 battle before delivering a resounding charge on their tormentors. The French infantry crumbled before the fusiliers' spirited charge and panic spread along its flanks to save the day for the British line, but at a cost: the 2nd Battalion had been destroyed and its cadre was returned home to recruit back to strength.

Minden Day (1 August) remembers the 20th Foot in Germany in 1759. Their motto *Omnia audax* (Daring everything) was never more true than at the Battle of Minden, when they were known as 'Kingsley's Stand' after refusing to retire from the firing line when ordered to, in view of their heavy casualties. A laurel wreath awarded to the regiment after the battle in respect of its courage is the origin of the wreath on the RRF badge today. The Lancashire Fusiliers observed Minden Day by wearing red and yellow roses in the tradition of most 'Minden' regiments. LF custom demands that officers new to the mess eat a rose from a silver bowl of champagne.

Gallipoli Day (25 April) commemorates the beach landings on the Dardenelles in 1915, where the Lancashire Fusiliers won 'six VCs before breakfast'. The ship's bell from HMS *Euryalus*, which delivered the Lancashire battalions to the beaches, was used to sound time in barracks. Gallipoli Day in Bury now remembers all Lancashire Fusiliers who gave their lives in the service of their country.

Normandy Day (6 June) marks the part played by the Royal Warwickshire Regiment

colours. Roses were emblazoned on the colours of all the antecedent regiments in one guise or another. The RNF and RWF displayed a united red and white rose 'slipped', that is, with stalk attached as if torn from the main stock, a symbol used by the old regiments in Dutch service to show loyalty to Mother England across the sea. The Tudor rose on the RF badge was taken from the emblem stamped into the guns they used to guard in the seventeenth century. The Red Rose of Lancaster came from the Royal Lancashire Militia via the colours of the Lancashire Fusiliers to the regimental colour today. A drummer's colour of gosling green silk is allowed to be paraded on St George's Day, a privilege given to the 5th (Northumberland) Regiment in 1836 with its unique battle in the massive operation of 1944, and the losses sustained in the assault on the German stronghold at Lebissey.

The regiment's foothold in the Wolfe Society comes via the LF. James Wolfe assumed command of the 20th Regiment in 1750 and stayed with it until 1756, when the outbreak of war moved him on to higher command.

THE ROYAL ANGLIAN REGIMENT

The first of the Army Council's 'large regiments' was created in 1964 by bringing together old county regiments of East Anglia and the east Midlands, most of which had a history dating back to the seventeenth century and the reign of James II.

By 1970 battalion titles were giving way to battalion nicknames. The 2nd became known as 'The Poachers' because of its Lincolnshire content and its march of the same name, and the 3rd as 'The Pompadours', an old name of the Essex inherited from the 56th Foot, whose rose purple facings happened to be the favourite colour of Madame de Pompadour. The 1st Battalion, lacking a suitable nickname, chose to be 'The Vikings', a convenient warrior appellation drawn from east coast history.

Regimental headquarters are at Gibraltar Barracks in Bury St Edmunds, the former depot of the Suffolk Regiment.

Royal Anglians band and drums, *c.* 1990. Note the eccentric brass edging on the helmets of the bandsmen behind the drummers.

The Royal Anglian Regiment
1964

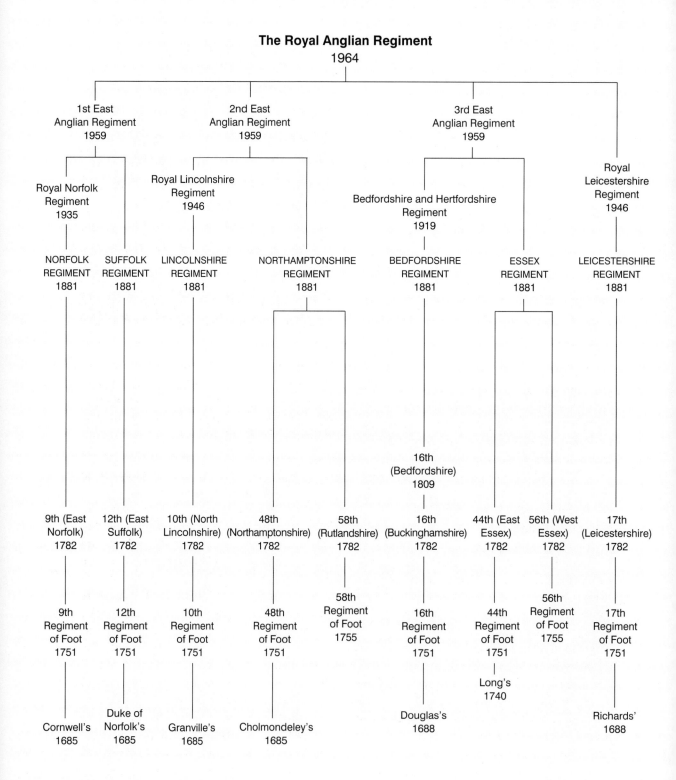

DRESS DISTINCTIONS

The blue peaked cap with scarlet band bears the regimental badge, the castle and key of Gibraltar on an eight-pointed star, basically the badge of the East Anglian Brigade prior to 1964 in the smaller form favoured by the officers. The castle and key emblem was worn as a battle honour by four regiments of the British Army, three of which were destined for the Anglians: the Suffolk, Essex and Northamptons. The castle's accompanying motto, *Montis insignia Calpe* (By the sign of the Rock), was also included in the badge of the Suffolk Regiment. The castle and its motto were originally allowed to be borne by the 12th (Suffolk), 56th (West Essex) and the 58th (Rutlandshire) Regiments in 1836 to affirm their battle honour 'Gibraltar 1779–83', awarded just after the great siege in which a handful of British regiments held out against the combined French and Spanish armies and navies for four years. The star part of the badge, minus a cross and hart, was taken from the 'Beds and Herts' badge and resembles the Star of the Order of the Bath which appeared (with laurel wreath) on officers' belt plates of the 16th (Bedfordshire) Regiment from 1830.

Collar badges are worn to battalion pattern in this regiment. Members of the 1st Battalion wear the Suffolks' castle badge with the Norfolks' figure of Britannia superimposed, whereas soldiers of the 2nd sport the Lincolns' sphinx with the Northamptons' 'Talavera' scroll.

Royal Anglian Regiment (RAR) buttons were impressed with the regimental castle and star until the demise of the 4th (Leicestershire) Battalion in 1970, when it was decided to perpetuate the memory of the Leicestershire Regiment by showing its tiger and wreath badge on the buttons. The complete laurel wreath dates back to 1777 and represents the encirclement of the 17th Foot by Washington's army at Princeton,

Minden roses fixed to the beret on 1 August. The black patch behind the badge is said to commemorate the death of Sir John Moore at Corunna in 1809. He was buried by men of the 9th (East Norfolk) Regiment 'darkly and at dead of night'. *(Grenadier Publishing)*

and Lt-Col Mawhood's reckless charge to break out of the Americans' cordon.

With the passing of the 3rd Battalion in 1992 its eagle badge, inherited from the Essex Regiment, was transferred to the remaining battalions in the form of a sleeve badge, worn near the left shoulder in the style of that of the Blues and Royals'. The Imperial Eagle, displayed on buttons of the Essex Regiment from 1902 and as a collar badge from 1954, is symbolic of the regimental eagle of the French 62nd Regiment captured by the 44th (East Essex) at the Battle of Salamanca in 1812.

1st Battalion uniforms are identifiable by a red and yellow Minden flash on the right sleeve, worn to honour the memory of the 12th Regiment at the Battle of Minden in 1759.

Lanyards are worn in battalion colours: 1st Battalion wear a yellow lanyard to reflect the

Colours of the 1st and 2nd Battalions at Duxford in 1995. *(Grenadier Publishing)*

yellow facings of the 9th and 12th Regiments, a distinction restored to the Suffolks in 1899 and the Norfolks in 1905. The 2nd Battalion lanyards are black, the facing colour of the 58th from 1755 to 1881. Lanyards worn in the 3rd Battalion were rose purple, the facing colour of the 56th, returned to the Essex in 1936. TA battalions wear lanyards of two or three colours; companies based in Leicester wore the red/grey/black twist of the Royal Leicesters – grey for the old facings of the 17th Regiment, which were returned to the Leicesters in 1931, and black as a sign of mourning for the death of Gen Wolfe.

MUSIC

The regimental quick march, *Rule Britannia/Speed the Plough*, from the Norfolks and Suffolks respectively, is sometimes played with *The Lincolnshire Poacher*. In this instance, *Rule Britannia* is not evidence of a link with the Royal Navy; it was chosen for the Norfolk Regiment to complement its Britannia badge. *Speed the Plough*, particularly apt for a regiment sometimes known as 'The Carrot Crunchers', is based on a seventeenth-century East Anglian folk tune.

The regimental slow march is that formerly played in the Northamptonshire Regiment, whose custom it was to play *Rule Britannia* and *God Bless the Prince of Wales* in the officers' mess.

The waltz, *Destiny*, was regarded with sacred respect in the Bedfordshire and Hertfordshire Regiment because it was a favourite of the 1st Battalion band just before the embarkation to France in 1914, where its destiny was to witness the destruction of the regiment at Mons, Le Cateau, the Marne, the Aisne and Ypres. *The Pilgrim's Hymn* was adopted in 1941 to commemorate Bedford's link with John Bunyan, author of *A Pilgrim's Progress*.

The quick march, *A Hunting Call*, which evoked the fox-hunting traditions of Leicestershire, was played in the county militia from 1860 and adopted as the regimental march of the Leicesters in 1933. Their slow march, *General Monckton 1762*, indicated the colonel of the 17th Foot and the date he composed the piece.

TRADITIONS

Formation Day (1 September) celebrates the 1964 amalgamation, which brought the eastern county regiments together as Royal Anglian on parade grounds in England, Germany and Arabia.

The 1st Battalion anniversaries are headed by Minden Day (1 August), when roses are worn on headgear in the custom of the Suffolk Regiment, whose forebears stopped to pick roses for their hats en route to the battle line at Minden in 1759. A red and a yellow rose were worn in the Suffolk on Minden Day

The 44th Regiment re-enactment group in 2005, displaying drills and tactics of the 2nd Battalion the 44th (East Essex) Regiment in the Peninsular War.

in remembrance of this and also on the sovereign's birthday, a tradition that began in an earlier battle on German soil. At Dettingen, Duroure's Regiment (the 12th) accompanied King George II on the field and chose to remember the honour by wearing fern leaves on his birthday. Dettingen Day (27 June) is also celebrated in 1st Royal Anglian.

St Patrick's Day (17 March) and Salamanca Day (22 July) are observed in memory of the capture of a French eagle standard by the 2nd Battalion of the 44th (East Essex) Regiment at the Battle of Salamanca in 1812. It was customary for the Essex Regiment's Corps of Drums to play Irish airs at reveille in

honour of this Irish battalion, raised for war in 1804 and disbanded at its end, in 1816. The eagle trophy was consigned to the Royal Hospital at Chelsea and entrusted to the regiment in the twentieth century.

Almanza Day (25 April) was kept by the Norfolk Regiment in memory of the 324 men of the 9th Foot who were killed or wounded out of a field strength of 467 at the 1707 battle in Spain. It is popularly believed that the figure of Britannia was conferred on the regiment by Queen Anne for the courage displayed by the regiment in the battle. A century later the 9th were in Spain again, their belt plates shining with Britannia.

Royal Leicestershire Regiment drummers, *c.* 1963. Full-length tigerskin aprons were adopted for all drummers of the regiment in India during the 1920s to promote the regimental badge and nickname. *(Leicester Mercury)*

Locals mistook her for the Virgin Mary and other regiments took the opportunity to mock the 9th as 'The Holy Boys'.

Sobraon Day (10 February), from the Lincolns, celebrates the remarkable advance of the 10th Regiment on the Sikh artillery at Sobraon in 1846. It is said the battalion marched through a hail of shot and shell in perfect order and with a silent progress that chilled the enemy.

Hindoostan Day (25 June) is what the Leicesters knew as Royal Tigers Day. It celebrates the time in 1825 when King George IV approved a tiger emblem for the 17th (Leicestershire) Regiment to mark its nineteen years of active service in India

between 1804 and 1823. The tiger, superscribed HINDOOSTAN, became the cap badge of the Leicestershire Regiment, whose members revelled under the collective nickname of 'Tigers' as a result.

Talavera Day (27 July) honours the 48th (Northamptonshire) Regiment at the Battle of Talavera in 1809. In the heat of the battle the 1st Battalion was rushed forward to strengthen a weak point in the line and the Duke of Wellington afterwards wrote of how 'the battle was certainly saved by the advance, position and steady conduct of the 48th'. The Northamptonshire Regiment displayed the battle honour 'Talavera' on its cap badge, and on its collar badge in the form of a wreath around its Militia shield, which displayed the Rutland horseshoe. On Talavera Day in the officers' mess a silver cup, purchased in 1877, would be charged with champagne at dinner and passed round in a solemn toast to Col Donellan and his men who fell on that day.

Blenheim Day (13 August) remembers the 16th Regiment of Foot at the Battle of Blenheim in 1704, when it was registered among those sustaining the highest casualties. Blenheim was the regimental day of the Bedfordshire Regiment.

The Royal Anglians' membership of the Wolfe Society came through the Suffolks, Leicesters and Northamptons. James Wolfe and his brother Edward served as ensigns in the 12th of Foot, and carried Col Duroure's colour at Dettingen. His motto *Stabilis* (Steady) was adopted unofficially by the Suffolk Regiment. The 17th Foot fought under Wolfe at Louisburg in 1758 and the Leicestershire Regiment honoured his memory in several ways; the band played *Wolfe's Lament* on 1st Battalion church parade, the officers' grey mess waistcoat was heavily braided in black and the mess silver was encompassed by black crepe on guest nights. The Northamptons' connection lay with their 48th and 58th Regiments, both of which fought under Wolfe in his Canadian campaigns of 1758/9. When he fell mortally wounded at Quebec it was the surgeon of the 48th who attended him.

A regiment's drums are respected for the honours emblazoned on them, and consequently protected when danger threatens. The Bedfords' Mons drum was the sole survivor of a set that was urgently thrust into the care of French villagers during the Mons offensive of 1914. It was eventually traced and returned to a place of honour in the regiment where it was paraded on special occasions. The Cambridgeshire Regiment TA, which was seconded to the Suffolks in 1961, buried its drums in the jungle at the time of the fall of Singapore in 1941. They were recovered in 1945, but only paraded in silence thereafter as a solemn mark of respect for the 784 Cambridge lads who never returned from Malaya.

THE LIGHT INFANTRY

In 1968 the four regiments grouped together as the Light Infantry Brigade were amalgamated into one large regiment. The term

Light Infantry colour serjeant in the regiment's green No. 1 dress, with the 'wrong way round' sash and Inkerman chain. The use of the beret with ceremonial attire is a rare sight among infantry regiments without hackles. (*Grenadier Publishing*)

Drummers of the Devonshire and Dorset Regiment in full dress with the green pagri adopted to distinguish their helmets from those of the Royal Marines.

The back badge on the cap and cross-belt of Drum Maj Scaife (2nd Gloucesters), 1935.
(Gloucester Regiment Museum)

'light infantry' was first used in the eighteenth century for companies selected to operate in the rough country of North America like the natives, unfettered by parade ground uniforms and rigid martial doctrines. In 1802 Sir John Moore opened a training school at Shorncliffe, where he gave birth to the Light Division, a term still used today to embrace the Royal Green Jackets (RGJ) – as Moore's infantry became – and the Light Infantry (LI), which represents the English county regiments that were converted to the light role after 1808.

Regimental headquarters LI, first established at the KSLI barracks in Shrewsbury, were later moved to Winchester, the training base of the Light Division and traditional home of the 'Greenjackets'.

As a result of army restructuring announced in 2004, two infantry regiments from the Wessex region were converted into the Light Division – the Devonshire and Dorset (D&D) and the Royal Gloucestershire, Berkshire and Wiltshire (RGBW). In 2007 all battalions of the Light Division – Light Infantry, Green Jackets and Rifle Volunteers (TA) – will unite as one regiment under a title resurrected from Green Jackets' history: The Rifles.

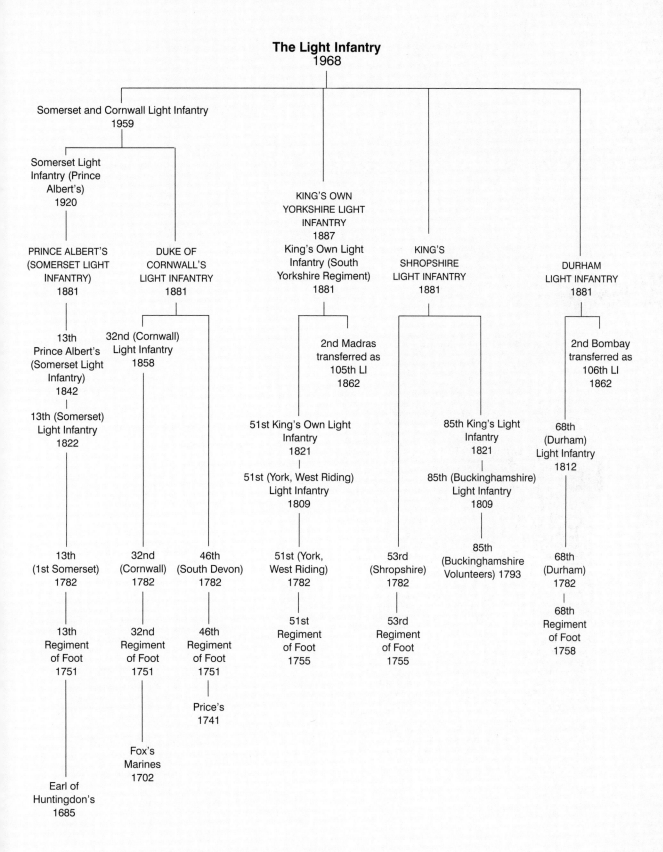

The Light Infantry
1968

Somerset and Cornwall Light Infantry
1959

Somerset Light
Infantry (Prince
Albert's)
1920

KING'S OWN
YORKSHIRE LIGHT
INFANTRY
1887

PRINCE ALBERT'S
(SOMERSET LIGHT
INFANTRY)
1881

DUKE OF
CORNWALL'S
LIGHT INFANTRY
1881

King's Own Light
Infantry (South
Yorkshire Regiment)
1881

KING'S
SHROPSHIRE
LIGHT INFANTRY
1881

DURHAM
LIGHT INFANTRY
1881

13th
Prince Albert's
(Somerset Light
Infantry)
1842

32nd (Cornwall)
Light Infantry
1858

2nd Madras
transferred as
105th LI
1862

2nd Bombay
transferred as
106th LI
1862

13th (Somerset)
Light Infantry
1822

51st King's Own Light
Infantry
1821

85th King's Light
Infantry
1821

68th
(Durham)
Light Infantry
1812

51st (York, West Riding)
Light Infantry
1809

85th (Buckinghamshire)
Light Infantry
1809

13th
(1st Somerset)
1782

32nd
(Cornwall)
1782

46th
(South Devon)
1782

51st (York,
West Riding)
1782

53rd
(Shropshire)
1782

85th
(Buckinghamshire
Volunteers) 1793

68th
(Durham)
1782

13th
Regiment
of Foot
1751

32nd
Regiment
of Foot
1751

46th
Regiment
of Foot
1751

51st
Regiment
of Foot
1755

53rd
Regiment
of Foot
1755

68th
Regiment
of Foot
1758

Price's
1741

Fox's
Marines
1702

Earl of
Huntingdon's
1685

Prince Alfred of Edinburgh in a rifles officer uniform of the 2nd Volunteer Battalion the Devonshire Regiment in 1895.

DRESS DISTINCTIONS

The Rifles' green peaked caps (officers) and berets (other ranks) follow a light infantry tradition that began in the years of the shako (1800–78), when light companies were distinguished by plumes or pom-poms of green.

The Victorian universal helmet, normally covered in blue cloth, was covered in dark green for regiments of light infantry.

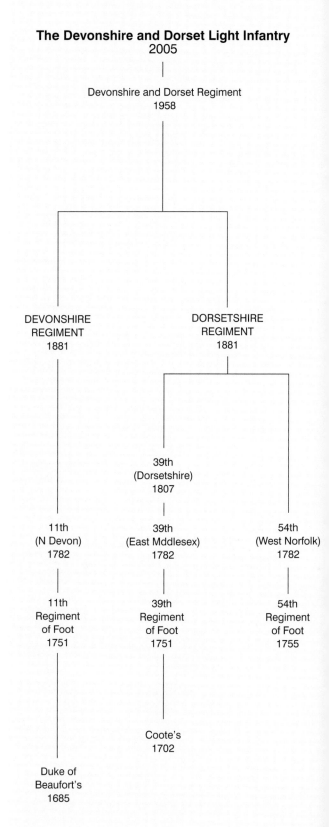

The Devonshire and Dorset Light Infantry
2005

|
Devonshire and Dorset Regiment
1958

DEVONSHIRE
REGIMENT
1881

DORSETSHIRE
REGIMENT
1881

39th
(Dorsetshire)
1807

11th
(N Devon)
1782

39th
(East Mddlesex)
1782

54th
(West Norfolk)
1782

11th
Regiment
of Foot
1751

39th
Regiment
of Foot
1751

54th
Regiment
of Foot
1755

Coote's
1702

Duke of
Beaufort's
1685

**The Royal Gloucestershire,
Berkshire and Wiltshire Light Infantry**
2005

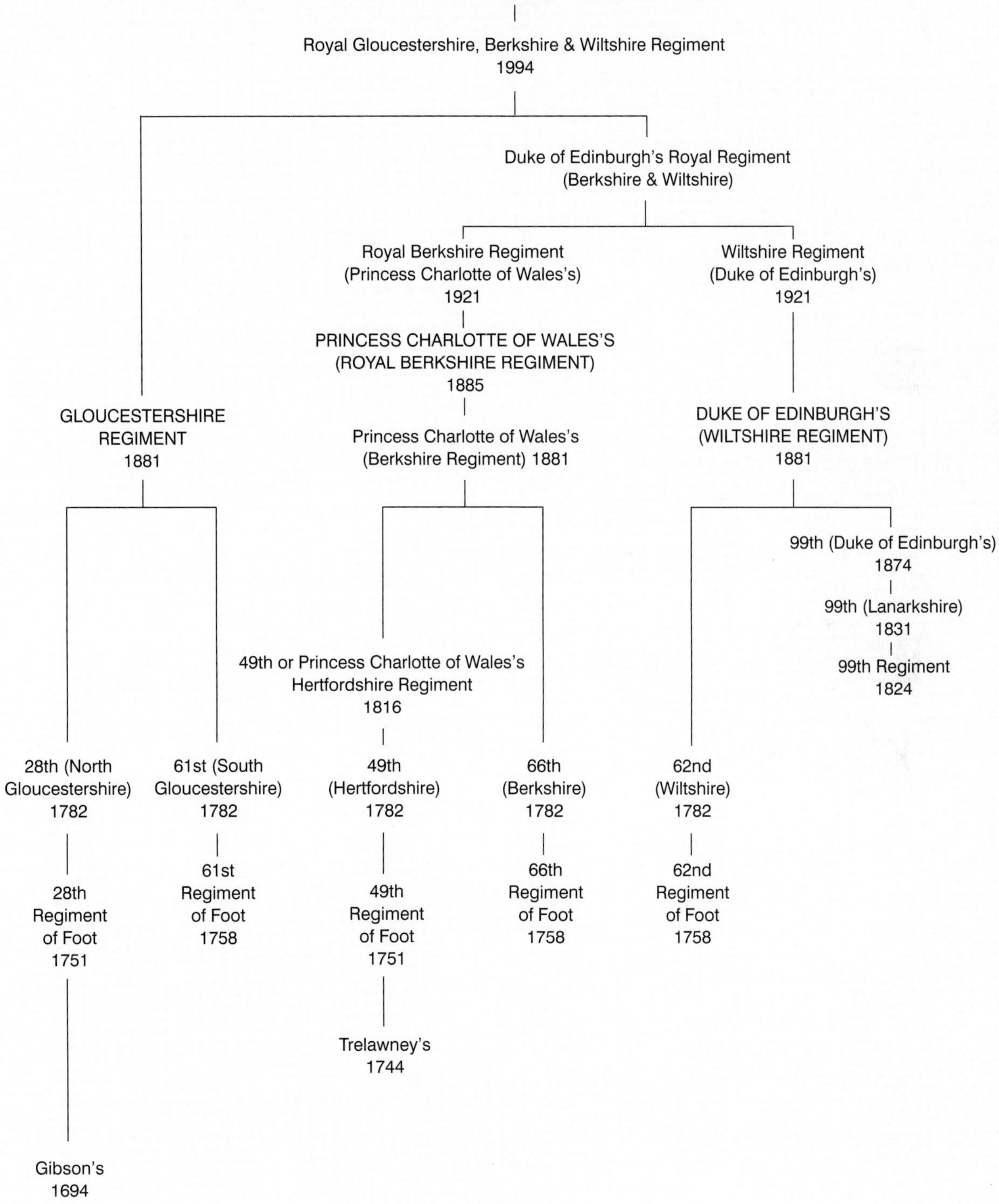

Royal Gloucestershire, Berkshire & Wiltshire Regiment
1994

Duke of Edinburgh's Royal Regiment
(Berkshire & Wiltshire)

Royal Berkshire Regiment
(Princess Charlotte of Wales's)
1921

Wiltshire Regiment
(Duke of Edinburgh's)
1921

PRINCESS CHARLOTTE OF WALES'S
(ROYAL BERKSHIRE REGIMENT)
1885

GLOUCESTERSHIRE
REGIMENT
1881

Princess Charlotte of Wales's
(Berkshire Regiment) 1881

DUKE OF EDINBURGH'S
(WILTSHIRE REGIMENT)
1881

99th (Duke of Edinburgh's)
1874

99th (Lanarkshire)
1831

99th Regiment
1824

49th or Princess Charlotte of Wales's
Hertfordshire Regiment
1816

28th (North
Gloucestershire)
1782

61st (South
Gloucestershire)
1782

49th
(Hertfordshire)
1782

66th
(Berkshire)
1782

62nd
(Wiltshire)
1782

28th
Regiment
of Foot
1751

61st
Regiment
of Foot
1758

49th
Regiment
of Foot
1751

66th
Regiment
of Foot
1758

62nd
Regiment
of Foot
1758

Trelawney's
1744

Gibson's
1694

The silver-strung bugle horn, which is worn on cap, beret, collar and buttons, is the same as that adopted by the light companies in the 1780s and maintained by the 'Light Bobs' ever since, in one form or another, with regimental embellishment. It emulates the old bugle horn used by hunters in the chase and by light infantry to sound communications in barracks, on the march and in the field. Known as 'half a cap badge' because of its semicircular form, the bugle is worn with a red ground between the horn and its strings, a distinction borrowed from the badge of the Duke of Cornwall's Light Infantry, who used it to symbolise a privilege of its 2nd Battalion, the old 46th Regiment. Drummers and light company men of the 46th were permitted a red pom-pom on their shakos to celebrate an audacious night attack by the light company of the 46th Regiment on an American camp by the Brandywine river during the American War of Independence. The victims swore vengeance on their 'surprisers' and the cocky lads who went to make up the light companies of the 46th and 49th Regiments duly obliged by wearing conspicuous red feathers in their caps to attract any unfinished business.

The RGBW badge, which is basically the Wiltshires' cross mounted with the Gloucesters' sphinx, is also worn on a red backing to echo the red feathers sported in North America, in this instance by the light company of the 49th. On the beret this takes the form of a long red triangle – the Duke of Edinburgh's Royal Regiment's (DERR) Brandywine flash.

A small sphinx badge, uniquely worn (within a laurel wreath) at the back of cap and beret, originated with the 28th (North Gloucestershire) Regiment, whose soldiers fitted a plate pressed with the sphinx on the back of their shakos to commemorate their back-to-back stand against a two-pronged attack in the Battle of Alexandria in 1801. The larger version of the back badge, struck during the First World War to mark a similar manoeuvre at Festubert, proved unpopular and a reversion to the small badge was made in 1935.

The D&D badge is made up of the Devons' Exeter castle and motto superimposed with the Dorsets' sphinx and motto. The sphinx, on a tablet marked EGYPT, was awarded to all the regiments involved in the 1801 campaign to rid Egypt of Napoleon. The sphinx displayed by the Dorset Regiment was different in that its tablet inscription was altered in 1841 to MARABOUT, a battle honour given to the 54th Regiment when its prized trophy, a gun taken at Fort Marabout (near Alexandria), was finally handed in, forty years after the battle. The Marabout Gun now resides in the Dorset Military Museum in Dorchester.

Warrant officers and serjeants of the LI are authorised by custom to two items of dress that commemorate battles in which sergeants had to take on the responsibilities of their officers. The red sash of rank is worn over the left shoulder, which is opposite to the regulation side for sergeants and warrant officers of the British Army. This distinction of the Somerset Light Infantry was adopted by sergeants of the 13th Regiment who had stood in for officers felled in battle and who wore their sashes like officers at that time, from the left shoulder with the knot on the right hip. The Inkerman chain, which is worn suspended from the sash, was inherited from the Durham Light Infantry. It attaches to a whistle used by light infantry officers and sergeants in the nineteenth century to marshal their companies about the battlefield. At the Battle of Inkerman in 1854 officers and sergeants of the 68th manoeuvred their men out of danger of a strong Russian flanking movement. Inkerman Day (5 November) was observed in the regiment up to the 1968 amalgamation.

The band of the Light Infantry, 1989.

Officers wear the whistle chain from a black leather cross-belt today, while other ranks wear a black leather waist belt, both accessories of rifle regiments now used throughout the Light Division.

Buglers are issued with light infantry No. 1 dress (green tunic with bright buttons and blue trousers with a green stripe) and a rifles busby that conforms to the type worn in the Royal Green Jackets, another concession to uniformity in the Light Division. Drummers of the Devon and Dorset Regiment wear traditional infantry scarlet but with white marine helmets to mark the regiment's close links to the sea and its history of marine duty: the 39th at Cape Passaro in 1718, the 54th at Gibraltar in 1756–65 and the 11th at Cape St Vincent in 1797.

The Shropshire and Herefordshire Battalion (TA) wear a *Croix de Guerre* cockade in No. 1 dress to honour the ribbon awarded to the 4th Battalion KSLI in recognition of their gallantry at La Montagne de Bligny on 6 June 1918. A *Croix de Guerre* ribbon granted to the Devonshire Regiment by the French government for bravery in battle at Bois des Buttes in 1918 is worn as a sleeve badge in the D&D, a custom begun in 1939. The blue rectangle worn by Gloucesters at the top of the sleeve represents a US Presidential Citation made to the regiment for its outstanding courage at the Battle of Imjin River in 1951.

LI officers and serjeants wear a lanyard of rifle green in barrack and service dress. Grass-green lanyards of the D&D reflect the facing colour of the regiment reauthorised to the Dorsets in 1904 and to the Devons in the following year. The colour had inspired nicknames like 'The Green Linnets' for the 39th and 'Popinjays' for the 54th in the eighteenth century. Stable belts are of corresponding greens, those of the D&D enlivened with a central stripe of tawny orange.

Light Infantry at the double with rifles at the trail, *c.* 1980.

MUSIC

The regimental quick march, *Light Infantry*, is a modern composition but the double past, *The Keel Row*, comes from an old Tyneside love song used by the Durham Light Infantry. Double marching is a fast-paced progression peculiar to light infantry and rifle regiments that simulates their historic role in running across the battlefield ahead of the main army.

Marches played on suitable occasions are *Prince Albert* and *Palace Guard* (SLI), *One and All* and *Trelawney* (DCLI), *Minden March* and *With a Jockey to the Fair* (KOYLI), *Old Towler* and *Daughter of the Regiment* (KSLI), and *The Light Barque* and *The Old 68th (The Prince Regent)* of the DLI.

The regimental quick march of the Devon and Dorsets is a composition of *Widecombe Fair, We've Lived and Loved Together* and *The Maid of Glenconnel*. The latter, a favourite of the wife of the founder of the 54th Regiment, was played in both quick

and slow time for the Dorset Regiment. The D&D slow march brings together *The Rose of Devon* and *The Maid of Glenconnel*.

The RGBW chose *Army of The Nile* for its quick march and *Scipio* as its slow march. *Army of The Nile*, in previous form, was a secondary march of the Gloucesters that was played to honour their sphinx tradition.

In 1959, the new Duke of Edinburgh's Royal Regiment adopted *The Farmer's Boy* as its quick march because it had associations with both the Berkshire and Wiltshire Regiments. The DERR slow march, *Auld Robin Grey*, came from the Wiltshires and, before 1881, the 99th Regiment. *The Wiltshires* was based on the old county fable which told of the Moonrakers who fooled excise officers by pretending to be simple yokels and sang 'The Vly be on the turmat but there bain't no vlies on we'. The regimental march of the Royal Berkshires was *The Dashing White Sergeant*.

Gloucestershire Regiment marches are headed by *The Kynegad Slashers* (based on a

Leinster jig and an old nickname of the 28th), *The Silver-tailed Dandies* (an old nickname of the 61st), *The Royal Canadian* (played from 1925 as a tribute to this allied regiment in the Canadian army) and *Salamanca Day* (written for the Corps of Drums).

TRADITIONS

The regimental day (22 July) is the anniversary of the Battle of Salamanca in 1812, Wellington's first large-scale battle and his masterpiece victory over the French in Spain. Four antecedents of the LI took part: the 51st (York, West Riding), the 68th (Durham), 32nd (Cornwall) and the 53rd (Shropshire), the last named both taking heavy casualties in the fighting. The Devonshire Regiment kept the day in memory of 'The Bloody Eleventh', who came up against a deadly resistance in the closing moments of the battle. In the Gloucestershire Regiment two privates replaced colour sergeants in the escort to the colour on Salamanca Day to honour Privates Crawford and Coulson of the 61st, who rescued their battalion colours in the battle.

The Wiltshire Regiment custom was to give its sergeants custody of the colours on Ferozeshah Day (21 December), the anniversary of a Sikh wars battle. In this case the 62nd (Wiltshire) Regiment was cut up to the extent that its colours, carried into battle by ensigns, had to be brought out by sergeants.

On Minden Day (1 August) white roses are worn in the custom of the King's Own Yorkshire Light Infantry (KOYLI) and other regiments that picked roses for hat decoration on the way to the battlefield.

The battle honour 'Jellalabad' is carried on the regimental colour with a mural crown, as on the bugle badge of the

R. Caton Woodville's painting of a breach in the walls of Badajoz and a British storming party.

68th (Durham) Light Infantry re-enactment team display light infantry tactics of the Peninsular War period.

Somerset Light Infantry. It was awarded to the 13th Regiment to mark the siege of the Indian border town, defended by Sir Robert Sale from November 1841 to April 1842 against the Afghan army of Akbar Khan. The regiment became famous at the time as 'The Illustrious Garrison' and 'The Jellalabad Heroes', while receiving the more lasting accolade of Prince Albert's title.

On Esla Day (31 May) the KOYLI would compete with the 15th/19th Hussars for a painting of the crossing of the Esla river in northern Spain. During this incident of the Peninsular War men of the 51st had to grab hold of stirrups of the 15th Hussars to avoid being swept away downriver.

Other important battle anniversaries are Lucknow Day (17 November) from the DCLI, Paardeberg (27 February) and Anzio (14 May) from the KSLI, and Hooge (9 August) and Inkerman (5 November) from the DLI. Vesting Day (10 July)

celebrates the day in 1968 when the four light infantry regiments came together as one. The Devonshire and Dorsets' Amalgamation Day (17 May) is observed with a major parade and regimental reunion.

Wagon Hill Day (6 January) remembers the recovery of Wagon Hill by three companies of the 1st Devons during the Siege of Ladysmith in 1900. Warrant officers and sergeants are invited to the officers' mess, a tradition of the regiment that acknowledges the debt owed to the sergeants who took the place of officers shot in the battle.

Bois des Buttes Day (27 May) commemorates the gallant resistance put up by the 2nd Devons during the German drive on Paris in 1918, when fighting in the woods ended with 551 battalion men killed. In 1921 the regiment erected a memorial to its dead in the village of La Ville-aux-Bois les Pontevert and a special toast to the French Army was introduced into the officers' mess

Detail from a painting of the 2nd Devons at Bois des Buttes in 1918. *(RHQ D&D)*

ritual. The D&D support a junior NCOs' dinner night on the day.

Sarah Sands Day (11 November) replays the fateful voyage of the SS *Sarah Sands* and its cargo of soldiers en route to India in 1857. Fire broke out on board ship in mid-ocean, which persuaded the crew to take to the boats, leaving men of the 54th to fight the terrifying inferno with their families. It took eighteen hours to bring the flames under control, a feat of endurance that was read out at the head of every regiment in the army. The day is marked with inter-company competitions and ends with the traditional Sarah Sands Ball in the warrant officers' and sergeants' mess.

The Vernon bell, which used to be placed at DERR barrack gates, was presented to the regiment in 1960 to cement the affiliation between HMS *Vernon* and the Wiltshire Regiment. In 1951 a naval crown, superscribed '2nd April, 1801', was granted

to the Royal Berkshire for its presence at the Battle of Copenhagen. A coiled rope in the badge of the regiment manifested this connection with the Royal Navy.

Plassey Day (23 June) records Clive's famous victory of 1757 in India, and the only British regiment present, the 39th Foot.

Back Badge Day (21 March) takes its theme from the Gloucesters' strange practice of wearing a badge on the back and front of its headgear, a commemoration of the back-to-back fighting at Alexandria in 1801. This custom of the 28th (North Gloucestershire) Regiment was eventually given official sanction in 1830. An army order of 1955 granted the 1st Battalion special permission to fly a streamer from the pikestaff of the regimental colour on Back Badge Day in the blue of the US Presidential Citation. The streamer is emblazoned with 'Solma-ri', the Korean valley in which the regiment made its name in 1951.

A newspaper report on the battle at the Imjin river in April 1951 hailed the stand made by 'The Glorious Glosters' against a Chinese army 30,000 strong as it crossed the Imjin and attacked the British 29th Infantry Brigade. The 'Glosters' fought back against impossible odds but by the evening of 24 April were pushed back on a hill where they fought desperately throughout the night. On the morning of the 25th the survivors attempted to break out but 526 men fell into enemy hands and were taken as prisoners of war.

The 66th (Berkshire) Regiment suffered a similar fate at the hands of the fanatical Ghazis of Afghanistan in 1880. The Royal Berkshires commemorated the battle on Maiwand Day (27 July) and a gigantic lion monument was erected in the heart of Reading to the memory of the 'last eleven' to succumb to the horde.

The LI has three mottoes on its blue regimental colours. *Aucto splendore resurgo* (Rise again with increased splendour) comes from the old Buckinghamshire Volunteers and relates to previous regiments that were ranked 85th in line. *Cede nullis* (Yield to none) came by way of the KOYLI from the 105th Regiment. *Faithful* was the family motto of Col Lambton of the old 68th, unofficially displayed on the caps of the regiment. The Devons' badge motto *Semper fidelis* (Always faithful) is now displayed with the Dorsets' *Primus in Indis* (First in India), an achievement of the 39th Regiment. *Montis insignia Calpe* (By the sign of the Rock) came with the castle and key badge of the Dorset Regiment and relates to its battle honour 'Gibraltar 1779–1783'.

The right to dispense with the necessity of drinking the loyal toast was inherited from two regiments. The Durhams' dispensation was given by King George III, possibly as a considered response to the official ban on its unofficial motto *Faithful*. The Shropshires were not required to drink the toast, nor to stand for the national anthem, a legacy of the 85th Regiment whose officers won the gratitude of George IV when they intervened to save him from a mob at the Theatre Royal in Brighton during an unpopular period in his reign. Officers of the Duke of Cornwall's made the toast just once a year, on the sovereign's birthday, a unique custom which began with the privations of the Siege of Lucknow in 1857, when the officers' wine ration in the hard-pressed 32nd dwindled to such an extent that a decision was taken to reserve what was left for the Queen's birthday toast. The loyal toast as practised by officers of the Gloucestershire Regiment seems to ignore everyone present except the mess president and vice-president, who propose and respond the toast between themselves. This custom began during the Peninsular War, after a battle that left just two officers of the 28th standing, with an obligation to toast the King's health in this way. The regiment's membership of the Wolfe Society originated at the Battle of Quebec, where Gen Wolfe fell, mortally wounded, at the head of the 28th Regiment.

Special toasts were given in at least two regiments. The officers' mess of the 1st KOYLI drank a toast to 'Dyas and his Stormers', after which members and guests would stand in silence. This re-creation of a Peninsular War toast in the 51st Regiment focused on Ensign Dyas, famed for his bravery in leading a forlorn hope of volunteers to scale the walls of the fortress Badajoz in the siege of 1812. A Bumper toast to the 1st Duke of Kent, originally the province of the 2nd Dorset Regiment and their forerunners, the 54th Regiment, began in 1802 when Prince Edward took over the governorship of Gibraltar. His harsh discipline proved so unpopular, however, that soldiers from the garrison marched on his residence with assassination in mind, only to be scattered by a volley from the more loyal 54th. The Duke gratefully presented a silver punch bowl to the

DWR colours and large honorary colours being marched through the streets of Huddersfield in the 1970s.

officers of the 54th, who have returned the consideration ever since by drinking the toast and inviting successive Dukes of Kent to be Colonel-in-Chief of the Regiment.

Officers of the King's Shropshire Light Infantry were reminded of the origins of the bugle badge with a mess dinner call taken from the French *Messe de St Hubert*, the patron saint of hunters.

THE YORKSHIRE REGIMENT

The regiment was formed in 2006 with the union of three regular infantry battalions: the Green Howards (regimental headquarters (RHQ) at Richmond with TA companies in Cleveland and North Yorkshire); the Duke of Wellington's Regiment (RHQ at Halifax with TA units in Keighley, Bradford and Huddersfield); and the Prince of Wales's Own Regiment of Yorkshire, the former West and East Yorkshire Regiments (RHQ in York with TA detachments at Leeds, Hull and Beverley). The 4th Battalion is Yorkshire's TA element.

DRESS DISTINCTIONS

The blue peaked cap and khaki beret carry the new badge, which is made up of the White Rose, worn by the Yorkshire Brigade in the 1950s and the Yorkshire Volunteers from 1967, and the demi-lion from the Duke of Wellington's cap badge. The Duke's crest and title were conferred on the 33rd (West Riding) Regiment after his death in 1852, in honour of the long association between man and regiment that began in 1793 when he purchased a lieutenant colonelcy in the 33rd. As a younger officer Arthur Wellesley served with the 76th Foot. The new badge is pinned to a square green patch on the beret, a custom of the Green Howards. Stable belts are green with a blue band and scarlet stripe in the centre.

Eighteenth-century re-enactment group in the vestments of a marching regiment of the line at the time of Gen Wolfe's campaigns.

The East Yorkshires' badge, a star with the white rose of York on black in the centre, was employed by the PWO as a collar badge. The black part of the badge echoes the black line in the regiment's maroon and buff side hats and stable belts, and in the officers' shoulder cords, an old distinction of the East Yorkshire Regiment (EYR) which commemorates the death of Gen Wolfe at Quebec. Buff was the old facing colour of the 14th Regiment, restored to the West Yorkshire Regiment (WYR) in 1900. PWO buttons, impressed with the West Yorks'

Prince of Wales's plume and the Horse of Hanover, omitted their button honours – the royal tiger within a circle inscribed INDIA and WATERLOO. The Prince of Wales's crest and title were bestowed on the 14th Regiment in 1876 after an inspection by His Royal Highness at Lucknow.

The Duke of Wellington's Regiment (DWR) badge had been worn on a scarlet backing since the Second World War. Scarlet was the facing colour of the 33rd and 76th Regiments that was returned to the DWR in 1905 and later extended to its stable belts,

The band of the Duke of Wellington's Regiment marching through the ranks prior to its amalgamation with other bands of the King's Division in 1994. *(Soldier)*

lanyards, ranking and bugle cords. The DWR collar badge, an elephant with howdah circumscribed HINDOOSTAN, was granted to the 76th Regiment in 1807 for distinguished service on Lord Lake's campaign of 1803, during which the regiment was known as 'The Old Immortals' from its remarkable ability to climb back to fighting strength after each devastating battle of the Mahratta Wars.

The Green Howards' badge brought together the coronet and A cypher of Princess Alexandra with the Dannebrog (Danish cross) of her homeland, above the regimental numeral XIX. The title Princess of Wales's Own was conferred on the 19th Regiment in 1875 after she had presented new colours at Sheffield. As a cap badge the design incorporated a scroll inscribed with the regiment's title, which was updated to the Green Howards in 1951. This curious title was invoked in 1920 from an old nickname which came about in 1744 when the regiment, then known as the Hon. Charles Howard's, found themselves on

campaign with another called Howard's. The two regiments had to distinguish between themselves and did so by the facings colours on their red coats, which produced 'Howard's Buffs' and 'Green Howards'. A few years after this all regiments were identified by a number based on their seniority in the line and the problem was eliminated.

The Leeds Rifles, a much-decorated TA battalion originally formed with the rifle volunteers in 1859, wore a green/yellow/blue ribbon on its shoulder straps, a silver metal maple leaf on the upper sleeve (marking service with the Canadians in the Second World War), a Croix de Guerre ribbon (for distinguished service at Bois de Petit Champ and Bligny in 1918) and an embroidered tank sleeve badge, representing a term spent with the Royal Tank Regiment in North Africa and Italy in 1942–5.

MUSIC

Maria Theresa, an arrangement of three funeral marches presented to Col Howard at

The Yorkshire Regiment
2006

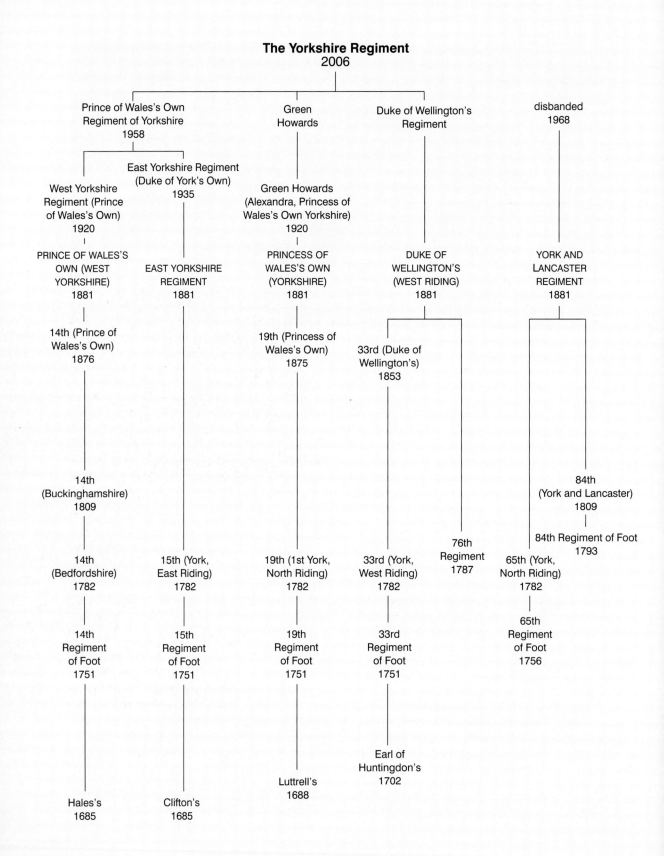

Prince of Wales's Own
Regiment of Yorkshire
1958

Green
Howards

Duke of Wellington's
Regiment

disbanded
1968

West Yorkshire
Regiment (Prince
of Wales's Own)
1920

East Yorkshire Regiment
(Duke of York's Own)
1935

Green Howards
(Alexandra, Princess of
Wales's Own Yorkshire)
1920

PRINCE OF WALES'S
OWN (WEST
YORKSHIRE)
1881

EAST YORKSHIRE
REGIMENT
1881

PRINCESS OF
WALES'S OWN
(YORKSHIRE)
1881

DUKE OF
WELLINGTON'S
(WEST RIDING)
1881

YORK AND
LANCASTER
REGIMENT
1881

14th (Prince of
Wales's Own)
1876

19th (Princess of
Wales's Own)
1875

33rd (Duke of
Wellington's)
1853

14th
(Buckinghamshire)
1809

84th
(York and Lancaster)
1809

84th Regiment of Foot
1793

14th
(Bedfordshire)
1782

15th (York,
East Riding)
1782

19th (1st York,
North Riding)
1782

33rd (York,
West Riding)
1782

76th
Regiment
1787

65th (York,
North Riding)
1782

14th
Regiment
of Foot
1751

15th
Regiment
of Foot
1751

19th
Regiment
of Foot
1751

33rd
Regiment
of Foot
1751

65th
Regiment
of Foot
1756

Earl of
Huntingdon's
1702

Luttrell's
1688

Hales's
1685

Clifton's
1685

A painting of the Battle of Famars in 1793 showing the 14th Regiment storming a redoubt to their drummers' stolen beat.

the Viennese court in 1742, is the oldest of this collection and stands as the regimental slow march of the Green Howards. Their quick march, *Bonnie English Rose*, was adopted by the 19th in 1868 and officially sanctioned to the regiment in 1881, when its badge was the white rose of York.

Ca Ira, the regimental quick march of the West Yorkshire Regiment, is unique in being the only march gained in battle. It was the Duke of York who ordered the 14th to adopt this French Revolutionary chant in 1793 following the action at Famars, where Lt-Col Doyle rallied his men with the command 'Drummers, strike up *Ca Ira* and break the scoundrels to their own damned tune!' The French were stunned and the day was won but the regiment's return to England was slightly marred by the good people of Dartford, who stoned the band for playing the enemy's music. Today the march is played with *Yorkshire Lass*, the regimental march of the East Yorkshires, arranged in 1881 from Egerton's 1875 composition *My Bonnie Yorkshire Lass*.

The PWO slow march, *God Bless the Prince of Wales/March of the XVth Regiment*, similarly unites the slow marches of the WYR and EYR. The *XVth von England* was used by the 15th (Yorks, East Riding) Regiment from 1790, along with the troop *The Duke Of York*.

The title Duke of York's Own was authorised to the EYR in 1935 on the occasion of the 250th anniversary of the regiment and the Silver Jubilee of King George V to honour the Duke of York, Colonel-in-Chief of the East Yorkshires since 1922.

The Wellesley, the old regimental march of the 33rd, was adopted by the Duke of Wellington's Regiment for its title, the family name of the 'Iron Duke' when he became colonel of the 33rd in 1806. The regiment's second march, *Scotland the Brave*, tells of the origins of the old 76th Regiment. On guest nights in the officers' mess *Rule Britannia* is traditionally played with a medley of rugby tunes, the West Riding being a strong rugby-playing area and 'The Dukes' very successful in the Army Challenge Cup.

The 19th Regiment re-enactment team in 2005; display of rifle drill and uniform of the Crimean War.

TRADITIONS

Formation Day (6 June) was chosen to fall on the anniversary of D Day, a battle honour shared by all three regiments.

'The Dukes' observe two anniversaries: St George's Day (23 April), when a white rose is worn in the cap, and Waterloo Day (18 June) to commemorate the heavy losses of the 33rd in the battle, under their former colonel the Duke of Wellington. During the Napoleonic Wars the 33rd became known as 'The Havercake Lads', after a West Riding oatcake used by recruiting sergeants to tempt hungry young men to the colours. The regiment is unique in being able to parade a pair of honorary colours in addition to the regulation pair. The originals were presented to the 76th Regiment on

Green Howards drummers wrapping the five Russian drums with oak leaves for Alma Day at Aldershot in 1934. *(Green Howards Regimental Museum)*

Jersey in 1808 on the wishes of Lord Lake, who had the 76th in his 1803 Hindustan campaign against the Mahrattas. Renewed in 1830, 1886, 1906 and 1969, the honorary colours carry the elephant with howdah and mahout, circumscribed HINDOOSTAN, and the battle honours 'Mysore, Nive, Corunna, Peninsula, Laswaree Nov. 1 1803, Deig Dec. 23 1804, Agra Oct. 10 1803, Delhi Sep. 11 1803 and Ally Ghur Sep. 4 1803'. The last three blazons are accredited to no other British regiment.

Imphal Day (22 June) celebrates the raising of the Siege of Imphal in Burma in 1944, in which the 1st and 2nd Battalions of the West Yorkshire Regiment fought the Japanese for four months without respite. The date is also significant in being the birth of the regiment in 1685.

Quebec Day (13 September) remembers the 15th Regiment in the Canadian campaign of 1759 and its association with the Wolfe Society. The East Yorkshire Regiment would decorate its colours with white roses on this day.

Alma Day (20 September) is observed in the Green Howards Battalion with a colour trooping and parade of Russian drums captured in the battle. The sergeants' mess honours the sergeants of the 19th Regiment who picked up their battalion colours as they fell and carried them forward into battle.

Generations of Green Howards have held military appointments in Norway and there exists a regimental alliance with the country's *Kongens Garde*. The regiment's relationship with the Norwegian royal family came through King Haakon VII, son-in-law of Queen Victoria and Colonel-in-Chief of the Green Howards from 1942. Soon after his death in 1957 King Olav V succeeded to the appointment, and King Harald V in 1992. The champion company goes under the title of King Harald's Company and bears his emblem. A special toast to the colonel-in-chief is followed by a silent toast to Queen Alexandra in the officers' mess. Mess protocol observes a number of interesting customs. The loyal toast was proposed only after three taps of the gavel, and the mess president and vice-president had bowed to each other and passed the port. Officers of the 2nd Battalion were wont to pass round a snuff box, once the gift of a grateful Napoleon to Marshal Ney. Subalterns new to the mess are faced with the Brights Cup and its formidable 14 pints capacity. Retiring officers are breakfasted out of the Green Howards instead of being dined out, a custom that originated in the Ulster 'troubles' of the 1970s, when security duties often altered normal procedures.

In the East Yorkshire Regiment the loyal toast was customarily proposed and seconded by the mess president, a nod to a certain dinner party at which the vice-president was found to be too inebriated to be able to voice his part of the toasting ritual. The PWO upheld the custom with the mess ignoring the president's first (seated) proposal to the vice-president. Only when the president stands and repeats it to the mess does everyone stop talking and respond with the toast. Orderly officers of the EYR wore their swords to dinner as a reminder of stormy days in Scotland during 1689, when arms were rarely laid aside because of the constant threat of Jacobite raids. In the PWO Battalion the orderly officer symbolises this readiness by wearing cap and sword when in the anteroom of the officers' mess before dinner.

Mess silver is the pride of any officers' mess and that polished up for the Duke of Wellington's Regiment includes two pieces of historical interest. The central section of King Theodore's Drum, taken at Magdala in 1868, is inscribed, 'This drum of gold from the Dejaj Match Oukie which he gave to Queen Meuvin in the year of St Mark 1737'. The Abyssinian Cup was made to duplicate the regiment's Cornwallis Cup of 1806. Lord Charles Cornwallis was colonel of the 33rd Regiment before the Duke of Wellington and is remembered for raising it to a level of excellence in the eighteenth century.

THE MERCIAN REGIMENT

Future Army Structures of 2004 nominated three county regiments of central England for amalgamation under the title of Mercian Regiment. Mercia was the kingdom that spread across the Midlands in Anglo-Saxon times. Battalions affected are 1st Cheshire (RHQ at Chester Castle), 1st Worcestershire and Sherwood Foresters (RHQ at Norton Barracks near Worcester) and 1st Staffordshire Regiment (RHQ at Whittington Barracks near Lichfield).

County attachments run deep. The 22nd (Cheshire) Regiment was raised on the Roodee at Chester in 1689 and the South Staffords were born of local volunteers, many from the county's militia. The 38th (1st Staffordshire) Regiment, formed in 1705 at the King's Head in Lichfield, was remembered on the tercentenary in 2005 when a regimental deputation revisited the King's Head to mark the occasion. The romantic term 'Sherwood Foresters' originated in 1814, when the Prince Regent approved the title Royal Sherwood Foresters to the Nottinghamshire Militia after it had guarded royal buildings in London during the previous year. The name also settled temporarily on the 45th (1st Nottinghamshire) Regiment around 1866.

DRESS DISTINCTIONS

Blue caps and berets currently display one of three badges: the Cheshires' star and acorn, the WFR's elongated star and cross, the Staffords' knot and plume. The Cheshires' Victorian star is characterised by an acorn and oak leaf centre, which came from King George II at the Battle of Dettingen

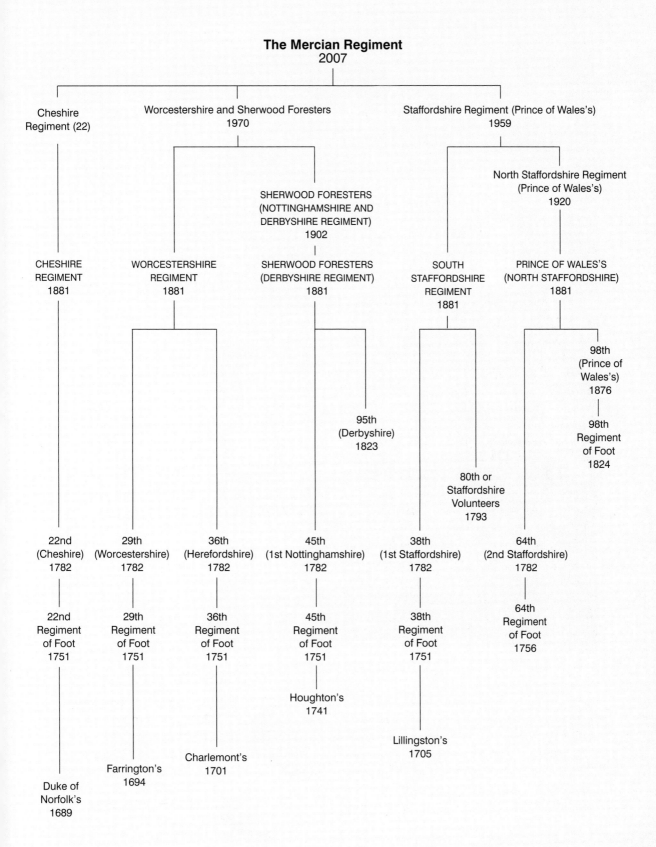

The Mercian Regiment
2007

Cheshire Regiment (22)

Worcestershire and Sherwood Foresters
1970

Staffordshire Regiment (Prince of Wales's)
1959

North Staffordshire Regiment
(Prince of Wales's)
1920

SHERWOOD FORESTERS
(NOTTINGHAMSHIRE AND
DERBYSHIRE REGIMENT)
1902

CHESHIRE
REGIMENT
1881

WORCESTERSHIRE
REGIMENT
1881

SHERWOOD FORESTERS
(DERBYSHIRE REGIMENT)
1881

SOUTH
STAFFORDSHIRE
REGIMENT
1881

PRINCE OF WALES'S
(NORTH STAFFORDSHIRE)
1881

98th
(Prince of
Wales's)
1876

98th
Regiment
of Foot
1824

95th
(Derbyshire)
1823

80th or
Staffordshire
Volunteers
1793

22nd
(Cheshire)
1782

29th
(Worcestershire)
1782

36th
(Herefordshire)
1782

45th
(1st Nottinghamshire)
1782

38th
(1st Staffordshire)
1782

64th
(2nd Staffordshire)
1782

22nd
Regiment
of Foot
1751

29th
Regiment
of Foot
1751

36th
Regiment
of Foot
1751

45th
Regiment
of Foot
1751

38th
Regiment
of Foot
1751

64th
Regiment
of Foot
1756

Houghton's
1741

Lillingston's
1705

Charlemont's
1701

Farrington's
1694

Duke of
Norfolk's
1689

Provost corporal of the Staffordshire Regiment in No. 1 dress 'blues' with the glider sleeve badge. *(Grenadier Publishing)*

according to legend, although it is known that the arms of the founder of the regiment, Henry Howard, 7th Duke of Norfolk, included a horse with 'in its mouth an acorn sprig with two leaves'.

The Dettingen theory has it that a detachment of the 22nd guarded the King on the field of battle in 1743 and was presented with a clutch of oak leaves plucked from a tree, which is why the Cheshires wear oak leaves on the cap in the presence of royalty and on special days.

The Stafford knot, from the arms of the earls of Stafford, has been used by regiments and departments associated with the county for over two centuries. The Staffordshire

Left: WFR officers in different orders of dress, 1996; the orderly officer, left, in mess kit complete with duty sword. *(Grenadier Publishing). Right:* At the Staffords' Tercentenary Weekend in 2005. A grenadier from the America-based 'Black Knots' re-enactment society (left) admiring the regimental mascot Watchman, with his handler and an expert of the 80th Regiment in the uniform of 1879 (centre). The 'Black Knots' represent the 64th Regiment in the American War of Independence.

Regiment wears the knot with the Prince of Wales's crest, a combination first seen in the North Staffordshire Regiment. The crest came from the 98th, which took the Prince's title in 1876 after he had presented new colours to the battalion on Malta, a compliment to the previous 98th, the Prince of Wales's Tipperary Regiment (1805–1815). The Stafford knot is worn with the buff holland backing that was added to the South Staffordshires' cap badge in 1935 to symbolise the sacking used to repair uniforms during the extraordinary span of service endured by the 38th Regiment in the West Indies from 1706 to 1766. Alliances with the Jamaica Defence Force and the Antigua

Barbuda Defence Force commemorate this period of the South Staffords' history.

The Worcestershire Regiment's elongated star with the Sherwood Foresters' badge superimposed – a Maltese Cross (from the former 95th Rifles) with a stag in the centre – forms the badge of the WFR. The elongated star is a copy of that worn by officers of the Coldstream Guards, a tradition of the 29th Regiment, whose founder, Thomas Farrington, was once a Coldstreamer. The 29th won special permission to wear their star (like the Coldstream) on the pouch and valise, by which custom they became known as 'The Guards of the Line'. The motto, *Firm*, which

Staffords' Corps of Drums in the 1980s.

has been a feature of the Worcesters' star since 1881, was sanctioned to the 36th Regiment some sixty years before, probably in recognition of its steadfast rearguard action at the Battle of Lauffeldt in 1747. TA units based at Nottingham are responsible for the old volunteer regiments of the county and are guardians of their traditions, which include the Robin Hood Battalion's 1939–45 Belgian *Croix de Guerre* ribbon.

The South Staffords' brass glider badge, awarded for their airborne landings on Sicily in 1943, is worn by all ranks at the top of the right sleeve.

Regimental colouring dominates the uniforms. The buff facings of the 22nd Regiment, restored to the Cheshires in 1904, now appear on drummers' scarlet jackets. No. 1 dress 'blues' imitate this with buff piping around the shoulder straps. After the 1960s, Cheshire Regiment drummers broke with accepted custom and adopted dress cords coloured cerise and buff. Sergeants

and above wear a cerise lanyard in No. 2 dress and cerise pullovers in barrack dress. Cerise- and buff-striped stable belts are fitted with a clasp fashioned with the numeral 22, a promotion of the pre-1881 title that is rarely seen in other regiments today.

WFR drummers wear scarlet tunics with facings of Lincoln green, a shade adopted by the Sherwood Foresters in 1913 and the Worcesters in 1920. Green facings had been a distinction of the 36th and 45th Regiments, and the Derbyshire Militia. The green theme is continued in WFR stable belts, lanyards and No. 1 dress piping.

Staffords' drummers have scarlet tunics embellished with the yellow facings returned to the South Staffords in 1936. No. 1 dress, likewise, has yellow piping, but their scarlet mess jackets bear the black facings of the 64th Regiment, ordered to the North Staffords in 1937. This is the preferred look in the Staffordshire Regiment, which now turns out in black belts, black jerseys for barrack dress and black shoes in service dress.

MUSIC

The Staffordshire Regiment is an arrangement of the former regimental marches *Come Lasses and Lads* (South Staffords, ex-Staffordshire Militia) and *The Days We Went a Gypsying* (North Staffords). *The 80th*, the Staffords' inspection march, the fifes and drums' *We'll Gang Nae Mair to Glasgow Toun*, and *The Gemel Jager Marsch*, adopted on the liberation of Norway in 1945; all come from the South Staffords.

God Bless the Prince of Wales was adopted by the North Staffords in support of their 1876 title. *Zakhmi Dil* or *The Afghan March* is from the same regiment.

Royal Windsor, now played with the Foresters' *Young May Moon*, was presented to the 29th Regiment by Princess Augusta at Windsor in 1791.

The Duchess of Kent, now the WFR slow march, is another legacy of the Worcestershire Regiment, whose custom it was to play *The Lincolnshire Poacher* before other marches to honour their affiliation to the Lincolnshire Regiment, and *Rule Britannia* at the conclusion in memory of their part in the great naval victory of 1 June 1794. Their assembly march, *Hearts Of Oak*, also dates from this episode in the regiment's history.

Crich Memorial, named after the Sherwood Foresters' war memorial, which stands on a high hill overlooking Derbyshire and Nottinghamshire, was adopted by the regiment as its slow march in 1957. The Foresters' call (played on a cornet) was based on a carillon of bells which used to be tolled at a nunnery in Spain during the Peninsular War. Legend tells the story of the mother superior presenting the score to the 45th Regiment in gratitude for sparing her charges 'the rights of the victor'.

Wha Wadna Fecht for Charlie, the unlikely quick march of the Cheshire Regiment, was an old Jacobite tune accepted by the 22nd Regiment in 1851 for its reference to the name Charles. The march is played in homage to Gen Sir Charles Napier, who led the 22nd (Cheshire) Regiment to victory against the emirs of Scinde in 1843. The Cheshires' slow march is *The 22nd Regiment 1772*, their assembly a combination of *A Hundred Pipers* and the traditional county song *The Miller of the Dee*.

Badajoz Day, 1964. Sherwood Foresters with ram mascot and red jacket ceremony.

Painting of the 22nd (Cheshire) Regiment at Meeanee in 1843. *(National Army Museum)*

TRADITIONS

The 1843 Scinde campaign is a proud chapter in the history of the Cheshire Regiment, not least because the 22nd (Cheshire) was the only British regiment under Napier's command when he defeated a Baluchi army 30,000 strong at Meeanee. The three battle honours 'Meeanee', 'Hyderabad' and 'Scinde' are unique to the Cheshires in the British Army and Meeanee Day (17 February) is celebrated annually.

The Cheshires' membership of the Wolfe Society came through the 22nd, which had joined Amherst's 1758 expedition to capture the port of Louisburg on Cape Breton Island. The grenadier company was detached for Wolfe's assault on Quebec in the following year when, at the height of battle, the general died in the arms of Henry Brown of the 22nd. The Foresters' place in the society came

courtesy of the 45th Regiment, which served at the Siege of Louisburg with James Wolfe.

Badajoz Day (6 April) is celebrated in the way of the Sherwood Foresters, with a red coat flown from a flagpole to mark the action of Lt McPherson in the siege of this Spanish border fortress in 1812. When the 45th Regiment reached the citadel, McPherson signalled his section's achievement by running his coat up the flagpole. The Foresters' colours would be trooped on this day and then given over to the sergeants' mess, which hosted a ball in memory of those 'Old Stubborns' who fell at the Siege of Badajoz.

On Alma Day (20 September) tradition dictates that the drums captured by the 95th (Derbyshire) at the Battle of the Alma in 1854 are paraded and the regimental colour is carried by a common soldier in memory of Pte Keenan, who took up the colour after several officers had been killed in the attempt to keep it flying. The dangerous position of colour parties in war led to an army order to the effect that colours would no longer be carried in battle after the Alma. The 95th, which had been in existence for thirty years at the time of the Crimean War, were known as 'The Hosiers' after Derbyshire's hosiery trade and 'The Nails' from the hard nature of the men.

The Glorious First of June was celebrated by Worcesters everywhere to honour the 29th Regiment and its tour of duty with Lord Howe's fleet in the naval victory of 1794. The naval crown borne on the regimental colour today was awarded to the Worcestershire Regiment in 1909 for this action. The loyal toast was made in naval fashion with a special procedure in which the mess president would both propose and make the toast.

The custom of wearing swords in the mess originated in 1746, when officers of the 29th were attacked at dinner by American Indians. For the next 104 years all officers of the regiment wore swords when dining, but from 1850 onwards only the orderly officer and the officer of the week were required to keep the custom. Today the WFR orderly officer and duty field officer wear their swords in the mess but all other officers wear their sword frogs on the Sam Browne belts as a matter of course.

Pte Derby is the regiment's ram mascot, a legacy of the Sherwood Foresters, who maintained the ram traditions of the 95th Regiment and the Derbyshire Militia – a custom probably inspired by the old Jacobite song that was once made into a regimental march, *The Derby Ram*. The first ram was acquired by the 95th during the Siege of Kotah in the Indian Mutiny of 1857. Notable successors were Derby VIII, presented by the Maharajah of Alwar, and Derby X (1900–7), given by the Duke of Devonshire, the first in a long line of Swaledale rams from the herd at Chatsworth. The Staffordshire Regiment

owns bull terrier mascots, each with the name Watchman, a custom begun in 1949 when the 6th Battalion North Staffordshire Regiment (TA) was presented with a Staffordshire bull terrier.

Ypres Day (31 July) commemorates the 1st North Staffords' attack on the first day of hostilities at Ypres in 1917.

Ferozeshah Day (21 December) celebrates the 80th Regiment at the Battle of Ferozeshah in 1845. It was the custom of the South Staffords for the colours to be handed over to the sergeants for the day in honour of Sgt Kirkland, who received a battlefield commission for his capture of a Sikh standard in the fray.

If neither of these anniversaries can be observed in any year then Anzio Day (22 January) or Arnhem Day (17 September) may be substituted. Whichever day is selected, the Ferozeshah sergeants' custom is employed.

THE ROYAL WELSH REGIMENT

The Royal Welsh Regiment (RWR) formed as three battalions on St David's Day 2006: the Royal Welch Fusiliers, the Royal Regiment of Wales and the Royal Welsh Regiment (TA).

The Royal Welch Fusiliers were born at Ludlow in 1689 under Lord Herbert of Chirbury. Although they recruited all over Wales, the Fusiliers annexed the militia regiments of north Wales in 1881 and established bases at Wrexham and Caernarvon.

The Royal Regiment of Wales (RRW), which also dates back to 1689 through its antecedent 24th of Foot, is an amalgamation of the South Wales Borderers (RHQ at Brecon) and the Welch Regiment (RHQ at Cardiff). The RRW headquarters were set up in the Cardiff barracks in 1969.

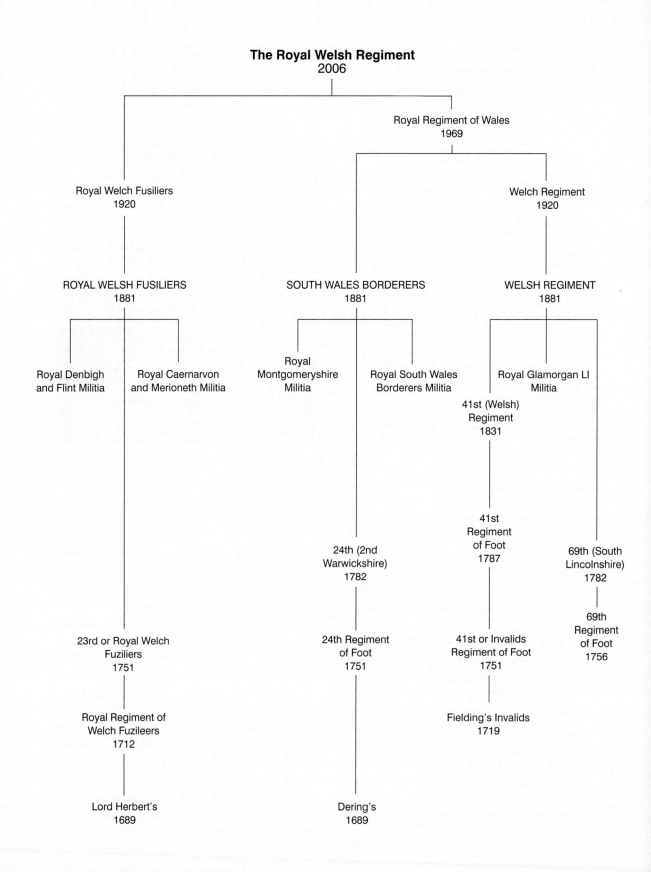

The Royal Welsh Regiment
2006

Royal Regiment of Wales
1969

Royal Welch Fusiliers
1920

Welch Regiment
1920

ROYAL WELSH FUSILIERS
1881

SOUTH WALES BORDERERS
1881

WELSH REGIMENT
1881

Royal Denbigh
and Flint Militia

Royal Caernarvon
and Merioneth Militia

Royal
Montgomeryshire
Militia

Royal South Wales
Borderers Militia

Royal Glamorgan LI
Militia

41st (Welsh)
Regiment
1831

41st
Regiment
of Foot
1787

69th (South
Lincolnshire)
1782

24th (2nd
Warwickshire)
1782

23rd or Royal Welch
Fuziliers
1751

24th Regiment
of Foot
1751

41st or Invalids
Regiment of Foot
1751

69th
Regiment
of Foot
1756

Royal Regiment of
Welch Fuzileers
1712

Fielding's Invalids
1719

Lord Herbert's
1689

Dering's
1689

Corporal and officer of the Royal Welch Fusiliers in No. 2 dress, the flash clearly visible on the officer's jacket. *(RWF Museum)*

DRESS DISTINCTIONS

The blue peaked cap with scarlet band was worn in the forming regiments, though the Fusiliers confined it to officers' uniforms. Other ranks of the RWR now conform to fusilier fashion and wear the regimental khaki beret with the Prince of Wales' badge on a green backing, with the white hackle of the Fusiliers. The Prince of Wales' crest, which was adopted by the RWF in 1714 and the 41st in 1831, became the cap badge of the Welsh Regiment in 1881 and the RRW in 1969. The beret hackle, adopted by the RWF after the Second World War, replicates the white plume that had been worn on their full dress caps since 1768.

RWR collar badges incorporate the wreath of immortelles that displaced the sphinx on Borderers' collar badges in 1958,

the Welsh dragon collar badge of the Welch Regiment (which was combined with the wreath for the RRW) and the Fusiliers' grenade. The ancient Welsh dragon badge was adopted by Welsh militia regiments and passed on to the Welsh regulars in 1881.

The unique flash of five black swallow-tail ribbons that hangs from the back of the collar in No. 1s, No. 2s and mess dress, is an eighteenth-century relic originally worn to tie the queue bag that kept the powdered wig from staining the red coat. When queues were abolished in 1808 officers of the 23rd Fusiliers continued to wear the ribbons, but Lt Col Harrison had to defend their use in 1834 and dashed off to seek permission from the King, who granted the flash as a 'peculiarity whereby to mark the dress of

De Neuville's painting of the 24th at Rorke's Drift, 22 January 1879.

that distinguished regiment'. The distinction was later extended to senior sergeants of the RWF, and to other ranks in 1900.

The green half of the regimental stable belt relates to the green belts of the RRW, which were based on the green facings of the 24th and 69th Regiments – and the SWB from 1905. Shoulder belts worn by ensigns, goat majors and drum majors bear the motto taken by Lt Col Williams from the Mackworths of Usk

Band and drums of the Royal Regiment of Wales, c. 1990. *(MoD)*

RWF goat major with regimental goat at Caernarvon Castle, the ceremonial pioneers on parade. *(RWF Museum)*

for his 41st Regiment in 1831 – *Gwell angau na chywillyd* (Death rather than dishonour).

Full dress scarlet is issued to drummers, goat handlers and RWF pioneers. A white Victorian tropical helmet adopted by the RRW around the 100th anniversary of the Zulu War of 1879 invokes a famous episode in the history of the South Wales Borderers brought to public attention in the film *Zulu*.

MUSIC

The British Grenadiers was imposed on all fusilier regiments around 1835 because of the grenadier bearskins which adorned these regiments at the time.

The War Song of the Men of Glamorgan together with *Forth to the Battle* form the RWF slow march. The contrary reference to southern Wales here vies with *Men of Harlech* in the RRW.

The Royal Welch Fusiliers, penned by John Philip Sousa, was presented to the regiment of that name in 1930 to mark its fellowship with the US Marine Corps forged in the Boxer Rebellion of 1900.

Men of Harlech, the RRW quick march, was inherited from the South Wales Borderers, who came by it through their militia battalions.

Scipio, written by Handel when the 41st was filling with disabled veterans from

The youngest private in the 1st Welch eating the leek on St David's Day, 1952, on active service in Korea; mascot Taffy VII held in check by Goat Maj Williams. *(RRW Museum)*

Marlborough's wars, was chosen to be the RRW slow march.

Other marches of the regiment are *God Bless the Prince of Wales*, *Ap Shenkin* (1st Welch), *The Lincolnshire Poacher* (2nd Welch, ex-69th) and *Warwickshire Lads* (24th Regiment).

On dinner nights hymns played in the 41st Regiment during the Afghan War of 1842 are traditionally aired. *Sun of my Soul*, *Spanish Chant* and *Vesper Hymn* were played by the band of the Welch Regiment on Sunday evenings.

TRADITIONS

All battalions keep a goat to take pride of place on parades. The earliest recorded example was that of the 23rd (Royal Regiment of Welch Fuziliers), whose goats preceded the mascots of other regiments by many decades. The first goat from the royal herd was presented to the 23rd by Queen Victoria in 1844, a decade before the 41st acquired its first. The animals are the essence of the regiment, and once accompanied their battalion on campaign and even into battle. The Borderers had few Welsh traditions and never took goats, but the RRW continued the Welch Regiment tradition and named its goats Taffy, Shenkin, Dewi or Sospan according to battalion custom.

St David's Day (1 March) is observed with the time-honoured ritual developed by the 23rd Fusiliers. Newcomers to the officers' mess, the sergeants' mess and the other ranks' dining hall are required to eat a raw leek in their respective venues to a drum roll under the watchful eye of the regimental goat. All ranks wear a leek in their headdress and in the Fusiliers a toast is made to 'Toby Purcell, His Spurs and St David'. This toast remembers a senior officer of the regiment, who fought at the Battle of the Boyne in 1690, and his spurs, which were passed on to successive seconds in command until lost to a fire in 1842. A dispensation from the need to drink the loyal toast or to stand for the national anthem on other days of the year came from the Prince Regent, who was cognisant of the 23rd Fusiliers' loyalty during the mutiny at the Nore in 1797. A RWF tradition in which officers ride in a five-mile steeplechase for the Red Dragon Cup was started on St David's Day, 1838.

Rorke's Drift Day (22 January) is when young recruits are initiated in the history of the regiment, principally the celebrated exploits of B Company, 2nd Battalion the 24th Regiment at the mission station at Rorke's Drift in South Africa. This small band of men stood alone against a Zulu army of some 4,000 warriors and held it at bay for two days and a night, just after the 1st Battalion had been annihilated by the same impi at nearby Isandhlwana. The 24th won a record number of Victoria Crosses, first to five men of the 2nd Battalion, who rescued a shore party from hostile natives on the Andaman Islands in 1867, and then to seven men of the same battalion for the defence of Rorke's Drift in 1879.

On Rorke's Drift Day the colours are paraded through barracks to let everyone see the silver wreath of immortelles that is permanently attached to the Queen's colour. This unique honour was approved by Queen Victoria in December 1880, some months after she had asked to see the Queen's colour of the 1st Battalion, which had been rescued from the bloodbath at Isandhlwana by Lts Melvill and Coghill.

They rushed it from the battlefield only to be slowed down by the strong current of the Buffalo river before being overpowered by Zulus. The colour was found the next day further downstream.

Gheluvelt Day (31 October) commemorates the 1914 battle in which both the Welsh Regiment and the South Wales Borderers had committed battalions to heavy loss. The Worcesters gave valuable support at the Chateau Gheluvelt and greetings are still exchanged with them.

Many infantry regiments have paraded ceremonial pioneers to commemorate the days when regimental pioneers went before the marching battalion to cut a path through natural obstacles with assorted tools, but only the RWF sought the proper authority to parade with ceremonial pioneers. They saw this as a privilege that required suitable representation and always made sure that a section of eight pioneers wearing a white buckskin apron and gauntlets marched at the head of the battalion, second only to the regimental goat. The pioneer sergeant's beard is a symbol of his experience, as his section's polished shovels, mattocks, axes and picks are symbols of their trade.

The RWF journal *Y Ddraig Goch* (the Red Dragon) testifies to the Welsh language spoken in the regiment, a skill that has proved useful on active service when radio messages have to be unintelligible to the enemy.

THE ROYAL IRISH REGIMENT

This large formation is the product of the 1992 amalgamation of the regular and TA battalions of the Royal Irish Rangers and the home service battalions of the Ulster Defence Regiment (UDR).

Royal Irish officers in the regiment's distinctive version of No. 2 dress, 1999. *(Grenadier Publishing)*

The Rangers were formed in 1968 when the three established infantry regiments of Northern Ireland were brought together. The UDR was created two years later as a direct response to the civil unrest in the province; its home service battalions vary in response to the level of sectarian violence in Ulster.

The Rangers title was previously used by a regiment of southern Ireland – the Connaught Rangers, raised in 1793. A previous Royal Irish Regiment – formerly the 18th of Foot, formed in 1684 – was disbanded with the Connaught Rangers and three other Irish regiments in 1922.

Regimental headquarters are in St Patrick's Barracks at Ballymena in County Antrim.

DRESS DISTINCTIONS

General service battalions continue to wear the Rangers' green *caubeen* with its green hackle, while the home service battalions keep to the green beret of the UDR, but the Angel harp and crown badge is worn throughout the regiment. The Fusiliers wore blue *caubeens* from around 1945, though their pipers had them in the 1920s, but the green *caubeen* and hackle, with the harp and crown badge, came from the Royal Ulster Rifles.

The collar badge, an Inniskilling scroll and castle with St George's flag flying from the battlements, came from the Royal Inniskilling Fusiliers. It commemorates the siege of Enniskillen in 1689, when the regiment was formed out of the town's Protestant defenders.

The general service battalions wear Rangers uniforms, which are based on those of the Royal Ulster Rifles: green No. 1 dress with the *caubeen*, black belt and buttons. Officers wear the Rifles' black leather pouch belt with a whistle and chain hanging from a shamrock boss, the pouch mounted with the Barrosa eagle of the former Royal Irish Fusiliers. This marks the capture of the imperial eagle of the French 8th Regiment by Sgt Masterson of the 87th at the Battle of Barrosa in 1811, when the Prince Regent showed his pleasure by conferring the eagle emblem on the regiment's insignia.

Green No. 1 dress with bright buttons is issued to the mascot handler, buglers, pipers and drummers. The pipers' version meets with a design first seen in the Royal

Irish Fusiliers around 1922: a green doublet with white edging tape and buttonhole loops, traditional saffron kilt, a black patent leather purse and green cloak chained across to a Celtic Tara brooch. Pipers of the Inniskillings wore grey jackets, acknowledging the grey coats worn by Tiffen's Regiment in 1689.

Mess jackets are scarlet with green facings, a reminder of the redcoat fusiliers.

MUSIC

The regimental quick march, *Killaloe*, was written around 1887 and is punctuated by yells from the ranks. The Irish Fusiliers' war cry *Faugh a Ballagh!* (Clear the way!) is now the regimental motto.

The slow march, *Eileen Alannagh*, was adopted in 1972. Regimental marches played prior to amalgamation, and now on suitable occasions, are *Sprig o' Shellalagh* and *Rory o' More* (Royal Inniskilling Fusiliers), *Off, Off Said the Stranger*, adopted by the 83rd around 1879 (Royal Ulster Rifles) and, from the Royal Irish Fusiliers, *St Patrick's Day*, *Garryowen*, *Barrosa* and *Norah Creina*.

TRADITIONS

Vesting, or Rangers' Day (1 July) commemorates the 1968 amalgamation, the 1881 amalgamations, and the day in 1916 when eighteen battalions of the Northern Irish Division fought in the opening Battle of the Somme.

Shamrock is worn on 'Paddy's Day', a custom of the old Irish regiments now lost to most natives of the Emerald Isle.

On Barrosa Day (5 March) the Rangers maintained a mess custom in which brandy, whiskey, curaçao and sherry were mixed together in the Barrosa Cup to celebrate an unfortunate direct hit on the liquor wagon, which resulted in a sudden drop in the 87th's drinks ration. A sad poem sung by officers at

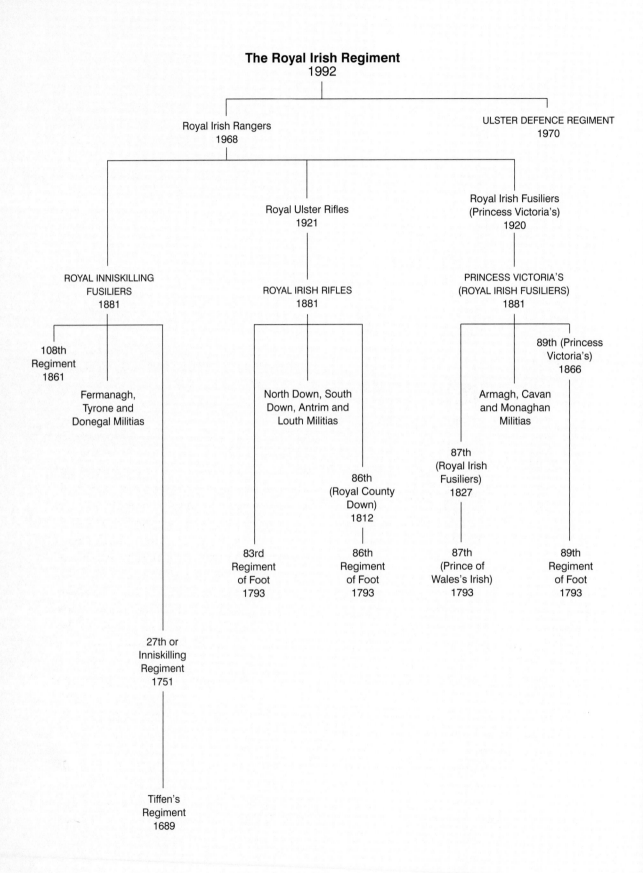

The Royal Irish Regiment
1992

Royal Irish Rangers
1968

ULSTER DEFENCE REGIMENT
1970

Royal Ulster Rifles
1921

Royal Irish Fusiliers
(Princess Victoria's)
1920

ROYAL INNISKILLING
FUSILIERS
1881

ROYAL IRISH RIFLES
1881

PRINCESS VICTORIA'S
(ROYAL IRISH FUSILIERS)
1881

108th
Regiment
1861

89th (Princess
Victoria's)
1866

Fermanagh,
Tyrone and
Donegal Militias

North Down, South
Down, Antrim and
Louth Militias

Armagh, Cavan
and Monaghan
Militias

87th
(Royal Irish
Fusiliers)
1827

86th
(Royal County
Down)
1812

83rd
Regiment
of Foot
1793

86th
Regiment
of Foot
1793

87th
(Prince of
Wales's Irish)
1793

89th
Regiment
of Foot
1793

27th or
Inniskilling
Regiment
1751

Tiffen's
Regiment
1689

Pipers of the Royal Irish Fusiliers in Tripoli, 1959. *(Regiment)*

THE PARACHUTE REGIMENT

Volunteers for parachute training were recruited during the early years of the Second World War, though parachute trials for military use had been pioneered by the Italians in 1927, the Russians in 1930 and the Germans in 1936. Parachute battalions formed in 1942 were put together as a regiment seven years later.

In 1950 King George VI presented colours to each battalion with the motto *Utrinque paratus* (Ready for anything) embroidered on. The Parachute Regiment recruited in its own right from 1952 from its base at Browning Barracks in Aldershot. Regimental headquarters are now located in the Colchester Garrison.

DRESS DISTINCTIONS

The maroon beret, which has been used to distinguish all airborne units since 1942, is worn by all personnel in most orders of dress. The regimental badge, a spread of wings with an open parachute and royal crest thereon, is worn on the beret, parade uniform collars, belts and buttons. Uniforms conform to standard infantry pattern except for the smock, which is designed for parachuting.

All trained members wear a wings emblem at the top of the sleeve to show they have passed through training and made the required number of jumps, one of which is made at night.

Stable belts and distinguishing stripes on No. 1 dress 'blues' are maroon, though lanyards are worn to battalion colours.

MUSIC

The inspiring quick march *Ride of the Valkyries* was arranged for the regiment in 1950 from Wagner's *Die Walkurie*, which retold the Norse legend of Odin's *Valkyrja*,

the anniversary dinner recounted the battle's events, and a speech made by the newest subaltern related the story and order of battle.

On Waterloo Day (18 June) regimental custom dictates that officers fall in on parade and then fall out again to allow the sergeants command of their companies. This practice highlights the officer casualties of the 27th (Inniskilling) Regiment at the Battle of Waterloo.

A succession of Irish Wolfhound mascots has been maintained since 1971, all endowed with the name of the ancient Irish chieftain, Brian Boru.

Paras on Salisbury Plain
on 16 Air Assault Brigade's
exercise, 2003. *(MoD)*

the 'Choosers of the slain' who rode through the sky to the battle.

A shortened version of Elgar's *Pomp and Circumstance March No. 4* is the regimental slow march.

The three battalion bands formed in 1947–8 were amalgamated into one prior to the restructure of army bands in 1994.

TRADITIONS

'Paras' are short on regimental history but unsurpassed in regimental pride. Recruits learn about early operations at Bruneval, Normandy and Arnhem, as well as the more recent Falkland Islands conflict, while undergoing infantry training, which extends to P Company, the harsh pre-parachute selection test devised in the 1940s to produce soldiers that will be equal to the particular dangers faced by the paratrooper.

Para training looks for courage, peak physical fitness and a self-reliance that is unmatched by any other unit outside the airborne brotherhood. Soldiers who survive P Company are packed off to the RAF and Parachute Training School (motto *Knowledge dispels fear*) to qualify in their chosen role for the 'Maroon Machine'.

On Airborne Forces Day, veterans of the Parachute Regimental Association gather together. Individual battle anniversaries used to be observed within the battalions but representatives of the regiment are still sent to events on the Continent that commemorate wartime operations at the battle sites.

In 1955 the first of the regiment's Shetland pony mascots was adopted: Pegasus in 1 Para, Bruneval in 2 Para and Coed Goch Samswn in 3 Para.

THE GURKHA BRIGADE

The Gurkha Brigade is the collective term for the various Gurkha battalions and units that have been integrated into the British Army since four regiments of Gurkha Rifles (the 2nd, 6th, 7th and 10th) were transferred from the Indian Army after Indian independence in 1947.

Gurkhas come from the mountainous principality of Ghorka in Nepal. Their long relationship with the British Army began in northern India in 1813, when their warlike expansion into neighbouring lands clashed with British interests and a determined conflict ensued in which both sides grew to admire the other's bravery.

The army finally accepted the Gurkhas' offer of help in the Indian Mutiny and has sustained the bond ever since.

Brigade headquarters are at the airfield camp near Netheravon in Wiltshire.

DRESS DISTINCTIONS

The black Kilmarnock cap, adopted around 1860, is worn with No.1 dress; the Kashmiri, a stiff-brimmed hat based on the slouch hat worn from 1901 in hot climes, is reserved for service dress. In working dress the beret is worn, green for the Royal Gurkha Rifles and blue for the support regiments.

Badges are designed around the Gurkhas' heavy knife that is carried on the back of the belt on all orders of dress. The kukri is a close combat weapon with a curved blade which broadens to a point. The badge of the Royal Gurkha Rifles (RGR) and the brigade band has two crossed kukris with a crown above. The Queen's Gurkha Engineers' kukris are embellished with the RE grenade and motto within the RE

Subaltern in RGR No. 1 dress with the Queen's Truncheon in 2000. Note the Royal Green Jackets' badge on his black belt. *(Grenadier Publishing)*

crowned wreath, the Queen's Gurkha Signals' kukris lie between the Royal Signals' figure of Mercury and the motto, and the Queen's Own Gurkha Logistic Regiment wear the star of the Royal Logistic Corps badge with the crossed kukris thereon. On the Kashmiri, RGR wear their badge pinned to a patch of Hunting Stuart tartan, a distinction of 10GR worn to mark their affiliation to the Royal Scots.

No. 1 dress is rifle green in the RGR and the band, and blue in the support regiments. 'Blues' are distinguished by trouser stripes that correspond to those on the uniforms of the associated corps, Royal Engineers, Royal Signals or Royal Logistic Corps.

RGR uniform collars are underlined with scarlet piping, a peculiarity of 2GR worn to signify its special relationship with the King's Royal Rifle Corps, whose green jackets were regimentally coloured with scarlet facings. Belts and buttons conform to the Rifles' black pattern. The waist belt is worn over a black cummerbund in service

The Royal Gurkha Rifles
1994

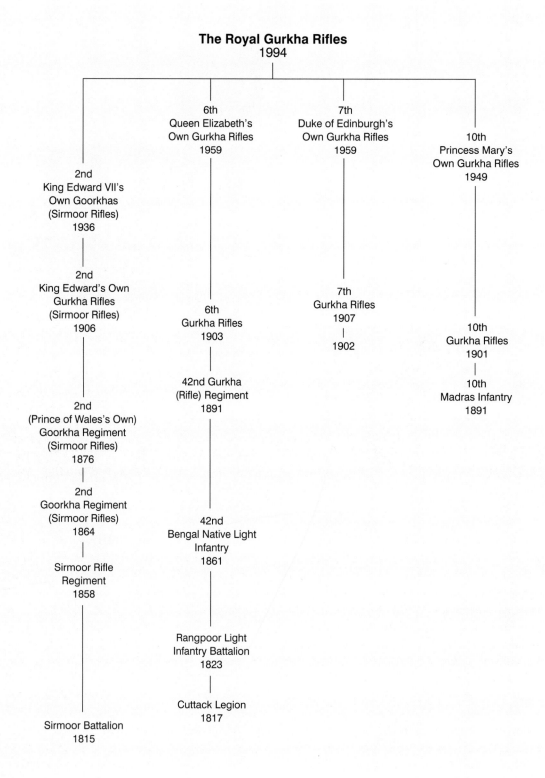

6th
Queen Elizabeth's
Own Gurkha Rifles
1959

7th
Duke of Edinburgh's
Own Gurkha Rifles
1959

10th
Princess Mary's
Own Gurkha Rifles
1949

2nd
King Edward VII's
Own Goorkhas
(Sirmoor Rifles)
1936

2nd
King Edward's Own
Gurkha Rifles
(Sirmoor Rifles)
1906

6th
Gurkha Rifles
1903

7th
Gurkha Rifles
1907

1902

10th
Gurkha Rifles
1901

42nd Gurkha
(Rifle) Regiment
1891

10th
Madras Infantry
1891

2nd
(Prince of Wales's Own)
Goorkha Regiment
(Sirmoor Rifles)
1876

2nd
Goorkha Regiment
(Sirmoor Rifles)
1864

42nd
Bengal Native Light
Infantry
1861

Sirmoor Rifle
Regiment
1858

Rangpoor Light
Infantry Battalion
1823

Cuttack Legion
1817

Sirmoor Battalion
1815

Recruits at the brigade depot (Malay Lines) in No. 6 warm weather dress.

dress. The black pouch belt, worn by officers across the shoulder, is ornamented with the badges of affiliated regiments: the Royal Green Jackets' on the front and the King's Royal Hussars' on the back pouch. The silver ram's head, from which hangs the whistle chain, commemorates the Sirmoor Battalion's assault on Fort Koonja in 1824.

Gurkha pipers date from the old days of Empire when Indian Army units liked to emulate the sounds of Scottish regiments stationed in India. Their uniforms are identified by tartans: McLecce in the Queen's Gurkha Engineers, Red Grant in the Queen's Gurkha Signals and McDuff in the Queen's Own Gurkha Logistic Regiment. Pipers of the Royal Gurkha Rifles wear the Douglas tartan of the Cameronians (Scottish Rifles), a legacy of their affiliated regiment the 7GR, whose uniform was marked out by Douglas tartan trews.

MUSIC

The Brigade quick march is *Yo Nepali*. The Rifles march to *The Bravest of the Brave* in quick time, *The Keel Row* in double time and *God Bless the Prince of Wales* in slow time. The slow march came from 2GR and relates to its 1876–1906 title. The RGR pipers' march is the traditional Scottish *Garb of Old Gaul*.

The Gurkha Band was made by merging the 2GR band, formed in 1859, with the Staff Band of the Brigade of Gurkhas, formed in 1958.

7th Gurkha Rifles sharpening kukris for the Falklands War, 1982.

TRADITIONS

The great respect with which Gurkhas are held in the army is generated by their conduct, efficiency and bravery, qualities that are underpinned by the RGR motto *Kafar hunnu bhanda marnu ramro* (It is better to die than be a coward).

No colours are carried in the brigade but the Rifles march behind their Queen's Truncheon, which was ordered to 2GR by Queen Victoria when it became a rifle regiment after the Indian Mutiny. As a rifle regiment, the 2nd had to lay up its colours, one of which was an honorary colour awarded for its bravery at Delhi, where the regiment formed an undying association with the 60th Rifles. The truncheon dismantles into five pieces to facilitate it being carried into battle by five soldiers. The crown is supported by three Gurkha figures on a ring of silver inscribed MAIN PICQUET, HINDOO RAO'S HOUSE, DELHI 1857. On a lower ring the inscription is repeated in Nagri script. In 2GR the men called the truncheon *Nishani Mai* (the Great Mother) and swore their oath of allegiance on it when joining the regiment. On anniversaries like Delhi Day (14 September) and the crossing of the Tigris in 1917, the truncheon would be put out for saluting.

THE ROYAL GREEN JACKETS

The Royal Green Jackets (RGJ) was formed in 1966 when the three battalions of the Green Jackets Brigade were brought together as a regiment. The brigade had been formed in 1958 from the regiments first trained in light infantry tactics – the Oxfordshire and Buckinghamshire Light Infantry (OBLI), the King's Royal Rifle Corps (KRRC) and the Rifle Brigade.

The royal title came from the old 60th, styled the Royal American Regiment in 1757. The regiment was raised in Pennsylvania two years earlier under a bill that allowed the King the right to grant commissions to foreign Protestants for military service in the Americas. Almost 200 years later, during the Second World War, the KRRC got special permission to train a cadre of Americans as officers in the regiment.

The term 'Green Jackets' was first applied to the experimental rifle battalions created at the end of the eighteenth century to operate in open skirmish order with the deadly Baker rifle. The first had a high proportion of German light troops and dressed its riflemen in the green jackets worn by German hunters and woodsmen, a distinction copied by successive rifle battalions. The concept prospered and riflemen became the subject of popular legend.

Regimental headquarters are at Peninsula Barracks in Winchester, the shared depot of the KRRC and the Rifle Brigade from 1858. Peninsula recalls the war in which the four original regiments successfully employed the specialist light infantry movements taught by Sir John Moore, the pioneer of the famous Light Division.

DRESS DISTINCTIONS

Caps and berets are rifle green, the colour of Rifles and Light Infantry headgear since the

An officer of the 95th Rifles re-enactment group with light infantry in the background in uniforms of the Napoleonic Wars.

Bugler of 1RGJ, *c.* 2002. *(MoD)*

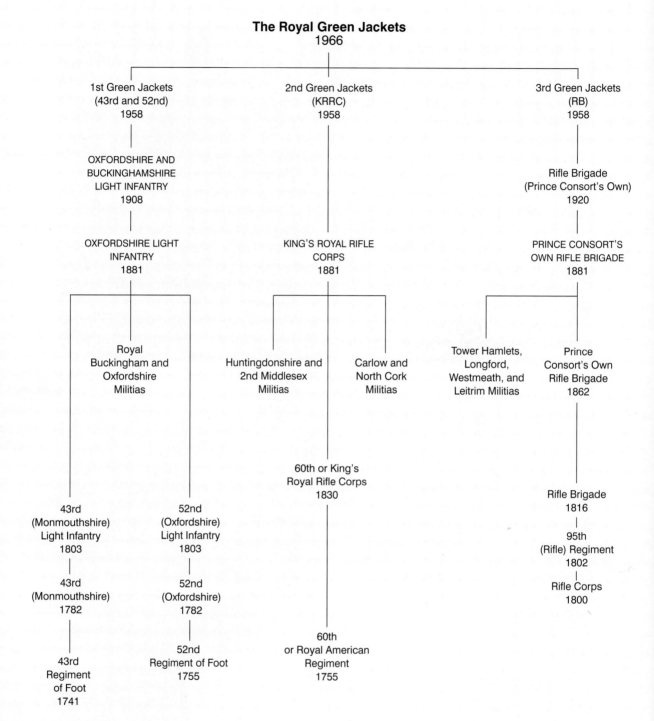

The Royal Green Jackets
1966

1st Green Jackets
(43rd and 52nd)
1958

2nd Green Jackets
(KRRC)
1958

3rd Green Jackets
(RB)
1958

OXFORDSHIRE AND
BUCKINGHAMSHIRE
LIGHT INFANTRY
1908

Rifle Brigade
(Prince Consort's Own)
1920

OXFORDSHIRE LIGHT
INFANTRY
1881

KING'S ROYAL RIFLE
CORPS
1881

PRINCE CONSORT'S
OWN RIFLE BRIGADE
1881

Royal
Buckingham and
Oxfordshire
Militias

Huntingdonshire and
2nd Middlesex
Militias

Carlow and
North Cork
Militias

Tower Hamlets,
Longford,
Westmeath, and
Leitrim Militias

Prince
Consort's Own
Rifle Brigade
1862

60th or King's
Royal Rifle Corps
1830

Rifle Brigade
1816

43rd
(Monmouthshire)
Light Infantry
1803

52nd
(Oxfordshire)
Light Infantry
1803

95th
(Rifle) Regiment
1802

43rd
(Monmouthshire)
1782

52nd
(Oxfordshire)
1782

Rifle Corps
1800

52nd
Regiment of Foot
1755

60th
or Royal American
Regiment
1755

43rd
Regiment
of Foot
1741

Riflemen operating the pairs system in the field, 1997. *(Grenadier Publishing)*

late Victorian era. The cap badge is based on that of the Rifle Brigade, a Maltese cross inscribed with battle honours within a crowned laurel wreath and naval crown marked COPENHAGEN 2ND APRIL 1801. An inscribed Maltese cross without a wreath, which formed the badge of the KRRC, originated on officers' pouch belts in the 5th Battalion of the 60th Rifles, raised in 1797 – the first of the regiment's Green Jackets. The cross is thought to have come from a German officer of the battalion (Hompesch), who was a Knight of Malta. The strung bugle horn at the centre of the cross, worn by all light infantry and rifle regiments, now appears on the front of the green side hat worn by RGJ officers.

No. 2 dress is worn with the green cap, the jacket distinguished with the Rifles' black belt and buttons, and a small, blackened bugle horn collar badge.

No. 1 dress and mess dress 'greens' have no collar badge – a regimental tradition.

Officers' tunics of 'Ox and Bucks' vintage have a button and length of braid sewn onto the collar, a unique distinction of the Oxfords' officers, who wore it as a relic of the eighteenth-century gorget which used to hang from buttons on the collar. Buglers wear gold-laced shoulder wings on the tunic and the plumed busby that was peculiar to rifle regiments from 1890. The bugle major is equipped with a traditional Rifles officers' braided tunic and the black pouch belt that goes with it. The regimental nickname, 'Black Mafia', stems from this dark order of dress and the regiment's well-connected officers.

MUSIC

The regimental march is made up of *Huntsman's Chorus* from the KRRC and *The Italian Song* adopted by 4th Battalion of the Oxfordshire and Buckinghamshire on campaign in Italy in 1943. Weber's *Huntsman's Chorus* (previously *Lutzow's Wild Chase*) speaks of the German *Jagers* who went to fill the ranks of the 60th Rifles' 5th Battalion in 1797 and Lutzow's German riflemen who fought against Napoleon in the ensuing wars.

The RGJ uphold the fast marching pace of their antecedent regiments and chose *The Road to the Isles* for their double past. Other regimental marches are *Nach Flager Von Grenada* (43rd) and *The Lower Castle Yard* (52nd) of the Ox and Bucks, and *I'm Ninety Five* of the Rifle Brigade, which held that number in the line before changing to brigade status.

TRADITIONS

Regimental anniversaries concern birth dates and battle days, mostly inherited; 1 January celebrates the formation of the Royal Green Jackets in 1966, but the regimental day is 25 July. In July 1968 battalion subtitles were abolished and a 'one regiment' spirit was encouraged.

The date 17 January marks the birth of the 43rd Regiment in 1741, 20 December the 52nd in 1755 and 25 December the 60th Regiment, also in 1755; 25 August commemorates the day in 1800 when the Rifle Corps first saw action, at Ferrol on the Spanish coast; 11 November remembers the KRRC at the Battle of Nonne Bosschen in 1914; 28 February the Relief of Ladysmith in 1900, which involved the KRRC and the RB; and 18 June the 52nd's defeat of the *Chasseurs de la Garde* at Waterloo, an important day in the Oxfordshires.

The date 14 September (Delhi Day) commemorates the struggle of the 52nd and the 60th against the Indian mutineers during the siege of 1857, and the start of the KRRCs' enduring friendship with 2nd Gurkha Rifles.

Membership of the Wolfe Society is inherited from the OBLI and the KRRC. At the Battle of Quebec in 1759 Gen Wolfe described the 60th as 'Swift and Bold', an acclamation the regiment later turned into a motto (*Celer et Audax*) and its ethos.

Green Jackets' drill has long differed from accepted army practice. The normal marching pace of 120 to the minute is upped to 140–180 per minute at the double, a reminder of the Napoleonic Wars when riflemen were trained to run ahead of the main body to skirmish with the enemy. This rapid deployment over wide areas of rough terrain meant that the Green Jackets had to be able to travel light, without the usual paraphernalia carried by the redcoats. Colours and drums, therefore, were dismissed from Green Jacket tradition and bugles replaced drums to convey orders across the battlefield. Today, buglers are seen in the RGJ where drummers are normally employed in other regiments. Rifles are traditionally carried down 'at the trail' with a loose sling, a throwback to days when light infantrymen had to march ready to give fire. Bayonets are referred to as swords because swords used to be issued instead of bayonets to extend the short Baker rifle to normal length. Emphasis is still placed on the Rifle regiments' old philosophy of discipline through encouragement and initiative.

THE SPECIAL AIR SERVICE REGIMENT

The Special Air Service Regiment (SAS) grew out of commando units formed in North Africa during the Second World War for raids behind enemy lines. Maj David Stirling of No. 8 Commando, who initiated parachute training for airborne attacks on German installations in the desert, was given command of the first special service regiment in 1942. After Stirling's capture in January 1943 a second 'special' regiment was created with his brother at its head. The word Special describes the units' departure from conventional tactics.

After the war SAS and commando units were disbanded but in 1947 the former was

Maj David Stirling with his Long Range Desert Group in North Africa, 1942. *(Imperial War Museum)*

reconstituted in a TA battalion when the Artists Rifles, a London volunteer unit raised in 1860, was transferred from the Rifle Brigade as 21SAS. During the Malayan emergency a need was identified for a special force that could survive in the jungle. Former Chindits and SAS soldiers were recruited to form the Malayan Scouts (SAS), which was admitted to the army list in 1952 as the Special Air Service. The regiment has been based at Hereford since 1960.

DRESS DISTINCTIONS

The beige beret and the winged dagger badge (with its motto *Who Dares Wins*) originated with Stirling and his men in 1942. The dagger symbolises the weapon used by commandos when operating by stealth, although it is officially described as a representation of Excalibur striking downwards.

The secretive nature of the regiment's work requires special clothing and kit, most famously black combats and balaclavas. Badges of rank are not worn on operational duties. The stable belt is blue.

No. 1 dress 'blues' are distinguished by a Pompadour (light blue) stripe on trousers and overalls. The CO and Officer of the Day traditionally wear a black leather pouch belt mounted with a silver whistle chain and the Mars and Minerva badge of the Artists Rifles.

MUSIC

The *Marche du Regiment Parachutist Belge* (quick) and *Lillie Marlene* (slow), are both reminiscent of the Second World War, when the regiment first made its mark on the world. The quick march refers to the year 1944 when the SAS Brigade embraced Belgian and Free French parachute squadrons.

TRADITIONS

Most countries keep a special force for covert operations but the SAS is world famous for its intensive training and efficiency. From the doctrine of small units tying down entire armies to damage and demoralise the enemy, often on its own territory, came the basic four-man patrol, composed of a leader, scout, signaller and medic. Stirling devised small operational patrols in the desert on the premise that they would be less noticeable than a large assault force. The regiment was the first to perfect the technique of abseiling from helicopters as a rapid-drop manoeuvre.

Officers and troopers work together to the highest standards, imbued with self-discipline, often disguised as natives of the region in which they operate. Individual identities and achievements are never publicly aired or celebrated.

THE SPECIAL RECONNAISSANCE REGIMENT

The Special Reconnaissance Regiment (SRR) was formed in 2005 as part of the special forces group for covert surveillance work in support of international expeditionary operations in the fight against terrorism.

DRESS DISTINCTIONS

A beige beret was adopted on formation, as worn in the SAS. The cap badge is an ancient Corinthian helmet on a special forces' upright dagger with a scroll labelled 'Reconnaissance'. The helmet, with its dark eye-holes, symbolises the unseen watcher.

MUSIC

The official march of the Reconnaissance Corps formed in the Second World War was *Away to the Mountain's Brow*.

TRADITIONS

The Reconnaissance Corps born in 1941 was employed to scout ahead of army divisions to determine enemy strength and movements, a hazardous task that required men with good survival skills.

THE ARMY AIR CORPS

The Army Air Corps (AAC) was formed in 1957 out of the Royal Artillery's Observation Post squadrons and the light liaison flights of the Glider Pilot Regiment, both created in 1942. The corps employs six regiments, five independent squadrons and various flights stationed around the globe to give helicopter support to land forces and an air assault capacity in battle. Corps headquarters and the School of Army Aviation are located at Middle Wallop in Hampshire.

DRESS DISTINCTIONS

A Cambridge blue beret is worn by all ranks, the badge pinned to a square patch of dark blue. The corps badge, a restyling of the eagle badge of the Glider Pilot Regiment, shows an eagle landing, contained within a crowned wreath.

The eagle alighting without the crown and wreath is worn on collars, buttons and on sergeants' sleeves above the chevrons.

No. 1 dress 'blues' are identified by the beret, Cambridge blue piping on the shoulder straps, and a broad scarlet stripe on the trousers like that worn by the Royal Artillery, which helped form the AAC, and the Royal Engineers, who pioneered army flying. Bandsmen wear a full dress blue tunic which is fashioned with a double-breasted plastron in the style of jackets of the Royal Flying Corps from 1912 to 1918.

MUSIC

The corps quick march is *Recce Flight*, the slow march, *Thievish Magpie*, a martial reworking of Rossini's opera score of 1817.

TRADITIONS

In the 1950s and '60s, pilots of the AAC were supported by ground crew supplied by

AAC soldiers grounding arms in front of a Lynx. *(MoD)*

the Royal Armoured Corps and the Royal Artillery. It wasn't until 1973 that the corps recruited its own air troopers, who, after promotion to corporal, may apply for pilot training; two-thirds of army pilots are non-commissioned officers.

The 2nd Regiment AAC is responsible for ground-crew training, which involves base protection, ground-to-aircraft communications, arming and fuelling.

Candidates for pilot training have to pass RAF selection tests and army flying grading on fixed-wing aircraft before ground school, which deals with basic principles of flight, meteorology, navigation, and aeromedical and survival training. After nine weeks at the Defence Helicopter Flying School, trainee pilots go for operational training at the School of Army Aviation for eighteen weeks before converting to type. Helicopter types range from

Officers' mess dinner night at Middle Wallop. Uniforms without Cambridge blue facings are guests from other corps. *(MoD)*

the general purpose Gazelle to the anti-tank Lynx and the sophisticated Apache attack.

Helicopters' traditional use, in observation, troop lifts and casualty evacuation, now extends to aerial command posts, fire support and

The regimental padre heads a service for three Staffords killed in Iraq, 2005.

missile strikes on heavy targets. Their extensive use in the army has transformed the way it operates in all situations and the AAC may now be recognised as the new combat arm.

The corps' cavalry-style guidons are emblazoned with the badges of the Royal Artillery and the Glider Pilot Regiment, with battle honours for the Falkland Islands and the Gulf conflicts.

THE ROYAL ARMY CHAPLAINS' DEPARTMENT

 An Army Chaplains' Department was set up in 1796 after an expedition to the West Indies had to leave without a single cleric on board to look after the soldiers' spiritual needs. Before this sudden decline in the support of civilian clergymen, British regiments had always sailed with a chaplain in the ranks. Presbyterian ministers were admitted to the department in 1827, followed by Roman Catholic in 1836, Wesleyan in 1881 and Jewish in 1892.

The 'Padres' lost 172 officers helping soldiers in the trenches during the First World War, and in 1919 the department was granted its Royal title.

DRESS DISTINCTIONS

The blue peaked cap is distinguished by a purple band and the RAChD badge, a Maltese cross on a crowned laurel and oak wreath with, in the centre, a voided quatrefoil with a circle inscribed IN THIS SIGN CONQUER, the exclamation of the Emperor Constantine who converted to Christianity after seeing a cross in the sky. Jewish chaplains wear a Star of David in place of the Maltese cross and no motto.

In service dress a white clerical collar is worn instead of shirt, and a black leather pouch belt with the badge is worn over the jacket. Buttons and rank pips are black. The blue mess dress has purple facings.

MUSIC

The RAChD march is Jeremiah Clark's *Trumpet Voluntary or the Prince of Denmark's March*, which is thought to have been written after he was appointed organist at St Paul's Cathedral in 1699.

TRADITIONS

Chaplains are appointed by the Parliamentary Under Secretary of State for the Armed Forces on the nomination of the named faiths. All members of the RAChD are commissioned officers ranked, since 1858, to a system where a Chaplain of the 1st Class is equal to Colonel, of the 2nd Class to Lieutenant Colonel, 3rd Class to Major and 4th Class to Captain. The senior officer is the Chaplain General.

These officers hold a unique position of approachability between the troubled soldier and the chain of command. On home stations padres give pastoral care and welfare to serving soldiers and their families. On active service they bring help and comfort to the wounded and the grieving, an essential support service to an army at war.

The Gurkha Brigade is exceptional and relies on its regimental pandits.

THE ROYAL LOGISTIC CORPS

The Royal Logistic Corps (RLC) was formed in 1993 by the amalgamation of four support corps, and elements of another, that kept the army moving, supplied, fed and operational. Put together their workload created a huge organisation that now embraces the largest single storage and haulage system in the country, a shipping line and a global post network. The title comes from the French *logistique*, which is 'the art of moving, lodging and supplying troops and equipment'.

Providing for armies has long been a problem, and many kings and nobles of history have been financially crippled in the

Ammunition wagon team struggling through a lunar landscape of the First World War.

A royal visit to 20 Squadron Royal Corps of Transport, keepers of the Queen's baggage train. *(Institution of the RASC and RCT)*

attempt. In the early part of the fifteenth century taxes were raised for a royal ordinance issued for the procurement and keeping of 'warlike stores'. The Office of Ordnance, formed in 1414 and named after this ordinance, was superseded in 1683 by the Board of Ordnance, which supplied arms and ammunition to the army and navy, built barracks and dockyards, and provided all stores to the services. A commissariat was formed to counter the problem of soldiers living off the land by dealing with their pay, victuals, forage and quartering. The Barrack Department of the eighteenth century administered and furnished living quarters.

In 1794 the Commissary General recommended that the inefficient baggage trains, with their hired wagoners, animals and sutlers, be replaced with a wagon train manned by soldiers under the discipline of their officers. The Royal Waggoners served throughout the Napoleonic Wars but succumbed to the long peace of the 1830s. The inadequacies of many army services were brought sharply into public focus through reports from the Crimean War, and in 1855 a Land Transport Corps (LTC) was instituted to alleviate the soldiers' suffering. The Board of Ordnance was dissolved in the same year.

After the Crimean War a permanent road transport regiment was created to support the army at home, on campaign and in barren lands. This Military Train absorbed the LTC, ranked as a cavalry regiment, and gained three battle honours in India and China. At this time transport, supply and stores were run by departments (officers) and worked by corps (other ranks). The Engineers, Artillery, and the Commissariat and Transport Corps relied on horse-drawn wagons, but the Royal Engineers were developing other forms of moving troops and *materiel*, notably by railways and canals. Their mechanical transport section was handed over to the Army Service Corps in 1902 in the shape of steam traction, and horse transport began its long phasing-out process.

In 1870 the Military Train was joined by the Stores Corps and Commissariat Corps to become a supply and transport organisation, but ten years on the stores companies were detached to pursue a separate career, providing vital supplies and armaments for an army that expanded with each great war.

The two global wars made unbelievable demands on the corps and saw the birth of the Pioneer Corps and the Army Catering Corps. The support of these five corps was as indispensable to the army then as the 'Loggies' are now.

RLC headquarters and training centre are at the Princess Royal Barracks at Deepcut in Surrey, the former base of the RAOC. The TA depot and training centre is at the Prince William of Gloucester Barracks in Grantham. The School of Catering is located at Aldershot, the ancestral home of the RASC/RCT. The School of Transport is at Leconfield in East Yorkshire and the School of Petroleum is in Dorset.

DRESS DISTINCTIONS

Blue caps and berets are graced with the crowned star of the Royal Army Service Corps (RASC) and the Royal Corps of Transport (RCT). On the star's laurel

Pioneers securing trackway for wheeled-vehicle access to a beach; 17 Port and Maritime Regiment RLC off-loading various vehicles and equipment from a Royal Fleet auxiliary ship, using landing craft and motorised rafts. *(MoD)*

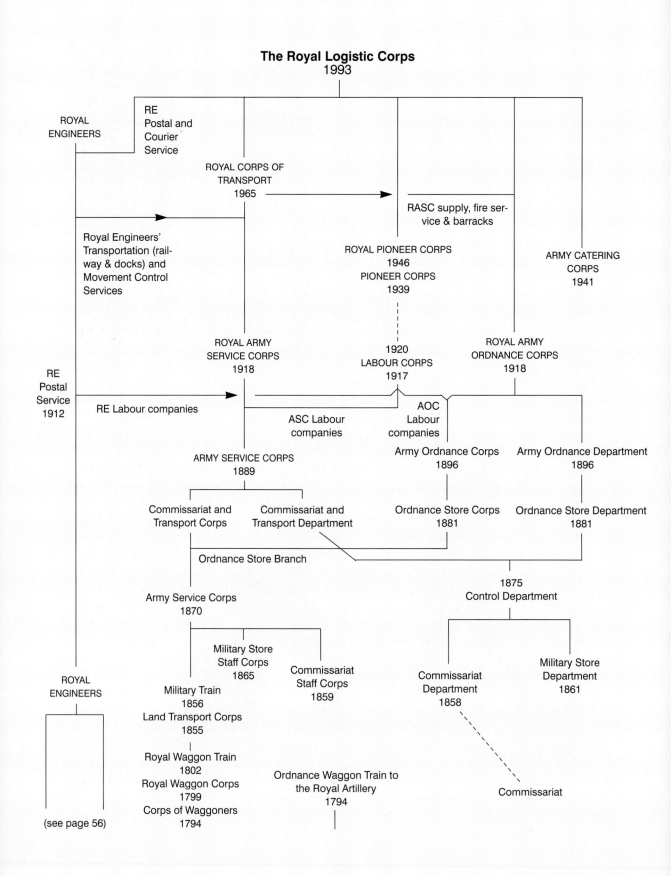

The Royal Logistic Corps
1993

ROYAL
ENGINEERS

RE
Postal and
Courier
Service

ROYAL CORPS OF
TRANSPORT
1965

RASC supply, fire ser-
vice & barracks

Royal Engineers'
Transportation (rail-
way & docks) and
Movement Control
Services

ROYAL PIONEER CORPS
1946
PIONEER CORPS
1939

ARMY CATERING
CORPS
1941

RE
Postal
Service
1912

ROYAL ARMY
SERVICE CORPS
1918

1920
LABOUR CORPS
1917

ROYAL ARMY
ORDNANCE CORPS
1918

RE Labour companies

ASC Labour
companies

AOC
Labour
companies

Army Ordnance Corps
1896

Army Ordnance Department
1896

ARMY SERVICE CORPS
1889

Commissariat and
Transport Corps

Commissariat and
Transport Department

Ordnance Store Corps
1881

Ordnance Store Department
1881

Ordnance Store Branch

1875
Control Department

Army Service Corps
1870

Military Store
Staff Corps
1865

Commissariat
Staff Corps
1859

Commissariat
Department
1858

Military Store
Department
1861

ROYAL
ENGINEERS

Military Train
1856
Land Transport Corps
1855

Royal Waggon Train
1802
Royal Waggon Corps
1799
Corps of Waggoners
1794

Ordnance Waggon Train to
the Royal Artillery
1794

Commissariat

(see page 56)

wreath lie two crossed axes from the badge of the Royal Pioneer Corps, and a Garter belt that encloses the shield of the Board of Ordnance, from the Royal Army Ordnance Corps (RAOC). Across the lower point of the star is a scroll with the Army Catering Corps' 1973 motto, *We Sustain*.

Service dress is worn with the cap by officers, the beret by other ranks and the RCT yellow/blue lanyard by all.

The blue overalls and trousers worn with No. 1 dress, mess dress and full dress are fashioned with the double scarlet seam stripe once seen in the RAOC. Otherwise these orders of dress are entirely blue, the uniform colour of both the ASC and the AOC before the general use of khaki in the early twentieth century.

Musicians' full dress uniform incorporates the Victorian helmet fitted with the ball top favoured by the ASC for safety when working near horses. The blue tunic has scarlet edging down the front in line with the buttons, which invoke this period with a design based on buttons worn by the Commissariat and Transport Staff and the Ordnance Store Department – the royal crest within a belt.

Working dress varies greatly according to occupation. Drivers, vehicle specialists, supply specialists and controllers, pioneers and movement controllers wear uniform barrack dress or combats offset by the corps stable belt, which is blue with yellow edging and a double scarlet stripe in the middle. Chefs are issued with the white hat, jacket and apron of their calling, but marine engineers and seamen/navigators wear the blue shirt of the Royal Navy. Pilots and air dispatchers of the airmobile squadrons have a flying suit, and soldiers of the Airborne Battalion, parachute equipment.

Protective clothing is given out to petroleum operators (rubber coveralls), railwaymen and port operators (hard hat and luminous jacket), couriers (motorcycle

Army Catering Corps chef, *c.* 1985.

gear) and ammunition technicians (padded explosive ordnance suit).

MUSIC

The corps march is Albert Elm's *On Parade*.

The RCT march *Wait for the Wagon*, an American song of 1851 based on an old English folk song, was adopted by the ASC in 1875 on a suggestion from the Commander-in-Chief, the Duke of Cambridge, at a review in Aldershot. As a march the tune was too short and in 1946 Bandmaster Dean rearranged it to include *The Trek Song* in homage to the many ASC companies that served in the Boer War of 1899–1902.

The Army Ordnance Corps served up to and through the First World War without a march to call its own, and in the 1920s the search was on for suitable music. *The Village Blacksmith* was chosen for its oblique reference to RAOC artificers' workshops, where guns and equipment were repaired and modified. As a march *The Village Blacksmith* had to be revised in 1941 and again in 1970.

Demuth's *Pioneer Corps* was adopted by that organisation in 1945. The Army Catering Corps' *Sugar and Spice* was an arrangement of Leveridge's *Roast Beef of Old England* and Dibdin's *Tight Little Island*.

In 1994 the RCT and RAOC bands were united to form the Band of the Royal Logistic Corps (RLC).

TRADITIONS

The 22 regular and 15 volunteer regiments of the RLC involve some 28,000 personnel, the largest of the army's corps. In battle logistic units supply and distribute ammunition, fuel, rations and spares, recover and repair damaged equipment, and treat and evacuate casualties.

Their web of responsibilities can be sourced through the corps' forerunners; the Royal Corps of Transport ('Truckies'): movement of personnel, distribution of food, oil and petrol worldwide, and ammunition to units in the field by road, air, rail, water and pack animal.

The Royal Army Ordnance Corps ('Providers'): supply of food, fuel, vehicles (from cycles to tanks), guns, ammunition, equipment, spare parts, accommodation and field bakeries; the maintenance of vehicles, guns, equipment, depots and stores complexes; technical support and bomb disposal.

The Royal Pioneer Corps ('Chunkies'): manual and mechanical materials handling; the maintenance, inspection and palletisation of fuel tanks; the loading of stores, equipment and ammunition; the defence of major headquarters with specialist dog-handling, and duties in recovering and identifying bodies prior to military/battlefield internment.

The Army Catering Corps ('Sustainers'): training and deployment of cooks to all army canteens, kitchens and field camps.

Air ambulance unit removing a casualty to hospital. *(MoD)*

RAMC re-enactment group with an ambulance of First World War vintage.

THE ROYAL ARMY MEDICAL CORPS

The Royal Army Medical Corps (RAMC) is descended from the Medical Staff Corps created in 1855 as a response to the poor treatment experienced by the sick and wounded in the Crimea. Prior to this soldiers in distress had to rely on the availability of the regimental surgeon.

In 1898 the surgeon officers of the Medical Staff were united with the orderlies of the Medical Staff Corps to produce the Royal Army Medical Corps. The Army Medical School at Netley was moved to Millbank in London four years later. RAMC headquarters are now with the Army Medical Services at the former Staff College in Camberley.

DRESS DISTINCTIONS

The blue peaked cap is distinguished by a band and welt of dull cherry, the colour of the trim on the blue uniform of the Medical Staff Corps from the 1860s, when it went under the title of Army Hospital Corps.

The RAMC badge is a laurel wreath with a crown on top and a scroll beneath inscribed *In arduis fidelis* (Faithful in adversity). Inside the wreath is the international emblem of medicine, the rod of Aesculopius (the Greek/Roman god of healing) with a serpent entwined. The badge has been worn on cap and collar since the birth of the RAMC in 1898. Today it is pinned to a cherry backing when worn on the beret.

No. 1 dress 'blues' have the dull cherry on shoulder straps and the trousers stripe. In mess dress the waistcoat and the facings of the blue jacket are also of this hue.

No. 2 dress is worn with a cherry lanyard and trade bars on the sleeve. This braid was introduced in 1886 and revived in 1956 for Class I and Class II tradesmen.

Dull cherry jerseys are available for officers and warrant officers in barrack dress.

MUSIC

The first march of the corps was Sousa's *Washington Post*, but in 1914 a change was made to *Her Bright Eyes Haunt Me Still*, an arrangement of an 1856 composition in honour of Florence Nightingale.

In 1923 *Bonnie Nell* was favoured, but replaced in 1948 by a seventeenth-century air, *Here's a Health unto His Majesty*. Shortly after this *Her Bright Eyes* was reintroduced as the corps slow march.

When HM Queen Elizabeth The Queen Mother was Colonel-in-Chief, *The Eriskay Love Lilt* would be played on officers' guest nights.

TRADITIONS

Corps Day (23 June) was set down in 1948, on the 50th anniversary of the formation of the RAMC, being the day on which the Medical Staff joined forces with the Medical Staff Corps in 1898.

The First World War had caused a rapid expansion of army medical services to cope with the vast numbers of casualties and new types of wound. Through impossible conditions members of the RAMC struggled and adapted to support the wounded on the front line, in the regimental aid posts, the dressing stations, casualty clearing stations, base hospitals, and the hospital ships and trains.

In spite of superhuman efforts to alleviate the suffering of soldiers and civilians in all corners of the globe, the RAMC suffered an abuse of its initials, with interpretations like 'Rob All My Comrades', 'Run Away Matron's Coming', 'Rather A Mixed Crowd' and, in reverse order, 'Can't Manage A Rifle'. Rifles haven't always been carried in the corps but arms are borne

today for personal protection. Medical services are subject to the Geneva Convention and although swords and bayonets are carried on parade they have to remain sheathed.

The corps continues to attend casualties and the sick in all situations, deploying field ambulance units, air ambulance, surgical teams, transfusion units, medical equipment depots, hygiene units and convalescent training depots.

THE CORPS OF ROYAL ELECTRICAL AND MECHANICAL ENGINEERS

The Royal Electrical and Mechanical Engineers (REME) was formed in 1942 by the collation of the engineering workshops of the Royal Engineers, Royal Army Service Corps and the Royal Army Ordnance Corps, to organise and rationalise engineering support for the army's vehicles, guns and technical equipment. The corps' skills were put to the test at El Alamein, from where they grew with each development in army equipment, and now extend to eight trades and nearly 10,000 personnel.

Headquarters are located at Arborfield in Berkshire, an engineering training establishment since 1942.

DRESS DISTINCTIONS

The blue peaked cap has the scarlet band of royal infantry regiments and the 1947 pattern badge – a horse, gorged with a coronet and chain reflexed over its back, rearing up on a globe and superimposed on a flash of lightning, all beneath a crown and scroll inscribed R.E.M.E. The horse with chain symbolises power under control, the lightning flash denotes electrical force.

The REME stable belt is blue with two yellow on red stripes, its clasp raised with the

Vehicle mechanics of a Light Aid Detachment in Kuwait. *(MoD)*

motto *Arte et marte* (By skill and by fighting). Trade emblems are worn on the sleeve.

Musicians were issued with full dress in 1979. It consists of a blue Victorian uniform and infantry pattern helmet, with scarlet facings and the Royal Engineers' broad scarlet stripe down the trousers' seams.

MUSIC

The corps quick march is a combination of the old army song, *Lillieburlero*, once used by the BBC News during the Second World War, and the French *Aupres de ma Blonde* for the trio section.

The REME band was formed in 1944 and became a major staff band in 1971.

TRADITIONS

REME suffered the usual misinterpretation of its initials through its early years. Old soldiers know them as 'Rarely Electrically or Mechanically Efficient', 'Rough Engineering Made Easy', etc. Today the efficiency of the corps in combat support is beyond doubt.

Soldiers below lance corporal hold the rank of craftsman and train for one of the corps' trades. Avionics technicians repair and maintain instrument systems on helicopters; aircraft technicians look after everything else on helicopters; electronics technicians maintain and repair all of the army's electronic systems, largely to be found in tanks, self-propelled guns and guided weapons; metalsmiths make tools and equipment parts, and repair vehicle bodywork; armourers repair and maintain the full range of weapons; vehicle mechanics work on heavy armoured track vehicles or light tracked and wheeled vehicles; recovery mechanics use cranes and lifting gear to rescue overturned and broken-down vehicles; and technical stores staff keep track of the thousands of REME special tools and test equipment. The best technicians are selected for artificer rank.

WRAC passing-out parade with a variety of cap badges showing destinations to which the women were being sent. They were employed as cooks, drivers, analysts, clerks, police, stewardesses, communications operatives and hairdressers.

THE ADJUTANT GENERAL'S CORPS

The Adjutant General's Corps (AGC) was formed in 1992 for the overall management of the army's human resources, through administration, education and discipline. The title comes from the chief administrative officer on the General Staff, whose office goes back to 1673.

The work of the AGC is carried out through four distinct branches, each of which has its own identity and history. The Staff and Personnel Support Branch (SPS) (62 per cent of the AGC) derives from the Royal Army Pay Corps (RAPC), the staff clerks of the Royal Army Ordnance Corps and the major part of the Women's Royal Army Corps (WRAC), which was dissolved in 1992. The large number of female clerks in the SPS Branch has led to AGC being read as 'All Girls Corps'. The Provost Branch (32 per cent) is made up of the Royal Military Police (RMP) and the Military Provost Staff Corps (MPSC). The Educational and Training Services Branch (ETS) (5 per cent) was formerly the Royal Army Educational Corps (RAEC) and the Army Legal Services Branch (ALS) (1 per cent), the Army Legal Corps (ALC).

AGC headquarters and training centre are at Worthy Down in Hampshire, the former home of the Royal Army Pay Corps.

DRESS DISTINCTIONS

A blue peaked cap with the royal scarlet band honours the four predecessor corps that held a royal title. The Royal Military Police, however, are allowed to keep their distinctive red caps (with black band) for recognition purposes. Berets of green, in a lighter shade than those worn in the WRAC, were chosen for the new corps, except the RMP again, which retains its scarlet berets.

The corps badge consists of a crowned laurel wreath (from the WRAC badge) with the royal crest within, on a scroll worded *Animo et fide* (With resolution and fidelity). The lion and crown that comprise the royal crest arrived by tradition of the Adjutant General's Department, the Pay Corps, the Provost Marshal and officers of the Military Police. The Provost Branch is allowed to deviate from corps insignia with the old crown and cypher badges of the RMP and the MPSC, though the new Military Provost Guard Service (MPGS) is represented by the royal crest and title scroll on crossed keys. The Army Legal Services retain the ALC badge – a blindfolded figure of Justice holding a sword and scales, superimposed on a globe and crossed swords surmounted by the royal crest, all contained in a circle inscribed JUSTITIA IN ARMIS. Members of the ETS Branch wear the old torch (of learning) collar badge of the RAEC.

In 1996 AGC musicians' uniform was laid down as infantry pattern: blue helmet and scarlet tunic with blue facings. Mess dress continues the theme with scarlet jackets and blue facings, the standing collar modelled on that worn in the AG Department of the 1890s.

MUSIC

The corps quick march, *A Pride of Lions*, written for the AGC in 1992, draws on the badges of the WRAC, RAPC, the former AG Department, the SPS Branch and the MPGS, all of which contain a lion emblem. The AGC slow march, *Greensleeves*, came from the WRAC, whose members wore uniforms of green.

The four branches of the corps manifest their independence with official marches of

AGC Field Admin Office.
(MoD)

The Adjutant General's Corps

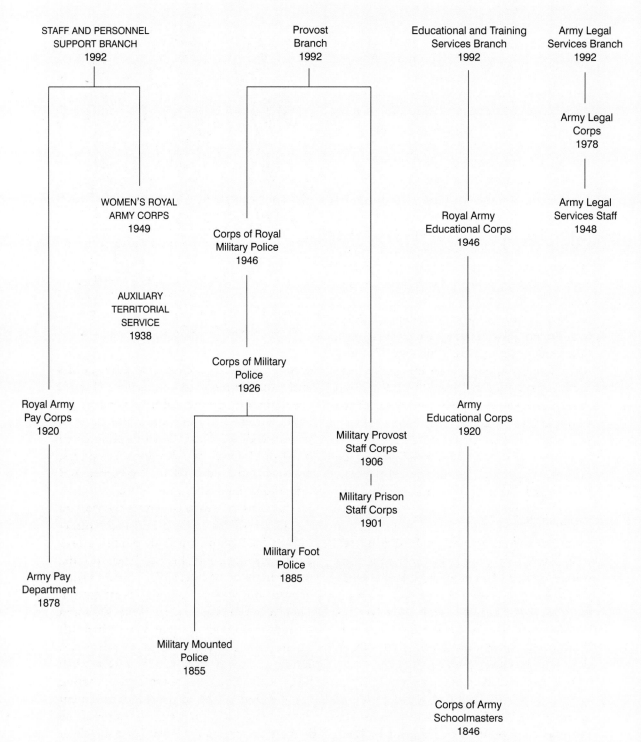

STAFF AND PERSONNEL
SUPPORT BRANCH
1992

Provost
Branch
1992

Educational and Training
Services Branch
1992

Army Legal
Services Branch
1992

WOMEN'S ROYAL
ARMY CORPS
1949

Corps of Royal
Military Police
1946

Army Legal
Corps
1978

Royal Army
Educational Corps
1946

Army Legal
Services Staff
1948

AUXILIARY
TERRITORIAL
SERVICE
1938

Corps of Military
Police
1926

Royal Army
Pay Corps
1920

Military Provost
Staff Corps
1906

Army
Educational Corps
1920

Military Prison
Staff Corps
1901

Military Foot
Police
1885

Army Pay
Department
1878

Military Mounted
Police
1855

Corps of Army
Schoolmasters
1846

their own. The SPS Branch uses Safroni's *Imperial Echoes*, the march of the Pay Corps from 1952. Before this date 'The Inkslingers' marched to *Primrose and Blue*, the poetic representation of corps colours. Former WRAC marches (authorised in 1959) number *The Lass of Richmond Hill, Early One Morning* and the pipe tune *Nut Brown Maiden*.

The Provost Branch has three marches: *The Watchtower* (RMP), *The New Colonial* (MPS) and *Steadfast and True* (MPGS).

The Educational and Training Services Branch lists *Gaudeamus Igitur* (RAEC from 1952) and *The Good Comrade*.

The ALS Branch is represented by the Army Legal Corps' *Scales of Justice*, an arrangement of the folk tunes *The Soldier Hath No Bedfellows* and *Stop Poor Sinner, Stop and Think*.

The Band of the Adjutant General's Corps was formed on a nucleus of musicians from the WRAC band in 1992, which was dissolved when female soldiers were integrated into the other corps of the army. The WRAC Staff Band was formed in 1949, shortly after the formation of the corps, and prided itself on being the only all-girl band. The first girl band was that of the ATS, formed during the Second World War, when the Royal Army Pay Corps managed to raise unofficial bands.

TRADITIONS

Corps Day (6 April) celebrates the time in 1992 when six corps came together under the colonel commandant of the Adjutant General's Corps. The custom of making a special toast to the corps commandant was inherited from the WRAC, where officers would drink a health to their Commandant-in-Chief, HRH Queen Elizabeth The Queen Mother.

The Staff and Personnel Support Branch (currently 4,500 all ranks) is composed of military clerks whose work embraces the various duties of army clerks prior to 1993. This involves the administration of field

'Redcaps' in service dress checking the papers of a Para corporal in battle dress, Aldershot during the 1950s. Mounted RMP patrols for training areas, military events and garrisons were stood down in 1995 in favour of motorcycle patrols. *(Aldershot Military Museum)*

records, soldiers' records, casualty reports and disciplinary documents; clerical detachments giving admin support to headquarters and other units; the issue of pay and allowances; the maintenance of MoD public accounts for local suppliers, agencies and Post Office receipts; and operational tasks with other units.

The Provost Branch continues the work of the Royal Military Police and the Military Provost Staff Corps, currently requiring over 2,000 personnel. The 'Redcaps' deal with the maintenance of discipline and crime prevention, detection and investigation. They need to possess interpersonal skills and professional integrity while being physically strong enough to handle harsh situations. RMP operational support duties range from large-scale traffic control to advising commanders in the field on the movement of front-line troops and supply columns. The Military Provost Staff are stationed mainly at the Military Corrective Training Centre at

Colchester Garrison, where they re-train 'soldiers under sentence' in the army's ways, and motivate their prisoners back to a mental and physical readiness for service life before their return to unit. The Military Provost Guard Service, formed in 1997, provides security guards for selected MoD sites.

The Educational and Training Services Branch combines the old teaching practices of the Royal Army Educational Corps with new developmental training, support and resettlement services. They assist all ranks to achieve their academic potential and cover international affairs, war studies, languages, and the general education of young soldiers and the children of service families.

The Army Legal Services Branch follows the duties of the commissioned solicitors and barristers of the Army Legal Corps that was set up after the Second World War. Its officers advise the chain of command on

disciplinary matters and prosecute/defend at courts martial. They give legal advice and assistance to serving soldiers and their families, instruct on military law and administer the army's legal system. Their skills cover the complex issues to be found in military, civil and operational law.

THE ROYAL ARMY VETERINARY CORPS

The Royal Army Veterinary Corps (RAVC) dates back to 1858 when veterinary surgeons attached to cavalry regiments were brought together as the Veterinary Medical Department (VMD). Prior to the Napoleonic Wars, care for army horses was entrusted to regimental farriers.

In 1881 the VMD was renamed Army Veterinary Department and ten years later

Dog-handlers from a variety of regiments and services at the Defence Animal Centre. *(MoD)*

its surgeons were given substantive military ranks. Lower ranks were recruited in 1903 for an Army Veterinary Corps and three years later the two factions were consolidated as one corps.

The First World War made great demands on army horses and the AVC grew in proportion to try to provide care for the huge number of animals used and injured in the conflict. In the last year of the war the 'Vets' were honoured with the royal prefix to their title.

In 1946 the RAVC was merged with the Army Remount Service (ARS) and moved from its base at Doncaster Racecourse to the Remount Depot at Melton Mowbray, where equines were to coexist with canines. RAVC headquarters are now located with the Army Medical Services in Camberley but the Melton depot still holds and trains dogs and horses as the Defence Animal Centre.

DRESS DISTINCTIONS

The blue peaked cap is distinguished with the maroon band first seen in the Army Veterinary Department of Queen Victoria's army. The field service cap is maroon with blue flaps and gold or yellow piping. No. 1 dress is similarly defined with a double maroon stripe down the overalls.

The crowned laurel wreath badge, which contained the corps' AVC monogram, was transplanted with the mythical man/horse figure of Chiron when the title was altered in 1918.

The corps stable belt is blue, with a central maroon band between yellow stripes.

MUSIC

The corps quick march is a combination of *Drink Puppy Drink* and *A Hunting We Will Go*, the latter a reference to the Leicestershire depot and the county sport, which was happily indulged in by ARS and RAVC alike. The slow march is *Golden Spurs*.

TRADITIONS

The corps deals with military dog care and training (detecting and guarding) and the procurement, stabling, schooling and caring of army horses. The old pack-horse techniques are learned for the odd occasion when the army needs to supply units in difficult and mountainous terrain.

THE SMALL ARMS SCHOOL CORPS

This small corps was created in 1919 with the Corps of Small Arms and Machine Gun Schools. The two were brought together in 1923 to give instruction in weaponry and assumed the Small Arms School Corps (SASC) title six years later. Corps headquarters were relocated from Hythe to the School of Infantry at Warminster in 1969.

DRESS DISTINCTIONS

Green berets are worn with the 1929 pattern badge, a pair of Lee-Enfield rifles crossed on a Vickers machine gun with a crown above, enclosed in a laurel wreath adorned with a title scroll. This badge superseded the simpler crown over crossed rifles.

MUSIC

March of the Bowmen was chosen for the SASC for its allusion to men and arms.

TRADITIONS

Corps Day (19 September) commemorates the opening of the School of Musketry at Hythe in 1854.

The corps is responsible for training instructors, the preparation of courses and the selection of firing-range managers. It trials new weapons, advises staff officers and instructs in the skills of weapons training. One in five SASC personnel are officers, promoted from within the corps.

Dentist at war, South Africa, 1900. *(NAM)*

THE ROYAL ARMY DENTAL CORPS

Awareness of the problems caused by a lack of dental health was acute in the days of the musket, when strong incisors and canines were needed to bite open cartridges when loading the firearm. When the musket was phased out in favour of the percussion rifle the army largely lost interest in its soldiers' teeth and neglect was the order of the day. The efficiency of the army was impaired by poor dental health, however, and dentists had to be shipped out to South Africa during the Boer War, but it wasn't until a front-line general got raging toothache in 1914 that dental surgeons were attached to the Royal Army Medical Corps on a permanent basis.

The Army Dental Corps was established in 1921 to treat soldiers and airmen at home and abroad, to enable them to be fit for service. Over 2,000 'Fang-snatchers' served in the Second World War and in 1946 the ADC received its royal title.

Corps headquarters, for a long time at Evelyn Woods Road in Aldershot, are now located with the Army Medical Services in Camberley.

DRESS DISTINCTIONS

The blue cap has a green band and welt, and the 1948 badge which features a dragon's head, with a sword between its teeth, within a crowned laurel wreath labelled *Ex dentibus ensis* (From the teeth a sword). The design was inspired by Greek mythology, in which Cadmus slew a dragon and sowed its teeth, which grew as the martial Sparti race. On the beret the badge is worn on a green backing.

Field service caps and stable belts are coloured emerald green, blue and cherry red. In service dress all ranks wear the green lanyard introduced in 1952. Green jerseys are supplied to officers and warrant officers for barrack dress.

MUSIC

The corps march, *Green Facings*, which conforms to RADC dress specifications, was arranged for the corps in 1953 and adopted in the following year. It brings together the old English airs *Green Broom* and *Greensleeves.*

TRADITIONS

The Corps Weekend in September is when members of the RADC Association can meet to march and remember in Aldershot. After the loyal toast has been taken another is made to the Colonel-in-Chief, HRH the Duchess of Gloucester. Like the RAMC the RADC bear arms for personal protection only, in accordance with the Geneva Convention. On parade, swords and bayonets are carried but not drawn.

Today, dental surgeons (officers) supported by technicians and surgery assistants (other ranks), serve in camp hospitals, field centres and laboratories, mobile teams and field ambulances. They are responsible for primary dental care for soldiers, entitled civilians and their dependants across the world.

THE INTELLIGENCE CORPS

The 'Int Corps' was formed in 1940 for the gathering and interpreting of intelligence concerning enemy movements in the Second World War. It soon expanded to employ 11,000 effectives, some of whom were required to work under cover in occupied countries. Members were not classed as Regular Army until 1957. HQ and training are at Chicksands in Bedfordshire.

DRESS DISTINCTIONS

No. 1 dress 'blues' have a Cypress green cap band, shoulder piping and trouser stripe. Berets are green also. The corps badge combines a crown and rose (the ancient symbol of silence and trust) flanked by laurel leaves and a title scroll.

MUSIC

The quick march, *The Rose and the Laurel*, based on two folk melodies, was adopted in 1954. The ancient *Trumpet Tune (and Ayre)* is the corps slow march.

TRADITIONS

The 'Int Corps' – motto *Manui dat cognito* (Knowledge gives strength to the arm) – builds on the code-breaking work initiated by Wellington's staff officers. Members specialise in linguistics, operational intelligence (the

Intelligence analysts following up a request for information, 2005.

gathering of knowledge about the adversary and its activities, capabilities and organisation), counter-intelligence, human intelligence, imagery analysis, signal intelligence and electronic warfare. Information has to be extracted from numerous sources, some believable, others not.

THE ARMY PHYSICAL TRAINING CORPS

The Army Physical Training Corps (APTC), formed in 1940, originated with the Army Gymnastic Staff of 1860, which provided the corps motto, *Mens sana in corpore sano* (A healthy mind in a healthy body). This staff, which comprised a major and twelve NCOs (the 'Twelve Apostles'), were so successful in

PT instructor attached to the King's Own Royal Border Regiment wearing the beret of that regiment and the dreaded kit of his own.
(Grenadier Publishing)

their work that a gymnasium was ordered for every garrison by 1862.

Headquarters established at Aldershot in 1940 are now to be found at Trenchard Lines near Pewsey in Wiltshire.

DRESS DISTINCTIONS

The blue peaked cap bears the corps badge: two swords, crossed and ensigned with a crown.

No. 1 dress 'blues' are distinguished by scarlet shoulder piping and trouser stripes. The twelve buttons on the officers' mess waistcoats immortalise the 'Twelve Apostles' of 1860.

MUSIC

The corps march, *Be Fit*, appeared in 1944 with words from Kipling's *Land and Sea Tales*.

TRADITIONS

The original disciplines of gymnastics, fencing and boxing are still taught alongside modern requirements. Instructors are drawn from all army units and trained for detachment to regiments stationed around the world, where they supervise sports programmes, PT sessions, route marches and combat obstacle courses.

QUEEN ALEXANDRA'S ROYAL ARMY NURSING CORPS

The Army Nursing Service, formed in 1881, gained the title Queen Alexandra's Imperial Military Nursing Service (QAIMNS) in 1902. In 1897 the first nursing reserves came into being, organised by Princess Christian, a daughter of the Queen. Both elements were sent out to South Africa in 1899 in support of army medical teams on campaign.

First World War medical
re-enactment group in 2005;
QAIMNS nurse making tea.

In 1949 the QAIMNS was combined with
the Territorial Army Nursing Service under
the title Queen Alexandra's Royal Army
Nursing Corps (QARANC), with headquarters
at Aldershot. Today they are with the Army
Medical Services at Camberley.

DRESS DISTINCTIONS

The blue peaked cap has a scarlet band with
a grey centre stripe. The badge, which was
designed by Queen Alexandra, is built
around the Dannebrog (Danish cross) of
her homeland, embossed with her cypher
and ensigned with a crown. The enclosing

laurel wreath is labelled with the motto *Sub
cruce candida* (Under the white cross) and
QARANC. The badge is worn on a red patch
for the grey beret. No. 1 dress cap, jacket
and skirt are grey, as is the ward dress,
which is traditionally worn with red cuffs
and tippet, and a white veil (officers) or cap
(other ranks).

MUSIC

The corps march, *Scarlet and Grey*, was
composed by the RAMC Director of Music
in 1950, an arrangement of Purcell's *King
Arthur* and the air *Gentle Maiden*.

Trainee musician in CAMus No. 1 dress 'blues'.
(*Grenadier Publishing*)

TRADITIONS

On Foundation Day (27 March) a guest dinner is held at which the loyal toast is followed by another toast to the colonel commandant. Queen Mary succeeded Queen Alexandra to the post in 1925.

Nursing officers, registered nurses and healthcare assistants can trace their origins back to Florence Nightingale, who led thirty-eight nurses to the hospital at Scutari in 1854 to help relieve the sufferings of the sick and wounded in the Crimea. The 'QAs' are known by their rank, which is preceded by the letter Q, as in QCpl.

THE CORPS OF ARMY MUSIC

The Corps of Army Music (CAMus) was formed at the Royal Military School of Music in 1994, to assume full responsibility for the recruiting and management of all army musicians. The corps coordinates the funding, tasking and manning of Regular Army bands.

Headquarters Directorate CAMus is at Kneller Hall at Twickenham, the centre of army music since 1857.

DRESS DISTINCTIONS

The blue cap has a royal scarlet band to comply with the royal status of the Military School of Music. The corps badge displays a crown and lyre within a wreath of oak and reeds, which bears the motto *Nulli secundus* (Second to none) – a comment on the high standard of army music. As a collar badge the motto is omitted. The ancient Greek lyre, the hand-held harp at the centre of the badge, has been worn as a sleeve emblem by army bandsmen for over a hundred years.

The corps stable belt is blue with a central band of three stripes that represent corps bands (light blue), infantry bands (red) and armoured cavalry bands (yellow).

MUSIC

The corps march is *The Minstrel Boy*, with its references to the musician going off to war.

The minstrels' earliest form of instrument was the lyre, as portrayed in the corps badge.

TRADITIONS

Corps Day (5 September) is now known as Duke of Cambridge Day in honour of the founder of the School of Military Music at Kneller Hall. The Duke of Cambridge took an interest in the reform of army music when commanding an infantry division in the Crimean War. At the Scutari Review of 1854 the massed bands played the national anthem together, but with different instrumentation, pitch and arrangement, it was a performance that convinced everyone present of the need for a standard form for all army bands to follow.

The school employs tutors for the eighteen different kinds of instrument used in the army, and academic professors to teach conducting, harmony, orchestration and the history of music.

Regimental bands have long been fostered for their value in raising morale in the ranks. They reached a peak of 191 in 1914, but had dropped to 30 on the regular establishment by 1994, when the small regimental bands were reorganised into sizeable bands that each represent a group of regiments.

TERRITORIAL ARMY (TA)

Territorial Army regiments have suffered a fragmented history of mergers, conversions, disbandings and re-formations. Study of their lineage is complex and unnecessary to this book. The current fifteen infantry and seventeen support regiments of the TA largely conform to the dress and customs of their affiliated regiments and corps in the regular army. The more independent and established regiments can be examined separately.

THE ROYAL MONMOUTHSHIRE ROYAL ENGINEERS (MILITIA)

This, the senior regiment of the Territorial Army, can trace its ancestry back to the Tudor levies. As the Monmouth and Brecon Militia it achieved its royal title in 1793. In 1852 it was listed as the Royal Monmouthshire (Light Infantry) Militia but in 1877 was converted (with the Anglesey Militia) to Royal Engineers, and accepted the present title in 1896.

Headquarters are at Monmouth, with squadrons at Newport, Swansea and Oldbury in the West Midlands.

DRESS DISTINCTIONS

Uniforms follow those of the Royal Engineers except for the badge, which is the Prince of Wales's crest flanked by the letters R and E, and the green militia flash of the stable belt.

MUSIC

The RMRE(M) supports a Corps of Drums in the full dress uniform of the Royal Engineers and parades to the marches of the corps.

TRADITIONS

The Monmouthshire Militia fought as royalist infantry in the Civil War and participated in the major wars that followed. During the withdrawal to Dunkirk in 1940 100 and 101 Field Companies were forced to revert to the infantry role, but spearheaded the thrust to the Rhine in 1944 as sappers once again. The regiment acquired the colours of the East Monmouthshire Militia in 1914, and remains the only RE unit to hold colours.

Tudor gunnery re-enactment.

THE HONOURABLE ARTILLERY COMPANY

The Honourable Artillery Company (HAC) was raised through a Charter of Incorporation granted by Henry VIII in 1537 for 'the Guylde of St George, to be overseers of the science of artillerie, that is to witt long bowes, cross bowes and hand gonnes'. The regiment developed with two distinct sides: infantry and artillery. Regimental headquarters are at Finsbury Barracks in London.

DRESS

The blue cap is distinguished by a red band with a blue strip in its centre. The infantry and band wear a grenade badge fashioned on that of the Grenadier Guards but with the monogram 'HAC' entwined on the bomb. The gun troop bears the gun badge of the Royal Artillery but with the motto scroll altered to read *Arma pacis fulcra* (Arms, the mainstay of peace). In 1953 the gunners adopted the crest from the ancient arms of the regiment for the beret: an arm embowered in armour, the gauntlet grasping a leading staff (presented to the company in 1693), between dragon's wings charged with the cross of St George.

It was King William IV who ordered the infantry section to adopt the uniform of the Grenadier Guards when he was Captain General of the HAC. Bearskins were introduced in 1855, but without the Grenadiers' plume. In 1890 the light cavalry squadron (formed in 1860) was converted to horse artillery and permitted to use the dress of the Royal Horse Artillery, although the tunic was kept and yellow cord tailored on.

In No. 1 dress 'blues' the gunners wear cavalry pattern shoulder chains and yellow cap lines. Musicians have the same uniform as Grenadier Guards musicians, except the cap has the HAC band, and lace on the scarlet tunic is silver, not gold.

MUSIC

The regimental quick march, *British Grenadiers*, and slow march, *Duke of York*, are borrowed from the Grenadier Guards; the gun troop's canter, *Bonnie Dundee*, trot, *The Keel Row* and walk, *Duchess of Kent*, are from the Royal Artillery.

The HAC Band has a long history and leads the company on state occasions. In orchestral mode it plays at dinners at Armoury House, the Mansion House, the Guildhall and certain livery halls in the City.

TRADITIONS

The company enjoys certain ancient privileges, not least of which are the royal gun salutes at the Tower of London and the Lord Mayor's parade.

Since 1611 serving members have their names entered in the Vellum Book. Toasting a member of the mess involves a custom from the eighteenth century, in which the assembly repeats 'Zay!' nine times.

THE ROYAL YEOMANRY

A Territorial armoured medium reconnaissance regiment established in 1967 from five Yeomanry regiments descended from troops formed in 1794. The royal title came courtesy of the Royal Wiltshire Yeomanry, who earned the privilege in 1830 by dispersing rioters at Pyt House in Tisbury. Other battle honours date from South Africa 1900.

Regimental headquarters are at the Duke of York's Barracks in Chelsea, with squadron offices in Swindon, Nottingham, Leicester and Croydon.

DRESS DISTINCTIONS

Each squadron is governed by its own traditions. A Squadron (Royal Wiltshire Yeomanry (PWO)) has a squadron in two regiments. Its distinctions can be found under the Royal Wessex Yeomanry.

B Squadron (Leicestershire and Derbyshire Yeomanry) has, for its badge, the crest of Prince Albert on the rose part of the Derbyshires' badge. The Leicestershire Yeomanry was awarded the title Prince Albert's Own in 1844, after escorting the Queen and Prince Consort to Belvoir Castle in the county.

Officers of the Sherwood Rangers in 1900.

A Daimler armoured car of the 2nd Derbyshire Yeomanry on active service in Holland 1944. *(Derby Museums & Art Gallery LFY 518)*

The C Squadron (Kent and Sharpshooters Yeomanry) badge is the White Horse of Kent on crossed carbines under a circlet inscribed KENT & COUNTY OF LONDON YEOMANRY. This squadron upholds a strange custom in which the officers attempt to parade in as many different varieties of dress as possible.

S Squadron (Sherwood Rangers Yeomanry) has a bugle horn badge and W Squadron (Westminster Dragoons) the arms of the City of Westminster.

The regimental band parades in the lancer uniform of the Inns of Court and City Yeomanry, the Edwardian pattern, French grey with purple facings, originally worn by the City of London (Rough Riders). Its badge portrays the four shields of the four Inns of Court supporting another from the arms of the City of London.

MUSIC

The regimental march, *Farmer's Boy*, is a reference to the farming stock from which yeomanry regiments originate. The Wiltshires laid claim to being the first in arms, in 1794, and paraded the motto *Primus in armis*.

TRADITIONS

The London-based squadrons date back to 1797 with the Westminster Troop and 1798 with the Islington Troop. These did not survive the Napoleonic Wars but a resurgence of volunteer cavalry in London took place at the time of the Boer War. In 1899 a battalion of Rough Riders was formed for South Africa, and in 1901 they returned to be transfigured into the City of London Yeomanry (the Rough Riders). Other London veterans of the war were re-formed as the 2nd County of London Yeomanry (Westminster Dragoons). This regiment subsequently played an active part in the social life of the city and received the Freedom of the City of Westminster in 1951. Ten years later the Westminsters were merged with the Berkshire Yeomanry and afterwards became HQ Squadron of the Royal Yeomanry. A battalion of sharpshooters, composed of men skilled with the rifle, was formed for the Boer War in 1900. After that conflict it continued as the 3rd County of London Yeomanry (the Sharpshooters).

THE ROYAL WESSEX YEOMANRY

The Royal Wessex Yeomanry was formed in 1971 from three yeomanry regiments of the West Country whose history goes back to 1794. The royal prefix was granted in 1979 and four years later the regiment was converted to a medium reconnaissance role in Landrovers.

Regimental headquarters are with the Dorset Yeomanry Squadron in Bovington. Other squadrons are at Salisbury, Cirencester, Barnstaple and Paignton.

DRESS DISTINCTIONS

Badges are worn to squadron tradition. The Royal Wiltshires (PWO) have the Prince of Wales's crest (since 1863) and the fern leaf emblem of the New Zealand Division, a sign of service with the 'Kiwis' in the North African desert during the Second World War.

The Royal Gloucestershire Hussars Squadron wear a portcullis and ducal crown badge, the Dorset Squadron a crowned Garter belt within a laurel wreath bearing scrolls inscribed SOUTH AFRICA and THE GREAT WAR. The Royal Devons Squadron wear the badge of the Royal 1st Devon Yeomanry, a circlet crowned with the royal crest encircling a crown and a hand clutching a parchment.

MUSIC

The Gloucesters chose the old hunting song, *D'ye Ken John Peel,* for their march in 1890, hosting, as they did, four masters of hounds and a field master. The Devons adopted *Widecombe Fair.*

The Royal Gloucestershire Hussars Band was first formed in 1834, when the regiment began its long association with Badminton and the dukes of Beaufort. It dresses in the old Beaufort blue uniform of that regiment.

TRADITIONS

In 1920 four West Country yeomanry regiments were converted to the artillery arm and served under the RA until 1967. The process involved amalgamation between the Royal 1st Devons and the Royal North Devons, and the Queen's Own Dorset

The Royal Wiltshire Yeomanry were seconded to XV Corps in 1916.

Yeomanry with the West Somerset Yeomanry and the Somerset Royal Horse Artillery. These TA regiments went into the Second World War as gunners and brought an added dimension to their arm of service.

THE ROYAL MERCIAN AND LANCASTRIAN YEOMANRY

This was formed in 1992 by the union of the Queen's Own Mercian Yeomanry and the Duke of Lancaster's Own Yeomanry, regiments that dated back to the 1790s. Regimental headquarters are at Telford, with squadrons at Dudley, Chester and Wigan.

DRESS DISTINCTIONS

The regimental badge is a Mercian eagle with a Saxon crown, superimposed on a Lancaster rose with the Duke of Lancaster's coronet. Other badges on the regimental guidon are the Warwicks' bear and ragged staff, the Worcesters' sprig of pear blossom, the Shropshires' loggerheads and the Staffords' knot and motto *Pro aris et focis*. The motto was used by many volunteer regiments in the 1790s and can be said to represent their purpose for rising up in the face of a threatened invasion – *For our hearths and homes*. In 1941 the red triangle sign of Bass Breweries at Burton upon Trent was adopted by the Stafford Yeomanry as a backing to their badge.

A print of 1799 depicting Warwickshire Yeomen at sword exercise. English troops had no actual enemy to contend with and enjoyed impressing locals with their military bearing. *(Warwickshire Yeomanry Museum)*

MUSIC

The quick march, *Light of Foot*, and slow march, *Scipio*, come from the QO Mercian Yeomanry. Other marches in the repertoire are *The Warwickshire Lads*, *Lillie Marlene* (ex-Staffords when serving as gunners in the Second World War) and *John o' Gaunt* (Duke of Lancaster's).

TRADITIONS

The title Duke of Lancaster's Own was bestowed on the Lancashire Corps of Yeomanry Cavalry by William IV in 1834. The title belongs to the monarchy, and successive sovereigns have presided over the regiment.

When Princess Victoria was crowned Queen in 1838 she acknowledged the cavalry escort on her visit to Shugborough six years before and made the SYC The Queen's Own Royal Regiment of Staffordshire Yeomanry Cavalry.

The yeomanry is remembered for its service in the Middle East during both world wars. All of the RM&LY's forming regiments fought there between 1915 and 1918, and the Warwickshires and Cheshires returned to Palestine in 1939. The Warwickshire and Worcestershire regiments, which amalgamated in 1956, took part in one of the last mounted charges against guns and entrenched infantry, at Gaza in 1917.

THE QUEEN'S OWN YEOMANRY

This was formed in 1971 from the Queen's Own Yorkshire Yeomanry, the Ayrshire Yeomanry, Cheshire Yeomanry and the Northumberland Hussars. The Cheshire was later moved to the Mercian Yeomanry and replaced by squadrons in Scotland and Northern Ireland. The Yorkshire and Scottish units date back to the 1790s.

Regimental headquarters are at Newcastle upon Tyne, with squadrons at York, Ayr, Cupar and Belfast.

DRESS DISTINCTIONS

The scarlet cap is worn with a fox badge. A running fox badge with a scroll marked FORRARD was worn by the East Riding Yeomanry until its merger with the Yorkshire Dragoons and Yorkshire Hussars in 1956.

MUSIC

D'ye Ken John Peel conforms to the fox badge and the hunting tradition of the regiment's officers, and was adopted as the regimental march.

TRADITIONS

The Yorkshire elements were first formed in 1794. In 1897 the Yorkshire Dragoons provided an escort for Queen Victoria's visit to Sheffield and in the same year accepted the Queen's Own title. Six years later the Yorkshire Hussars took on the title Alexandra, Princess of Wales's Own Imperial Yeomanry.

The Fife and Forfar Yeomanry/Scottish Horse Squadron claim a history that goes back to 1803, when troops formed in Fife were made into a regiment. The Fife Yeomanry enticed its recruits with red jackets like those worn by the local hunt.

A Squadron (Ayrshire (Earl of Carrick's Own) Yeomanry) takes its name from the Carrick district of Ayrshire where, in 1798, a group of farmers asked the local earl for his assistance in raising a troop of yeomanry cavalry to defend the area against invasion. The troop grew into a good regiment that served the crown continuously until the TA reductions of 1969.

The Scottish Horse, like the Irish Horse, dates from the start of the twentieth century. The battle honours 'South Africa 1900, 1901, 1902' head the regiment's list of honours.

THE LONDON REGIMENT

The 'Londons' are rooted in the rifle volunteers that formed in 1859–60 and attached to Home Counties regiments in the 1880s. When the Territorial Force was instituted in 1908 twenty-six of these volunteer battalions were brought together as the London Regiment. Some were sent to France in 1914 and by May of the following year the regiment had expanded to eighty-eight battalions. Many battle honours were earned but 1916 witnessed the break-up of the regiment as its battalions were dispersed back to their former regular regiments. Many were subsequently reorganised within the TA and in 1993 four of these companies were brought together again as the London Regiment. Regimental headquarters are at the TA Centre in Clapham Junction.

DRESS DISTINCTIONS

The Queen's Regiment Company wears the uniform of the successors to the Queen's Regiment, the Princess of Wales's Royal Regiment. The City of London Fusiliers Company similarly wears the uniform of its affiliated regulars, the Royal Regiment of Fusiliers. In both cases soldiers wear a London shield at the top of the left sleeve to distinguish them from their counterparts in the Regular Army.

The London Scottish Company parades in the grey kilt and hose adopted by the London Scottish Rifle Volunteers in 1872. Officers, pipers and drummers have the matching grey doublet (with blue facings). This Highland pattern of dress was fashioned out of the Elcho grey uniform worn by the Volunteers since its formation in 1859. The

A pioneer of the City of London Fusiliers Company in No. 2 dress. The beret is adorned with the RRF hackle and badge, the jacket with the London shield. *(Grenadier Publishing)*

blue glengarry is worn with the old badge: the Scottish lion on St Andrew's cross, a thistle wreath and circle lettered with STRIKE SURE. Labels across the top and bottom of the cross read LONDON and SCOTTISH.

The London Irish Rifles Company has a rifle green *caubeen* with a hackle of St Patrick's blue for the officers and senior NCOs, and green for other ranks. The harp and crown badge is worn over the right eye in the manner adopted with the *caubeen* in 1937. After service in the Second World War the

London Irish were attached to the Royal Ulster Rifles and came under the Royal Irish Rangers in 1968. The green No.1 dress (with black buttons and belts or silver buttons for the drummers and pipers), scarlet mess jackets and the green trousers worn in service dress, came from the Rangers' dress code.

MUSIC

The regimental march is *The Londons Return*, an obvious reference to the re-formation of the regiment in 1993. Company marches are more traditional: *Highland Laddie* (London Scottish Company), *Farmer's Boy/Soldiers of the Queen* (Queen's Regiment Company), *British Grenadiers* (Fusiliers Company) and *Garryowen* (London Irish Company).

TRADITIONS

The various companies that go to make up today's London Regiment originated in the many Middlesex Rifle Volunteer battalions raised in 1859–60 that bore titles such as the Civil Service Rifles, Bank of England Rifles and the Customs and Docks, etc. The 1st Tower Hamlets Rifle Volunteers served with the Rifle Brigade until 1904, when they transferred to the Royal Fusiliers (City of London Regiment), which gave up its four volunteer battalions to the London Regiment in 1908.

The London Scottish was attached to the Gordon Highlanders after the First World War. Its three battalions served in various TA formations in the Second World War and after.

THE ROYAL GIBRALTAR REGIMENT

The Gibraltar Regiment was created in 1958 out of the regular and volunteer factions of the Gibraltar Defence Force, which was set up at the beginning of the Second World War to help man the Rock's anti-aircraft guns. The royal title was granted on the 60th anniversary in 1999. Regimental headquarters are at Devil's Tower Camp in Gibraltar.

DRESS DISTINCTIONS

The blue peaked cap has the royal scarlet band and welt, and the regimental cap badge, which is based on that of the Gibraltar Defence Force of 1915–21: the castle and key, from the arms of Gibraltar, on a shield superimposed on a crowned decorative backing (depicting the Mediterranean) with a scroll labelled *Nulli expugnabilis hosti*, which roughly translates as 'Never taken by an enemy'.

Royal Artillery grenade collar badges and buttons are marked with the castle and key. The castle represents the fortified Rock, the key its strategic position – the gateway to the Mediterranean Sea.

Service dress is worn with a lanyard on the right shoulder, scarlet and grey for officers and RA white for other ranks. A cloth patch bearing the key emblem is worn on the upper sleeve.

Stable belts are scarlet with twin grey stripes running through.

Full dress uniform is infantry pattern, the helmet of the white, hot weather type. The scarlet tunic has slate grey facings.

MUSIC

Regimental marches were adopted when the force was largely Royal Artillery controlled: *British Grenadiers* and the *RA Slow March*.

TRADITIONS

The Regimental Day (28 April) celebrates the first parade by the volunteers of the Gibraltar Defence Force at the RA base on Europa Point. The men paraded in civilian clothes to begin their training in foot, rifle and gun drill.

Sortie Day (27 November) commemorates an episode in 1781 when Gibraltarian volunteers joined British units in action during the Great Siege.

The port sergeant of the Gibraltar Regiment in No. 3 dress, 2004, holding the keys to the garrison. *(Grenadier Publishing)*

The Ceremony of the Keys originated in the Great Siege of 1779–83, when the governor's daily routine was to commend the keys of the garrison to the safe-keeping of his port sergeant at the sound of the sunset gun. After the siege the custom continued with a ceremony that involved fifes and drums to warn aliens to leave before the gates were locked for the night. In 1978 the governor suggested that the post of port sergeant be found in a senior NCO of the Gibraltar Regiment. At official banquets the sergeant reports to the governor's table with the assurance 'Your Excellency, the fortress is secure and all's well', before passing the keys over.

Alliances were made with four regiments whose connection with Gibraltar go back to the eighteenth century: the Royal Anglian in 1968, the Royal Artillery in 1993, the Royal Engineers in 1996 and the Royal Irish in 1999.

When the last RA units left the Rock in 1958 the gunner troop of the Gibraltar Regiment inherited two responsibilities – the firing of royal salutes and the care of the Rock's apes. The gun troop is the only unit able to exchange gun salutes with the Honourable Artillery Company in London.

THE ROYAL MARINES

Although the Royal Marines (RM) have not been a part of the army for over 250 years, their army roots strike down deep and are evident today.

'Marine' is defined as 'of the sea', and the first regiment of marines was formed during the Second Anglo-Dutch Maritime War of 1664–6, to serve aboard navy ships. Subsequent wars brought new regiments of sea soldiers 'to make landings or otherwise', but these too were disbanded at the end of each conflict.

In 1755 a permanent Corps of Marines was established under the Admiralty. It achieved the royal title in 1802.

Royal Marines drummers in full dress, 1995.

Twenty-first-century marines are regarded as an elite fighting force with their feared commando units. The Special Boat Squadron was formed for covert raiding operations.

The Royal Marines have special connections with Deal, Chatham, Plymouth, Portsmouth and Poole.

DRESS DISTINCTIONS

The white naval peaked cap is worn with a scarlet band and the 1827 globe and laurel wreath badge surmounted by the royal crest. The globe represents the marines' worldwide service, the laurel their achievements in Britain's affairs in nearly every country on the globe. As a crest the badge is combined with its eighteenth-century forerunners, a fouled anchor, the motto *Per mare per terram* (By sea by land), and the single battle honour *Gibraltar 1704*.

Full dress is issued to musicians and drummers. It consists of the white 1912 Wolseley helmet, and the blue uniform of the Royal Marine Artillery with the cuffs of the Royal Marine Light Infantry. These two sections developed in the nineteenth century and came together in 1923.

No. 1 dress may be worn with cap or helmet. The officers' jacket, adopted after the First World War, is Royal Navy pattern with an open neck collar to reveal a shirt and tie. Members of the King's Squad, the title given to the senior training unit by George V, wear a white lanyard, and the helmet chinstrap down.

MUSIC

The quick march, *A Life on the Ocean Wave*, was taken in 1882 to replace less appropriate scores dating from the 1830s. The slow march, *Globe and Laurel*, was used from 1935 and in 1952 RM commandos adopted the trekking song of the Boer commandos, *Sarie Marais*. *The Preobrajensky March* was introduced by Earl Mountbatten in 1964.

TRADITIONS

On the tercentenary of the first marine regiment, in 1964, HM The Queen granted RM officers permission to make the loyal toast when seated, in naval fashion.

RM anniversaries are cited in daily orders on these dates:

23 April – the raid on Zeebrugge in 1918.

28 April – the landing at Gallipoli in 1915.

6 June – the Normandy landings, 1944.

7 June – the assault on Belleisle in 1761.

14 June – the recapture of the Falklands in 1982.

17 June – the Battle of Bunker Hill in 1775.

24 July – the capture of Gibraltar in 1704.

21 October – the Battle of Trafalgar in 1805.

28 October – the formation of the Duke of Yorke and Albany's Maritime Regiment, 1664.

1 November – the assault on Walcheren in 1944.

3 October – the landing at Termoli in 1943 (40 Commando).

23 January – the attack on Montforterbeek in 1945 (45 Commando).

31 January – the Battle of Kangdaw in 1945 (42 Commando).

2 April – the Battle of Comacchio in 1945 (Fleet RM Protection Group).

11/12 June – the attack on Mount Harriet (42 Commando) and the Two Sisters (45 Commando) in 1982.

22 May – the landing at Ajax Bay in 1982 (Commando Logistic Regiment).

21 May – the landings at San Carlos Water in 1982 (3 Commando Brigade, HQ and Signal Squadron, and operational landing craft squadrons).

BATTLE HONOURS

Battle honours are awarded to regiments that have seen active service in a significant engagement or campaign, generally with a victorious outcome.

Early awards for outstanding service in battle revolved around new titles (seventeenth century) and laurel wreaths (eighteenth century). The first battle honour in the shape of a label, with the name of battle/campaign thereon, came in 1768, when Emsdorff was taken from the caps of the 15th Light Dragoons and emblazoned on their guidon. Sixteen years later Gibraltar was put on the second colour of four infantry regiments which defended the Rock in a siege that lasted from 1779 to 1783. These colours, guidons and standards are regarded as sacred for the honours they bear and the lives lost in their name.

The first campaign honour came in 1802, when thirty-three regiments received permission to display a sphinx emblem to represent their part in the expedition to rid Egypt of Napoleon in the previous year. The year 1815 saw Peninsula awarded to eighty-seven regiments for the war of 1808–14 in Portugal, Spain and southern France, and Waterloo to thirty-eight regiments for their part in the great victory of the same year that brought the French wars to an end. Twenty-three battles of the Peninsular War were honoured to the regiments concerned on a fairly ad hoc basis from 1817 on.

Colonial wars were recognised spasmodically and in 1882 a review of battle honours put the great victories of Marlborough and Wolfe on the map. The 1909 review belatedly recognised seventeenth-century campaigns and some forgotten battles of the eighteenth century. After this, battle honours were awarded on a more efficient basis.

The First World War threw up 163 battle honours for regiments that had had battalions serving on all fronts. The resulting numbers of honours per regiment, therefore, were so great that a limit of ten was imposed for display on colours, standards and guidons. The same situation occurred after the Second World War, though on a slightly smaller scale, and the ten honours limit was applied again. A regiment would select its ten most important battle honours of the war, often those that commemorated the greatest loss of life. On average its actual list of battle honours would be about twice the size of its displayed honours.

A regiment's list of honours is a measure of distinction among its peers, but the modern regiment's long list of amalgamated honours can appear anonymous and repetitive, with regimental origins obscure.

A survey of the regiments of the Regular Army in order of precedence, before the many changes that took place in the reign of Elizabeth II, gives a clearer view of the origins of the modern regiments' honours.

THE DISPLAYED BATTLE HONOURS

The Life Guards: Dettingen, Peninsula, Waterloo, Tel el Kebir, Egypt 1882, Relief of Kimberley, Paardeberg, South Africa 1899–1902.

Mons, Le Cateau, Marne 1914, Aisne 1914, Messines 1914, Ypres 1914, 1915, 1917, Somme 1916, 1918, Arras 1917, 1918, Hindenburg Line, France and Flanders 1914–18. Souleuvre, Brussels, Nederrijn, North-west Europe 1944–5, Iraq 1941, Palmyra, Syria 1941, El Alamein, North Africa 1942–3, Italy 1944.

The Royal Horse Guards: Dettingen, Warburg, Beaumont, Willems, Peninsula, Waterloo, Tel el Kebir, Egypt 1882, Relief of Kimberley, Paardeberg, South Africa 1899–1902.

Le Cateau, Marne 1914, Messines 1914, Ypres 1914, 1915, 1917, Gheluvelt, Frezenberg, Loos, Arras 1917, Sambre, France and Flanders 1914–18.

Souleuvre, Brussels, Nederrijn, North-west Europe 1944–5, Iraq 1941, Palmyra, Syria 1941, El Alamein, North Africa 1942–3, Italy 1944.

1st King's Dragoon Guards: Blenheim, Ramillies, Oudenarde, Malpalquet, Dettingen, Warburg, Beaumont, Waterloo, Sevastopol, Taku Forts, Pekin, South Africa 1901–2.

Somme 1916, Morval, France and Flanders 1914–17.

Beda Fomm, Defence of Tobruk, Defence of Alamein Line, Advance on Tripoli, Tebaga Gap, Tunis, North Africa 1941–3, Monte Camino, Gothic Line, Italy 1943–4.

The standard of the 1st King's Dragoon Guards at Tidworth, 1958.

The Queen's Bays (2nd Dragoon Guards): Warburg, Willems, Lucknow, South Africa 1901–2.

Mons, Le Cateau, Marne 1914, Messines 1914, Ypres 1914, 1915, Somme 1916, 1918, Scarpe 1917, Cambrai 1917, 1918, Amiens, Pursuit to Mons.

Somme 1940, Gazala, El Alamein, El Hamma, Tunis, North Africa 1941–3, Coriano, Lamone Crossing, Rimini Line, Argenta Gap.

3rd Dragoon Guards (Prince of Wales's): Warburg, Beaumont, Willems, Talavera, Vittoria, Albuhera, Peninsula, Waterloo, Abbysinia, South Africa 1901–2.

Ypres 1914, 1915, Loos, Arras 1917, Scarpe 1917, St Quentin, Avre, Amiens, Hindenburg Line, Pursuit to Mons, France and Flanders 1914–18.

4th Royal Irish Dragoon Guards: Peninsula, Balaklava, Sevastopol, Tel el Kebir, Egypt 1882.

Mons, Le Cateau, Retreat from Mons, Marne 1914, Aisne 1914, Messines 1914, Ypres 1914, 1915, Somme 1916, Cambrai 1917, Pursuit to Mons.

5th Dragoon Guards: Blenheim, Ramillies, Oudenarde, Malplaquet, Beaumont, Salamanca, Vittoria, Toulouse, Peninsula, Balaklava, Sevastopol, Defence of Ladysmith, South Africa 1899–1902.

Mons, Le Cateau, Marne 1914, Messines 1914, Ypres 1914, 1915, Bellewaarde, Somme 1916, 1918, Cambrai 1917, 918, Amiens, Pursuit to Mons.

The Carabiniers (6th Dragoon Guards): Blenheim, Ramillies, Oudenarde, Malplaquet, Warburg, Willems, Sevstopol, Delhi 1857, Afghanistan 1879–80, Relief of Kimberley, Paardeberg, South Africa 1899–1902.

Retreat from Mons, Marne 1914, Aisne 1914, Messines 1914, Ypres 1915, Cambrai 1917, 1918, Somme 1918, Amiens, Sambre, France and Flanders 1914–18.

7th Dragoon Guards: Blenheim, Ramillies, Oudenarde, Malplaquet, Dettingen, Warburg, South Africa 1846–7, Tel el Kebir, Egypt 1882, South Africa 1900–2.

La Bassee 1914, Givenchy 1914, Somme 1916, 1918, Bazentin, Cambrai 1917, 1918, St Quentin, Avre, Amiens, Hindenburg Line, Pursuit to Mons.

The 1st Royal Dragoons: Tangier 1662–80, Dettingen, Warburg, Beaumont, Willems, Fuentes d'Onor, Peninsula, Waterloo, Balaklava, Sevastopol, Relief of Ladysmith, South Africa 1899–1902.

Ypres 1914, 1915, Frezenburg, Loos, Arras 1917, Somme 1918, Amiens, Hindenburg Line, Pursuit to Mons, France and Flanders 1914–18.

Nederrijn, Rhine, North-west Europe 1944–5, Syria 1941, Knightsbridge, El Alamein, Advance on Tripoli, North Africa 1941–3, Sicily 1943, Italy 1943.

The Royal Scots Greys: Blenheim, Ramillies, Oudenarde, Malplaquet, Dettingen, Warburg, Willems, Waterloo, Balaklava, Sevastopol, Relief of Kimberley, Paardeberg, South Africa 1899–1902.

Retreat from Mons, Marne 1914, Aisne 1914, Ypres 1914, 1915, Arras 1917, Amiens, Somme 1918, Hindenburg Line, Pursuit to Mons, France and Flanders 1914–18.

Hill 112, Falaise, Hochwald, Aller, Bremen, Merjayun, Alam el Halfa, El Alamein, Nofilia, Salerno, Italy 1943.

3rd King's Own Hussars: Dettingen, Salamanca, Vittoria, Toulouse, Peninsula, Cabool, Moodkee, Ferozeshah, Sobraon, Chillianwallah, Goojerat, Punjaub, South Africa 1899–1902.

Retreat from Mons, Marne 1914, Aisne 1914, Messines 1914, Ypres 1914, 1915, Arras 1917, Cambrai 1917, 1918, Somme 1918, Amiens, France and Flanders 1914–15.

Sidi Barrani, Buq Buq, Beda Fomm, Sidi Suleiman, El Alamein, North Africa 1940–2, Citta del Pieve, Citta di Castello, Italy 1944, Crete.

4th Queen's Own Hussars: Dettingen, Talavera, Salamanca, Albuhera, Vittoria, Toulouse, Peninsula, Ghuznee, Afghanistan 1839, Alma, Balaklava, Inkerman, Sevastopol.

Mons, Le Cateau, Marne 1914, Aisne 1914, Ypres 1914, 1915, St Julien, Arras 1917, Cambrai 1917, Somme 1918, Amiens.

Ruweisat, Alam el Halfa, El Alamein, Coriano, Senio Pocket, Rimini Line, Argenta Gap, Proasteion, Corinth Canal, Greece 1941.

5th Royal Irish Lancers: Blenheim, Ramillies, Oudenarde, Malplaquet, Suakin 1885, Defence of Ladysmith, South Africa 1899–1902.

Mons, Le Cateau, Retreat from Mons, Marne 1914, Aisne 1914, Messines 1914, Ypres 1914, 1915, Cambrai 1917, St Quentin, Pursuit to Mons.

The 6th (Inniskilling) Dragoons: Dettingen, Warburg, Willems, Waterloo, Balaklava, Sevastopol, South Africa 1899–1902.

Somme 1916, 1918, Morval, Cambrai 1917, 1918, St Quentin, Avre, Amiens, Hindenburg Line, St Quentin Canal, Pursuit to Mons, France and Flanders 1914–18.

7th Queen's Own Hussars: Dettingen, Warburg, Beaumont, Willems, Orthes, Peninsula, Waterloo, Lucknow, South Africa 1900–2.

Khan Baghdadi, Sharqat, Mesopotamia 1917–18.

Egyptian frontier 1940, Beda Fomm, Sidi Rezegh 1941, North Africa 1940–1, Ancona, Rimini Line, Italy 1944–5, Pegu, Paungde, Burma 1942.

8th King's Royal Irish Hussars: Leswaree, Hindoostan, Alma, Balaklava, Inkerman, Sevastopol, Central India, Afghanistan 1878–80, South Africa 1900–2.

Givenchy 1914, Somme 1916, 1918, Cambrai 1917, 1918, Bapaume 1918, Rosieres, Amiens, Albert 1918, Beaurevoir, Pursuit to Mons, France and Flanders 1914–18.

Villers Bocage, Lower Maas, Roer, Rhine, North-west Europe 1944–5, Buq Buq, Sidi Rezegh 1941, Gazala, El Alamein, North Africa 1940–2.

Imjin, Korea 1950–1.

9th Queen's Royal Lancers: Peninsula, Punniar, Sobraon, Punjaub, Chillianwallah,

Goojerat, Delhi 1857, Lucknow, Charasiah, Kabul 1879, Kandahar 1880, Afghanistan 1878–80, Modder river, Relief of Kimberley, Paardeberg, South Africa 1899–1902.

Retreat from Mons, Marne 1914, Aisne 1914, Messines 1914, Ypres 1914, 1915, Somme 1916, 1918, Arras 1917, Cambrai 1917, 1918, Rosieres, Pursuit to Mons.

Somme 1940, North-west Europe 1940, Gazala, Ruweisat, El Alamein, El Hamma, North Africa 1942–3, Lamone Bridgehead, Argenta Gap, Italy 1944–5.

10th Royal Hussars: Warburg, Peninsula, Waterloo, Sevastopol, Ali Masjid, Afghanistan 1878–80, Relief of Kimberley, Paardeberg, South Africa 1899–1902.

Ypres 1914, 1915, Rezenberg, Loos, Arras 1917, 1918, Somme 1918, Avre, Amiens, Drocourt-Queant, Pursuit to Mons, France and Flanders 1914–18.

Somme 1940, Saunnu, Gazala, El Alamein, El Hamma, Tunis, Coriano, Santarcangelo, Valli di Comacchio, Argenta Gap.

11th Hussars: Warburg, Beaumont, Willems, Salamanca, Peninsula, Waterloo, Bhurtpore, Alma, Balaklava, Inkerman, Sevastopol.

Le Cateau, Retreat from Mons, Marne 1914, Aisne 1914, Messines 1914, Ypres 1914, 1915, Somme 1916, 1918, Cambrai 1917, 1918, Amiens, France and Flanders 1914–18.

Villers Bocage, Roer, Rhine, Egyptian frontier 1940, Sidi Barrani, Beda Fomm, Sidi Rezegh 1941, El Alamein, Tunis, Italy 1943.

12th Royal Lancers: Salamanca, Peninsula, Waterloo, South Africa 1851, 1852, 1853, Sevastopol, Central India, Relief of Kimberley, Paardeberg, South Africa 1899–1902.

Mons, Retreat from Mons, Marne 1914, Aisne 1914, Messines 1914, Ypres 1914,

1915, Arras 1917, Cambrai 1917, 1918, Somme 1918, Sambre.

Dyle, Dunkirk 1940, North-west Europe 1940, Chor es Sufan, Gazala, El Alamein, Tunis, North Africa 1941–3, Bologna, Italy 1944–5.

13th Hussars: Albuhera, Vittoria, Orthes, Toulouse, Peninsula, Waterloo, Alma, Balaklava, Inkerman, Sevastopol, Relief of Ladysmith, South Africa 1899–1902.

France and Flanders 1914–16, Kut al Amara 1917, Baghdad, Sharqat, Mesopotamia 1916–18.

14th King's Hussars: Douro, Talavera, Fuentes d'Onor, Salamanca, Vittoria, Pyrenees, Orthes, Peninsula, Goojerat, Chillianwallah, Punjaub, Persia, Central India, Relief of Ladysmith, South Africa 1900–2.

Tigris 1916, Kut al Amara 1917, Baghdad, Mesopotamia 1915–18, Persia 1918.

15th The King's Hussars: Emsdorff, Viller-en-Cauchies, Egmont-op-Zee, Sahagun, Vittoria, Peninsula, Waterloo, Afghanistan 1878–80.

Retreat from Mons, Marne 1914, Aisne 1914, Ypres 1914, 1915, Bellewaarde, Somme 1916, 1918, Cambrai 1917, 1918, Rosieres, Pursuit to Mons, France and Flanders 1914–18.

16th The Queen's Lancers: Beaumont, Willems, Talavera, Fuentes d'Onor, Salamanca, Vittoria, Nive, Peninsula, Waterloo, Bhurtpore, Ghuznee 1839, Afghanistan 1839, Maharajpore, Sobraon, Aliwal, Relief of Kimberley, Paardeberg, South Africa 1900–2.

Mons, Le Cateau, Marne 1914, Aisne 1914, Messines 1914, Ypres 1914, 1915, Bellewaarde, Arras 1917, Cambrai 1917, Somme 1918.

A sergeant of the 14th/20th King's Hussars with a guidon of the 14th Light Dragoons, showing its painted Peninsular War battle honours.

17th Lancers: Alma, Balaklava, Inkerman, Sevastopol, Central India, South Africa 1879, South Africa 1900–2.

Festubert 1917, Somme 1916, 1918, Morval, Cambrai 1917, 1918, St Quentin, Avre, Hazebrouck, Amiens, Pursuit to Mons, France and Flanders 1914–18.

18th Royal Hussars: Peninsula, Waterloo, Defence of Ladysmith, South Africa 1899–1901.

Mons, Marne 1914, Aisne 1914, Messines 1914, Ypres 1914, 1915, Somme 1916, 1918, Cambrai 1917, 1918, Amiens, Hindenburg Line, France and Flanders 1914–18.

19th Royal Hussars: Assaye, Niagara, Tel el Kebir, Egypt 1882–4, Abu Klea, Nile 1884–5, Mysore, Defence of Ladysmith, South Africa 1900–2.

Le Cateau, Retreat from Mons, Marne 1914, Aisne 1914, Armentieres 1914,

Ypres 1915, Somme 1916, 1918, Cambrai 1917, 1918, Amiens, Pursuit to Mons.

20th Hussars: Peninsula. Mons, Retreat from Mons, Marne 1914, Aisne 1914, Messines 1914, Ypres 1914, 1915, Cambrai 1917, 1918, Somme 1918, Amiens, Sambre.

21st Lancers: Khartoum. North-West Frontier India 1915–16.

The Royal Tank Regiment: Somme 1916, 1918, Arras 1917, 1918, Messines 1917, Ypres 1917, Cambrai 1917, Villers Bretonneux, Amiens, Bapaume 1918,

A standard of the Royal Tank Regiment, with battle honours emblazoned on the standard and the bearer's belt.

Hindenburg Line, France and Flanders 1916–18.

Rhine, North-west Europe 1940, 1944–5, Abyssinia 1940, Tobruk 1941, El Alamein, North Africa 1940–3, Sicily 1943, Italy 1943–5, Greece 1941, Burma 1942. Korea 1951–3.

The Grenadier Guards: Tangier 1680, Namur 1695, Gibraltar 1704–5, Blenheim, Ramillies, Oudenarde, Malplaquet, Dettingen, Lincelles, Egmont op Zee, Corunna, Barrosa, Nive, Peninsula, Waterloo, Alma, Inkerman, Sevastopol, Tel el Kebir, Egypt 1882, Suakin 1885, Khartoum, Modder river, South Africa 1899–1902.

Marne 1914, Aisne 1914, Ypres 1915, 1917, Loos, Somme 1916, 1918, Cambrai 1917, 1918, Arras 1918, Hazebrouck, Hindenburg Line, France and Flanders 1914–18.

Dunkirk 1940, Mareth, Medjez Plain, Salerno, Monte Camino, Anzio, Mont Pincon, Gothic Line, Nijmegen, Rhine.

The Coldstream Guards: Tangier 1680, Namur 1695, Gibraltar 1704–5, Oudenarde, Malplaquet, Dettingen, Lincelles, Talavera, Barrosa, Fuentes d'Onor, Salamanca, Nive, Peninsula, Waterloo, Alma, Inkerman, Sevastopol, Tel el Kebir, Egypt 1882, Suakin 1885, Modder river, South Africa 1899–1902.

Retreat from Mons, Marne 1914, Aisne 1914, Ypres 1914, 1917, Loos, Somme 1916, 1918, Cambrai 1917, 1918, Arras 1918, Hazebrouck, Hindenburg Line.

Dunkirk 1940, Mont Pincon, Rhineland, North-west Europe 1940, 1944–5, Sidi Barrani, Tobruk 1941, 1942, Tunis, Salerno, Monte Ornito, Italy 1943-45.

The Scots Guards: Namur 1695, Dettingen, Lincelles, Talavera, Barrosa, Fuentes d'Onor, Salamanca, Nive, Peninsula, Waterloo, Alma, Inkerman, Sevastopol, Tel

Regimental colour of the Coldstream Guards, revealing their sphinx and battle honour blazons.

el Kebir, Egypt 1882, Suakin 1885, Modder river, South Africa 1899–1902.

Retreat from Mons, Marne 1914, Aisne 1914, Ypres 1914, 1917, Festubert 1915, Loos, Somme 1916, 1918, Cambrai 1917, 1918, Hindenburg Line, France and Flanders 1914–18.

Gazala, Medenine, Djebel Bou Aoukaz I 1943, North Africa 1941–3, Monte Camino Anzio, Italy 1943–5, Quarry Hills, Rhineland, North-west Europe 1944–5.

The Irish Guards: Retreat from Mons, Marne 1914, Aisne 1914, Ypres 1914, 1917, Festubert 1915, Loos, Somme 1916, 1918, Cambrai 1917, 1918, Hazebrouck, Hindenburg Line.

Norway 1940, Boulogne 1940, Mont Pincon, Neerpelt, Nijmegen, Rhineland, North-west Europe 1944–5, Djebel Bou Aoukaz 1943, North Africa 1943, Anzio.

The Welsh Guards: Loos, Ginchy, Flers-Courcelette, Morval, Pilckem, Poelcappelle, Cambrai 1917, 1918, Bapaume 1918, Canal du Nord, Sambre.

Defence of Arras, Boulogne 1940, Mont Pincon, Brussels, Hechtel, Fondouk, Hammam Lif, Monte Ornito, Monte Piccolo, Battaglia.

The Royal Scots: Tangier 1680, Namur 1695, Blenheim, Ramillies, Oudenarde, Malplaquet, Louisburg, Havannah, Egmont op Zee, St Lucia 1803, Corunna, Busaco, Salamanca, Vittoria, St Sebastian, Nive, Peninsula, Niagara, Waterloo, Nagpore, Maheidpore, Ava, Alma, Inkerman, Sevastopol, Taku Forts, Pekin 1860, South Africa 1899–1902.

Le Cateau, Marne 1914, 1918, Ypres 1915, 1917, 1918, Loos, Somme 1916, 1918, Arras

1917, 1918, Lys, Struma, Gallipoli 1915–16, Palestine 1917–18.

Defence of Escaut, Odon, Aart, Flushing, Rhine, North-west Europe 1940, 1944–5, Gothic Line, Italy 1944–5, Kohima, Burma 1943–5.

The Queen's Royal West Surrey Regiment: Tangier 1662–80, Namur 1695, Vimiera, Corunna, Salamanca, Vittoria, Pyrenees, Nivelle, Toulouse, Peninsula, Ghuznee 1839, Khelat, Afghanistan 1839, South Africa 1851–3, Taku Forts, Pekin 1860, Burma 1885–7, Tirah, Relief of Ladysmith, South Africa 1899–1902.

Retreat from Mons, Ypres 1914, 1917, 1918, Somme 1916, 1918, Messines 1917, Hindenburg Line, Vittorio Veneto, Gallipoli 1915, Palestine 1917–18, Mesopotamia 1915–18, North-West Frontier India 1916–17. Afghanistan 1919.

Villers Bocage, Tobruk 1941, El Alamein, Medenine, Salerno, Monte Camino, Anzio, Gemmano Ridge, North Arakan, Kohima.

The Buffs (Royal East Kent Regiment): Blenheim, Ramillies, Oudenarde, Malplaquet, Dettingen, Guadaloupe 1759, Belleisle, Douro, Talavera, Albuhera, Vittoria, Pyrenees, Nivelle, Nive, Orthes, Toulouse, Peninsula, Punniar, Sevastopol, Taku Forts, South Africa 1879, Chitral, Relief of Kimberley, Paardeberg, South Africa 1900–2.

Armentieres 1914, Ypres 1915, 1917, Loos, Somme 1916, 1918, Arras 1917, Amiens, Hindenburg Line, Struma, Jerusalem, Baghdad.

North-west Europe 1940, Alem Hamza, El Alamein, Robaa Valley, Sicily 1943, Trigno, Anzio, Argenta Gap, Shweli.

The King's Own Royal Lancaster Regiment: Namur 1695, Gibraltar 1704–5, Guadaloupe 1759, St Lucia 1778, Corunna, Badajoz, Salamanca, Vittoria, St Sebastian, Nive,

Peninsula, Bladensburg, Waterloo, Alma, Inkerman, Sevastopol, Abyssinia, South Africa 1879, Relief of Ladysmith, South Africa 1900–2.

Marne 1914, Ypres 1915, 1917, Somme 1916, 1918, Arras 1917, 1918, Messines 1917, Lys, France and Flanders 1914–18, Macedonia 1915, 1918, Gallipoli 1915, Mesopotamia 1916–18.

Dunkirk 1940, North-west Europe 1940, Defence of Habbaniya, Merjayun, Tobruk sortie, North Africa 1940–2, Montone, Lamone Bridgehead, Malta 1941–2, Chindits 1944.

The Royal Northumberland Fusiliers: Wilhelmstahl, St Lucia 1778, Rolica, Vimiera, Corunna, Busaco, Ciudad Rodrigo, Badajoz, Salamanca, Vittoria, Nivelle, Orthes, Toulouse, Peninsula, Lucknow, Afghanistan 1879–80, Khartoum, Modder river, South Africa 1900–2.

Mons, Marne 1914, Ypres 1914, 1915, 1917, 1918, St Julien, Somme 1916, 1918, Scarpe 1917, 1918, Selle, Piave, Struma, Suvla.

Dunkirk 1940, Caen, Rhineland, Sidi Barrani, Defence of Tobruk, Tobruk 1941, Cauldron, El Alamein, Salerno, Cassino II.

Imjin, Korea 1950–1.

The Royal Warwickshire Regiment: Namur 1695, Martinique 1794, Rolica, Vimiera, Corunna, Vittoria, Pyrenees, Nivelle, Orthes, Peninsula, Niagara, South Africa 1846–7, 1851, 1852, 1853, Atbara, Khartoum, South Africa 1899–1902.

Le Cateau, Marne 1914, Ypres 1914, 1915, 1917, Somme 1916, 1918, Arras 1917, 1918, Lys, Hindenburg Line, Piave, Sari Bair, Baghdad.

Defence of Escaut, Wormhoudt, Ypres–Comines canal, Normandy Landing, Caen, Mont Pincon, Venrail, Bremen, North-west Europe 1940, 1944–5, Burma 1945.

The Royal Fusiliers: Namur 1695, Martinique 1809, Talavera, Busaco, Albuhera, Badajoz, Salamanca, Vittoria, Pyrenees, Orthes, Toulouse, Peninsula, Alma, Inkerman, Sevastopol, Kandahar 1880, Afghanistan 1879–80, Relief of Ladysmith, South Africa 1899–1902.

Mons, Marne 1914, Ypres 1914, 1915, 1917, 1918, Somme 1916, 1918, Arras 1917, 1918, Cambrai 1917, 1918, Hindenburg Line, Struma, Landing at Helles, Palestine 1918.

Dunkirk 1940, Keren, North Africa 1940, 1943, Mozzagrogna, Salerno, Garigliano Crossing, Anzio, Cassino II, Gothic Line, Coriano.

Korea 1952–53.

The King's Liverpool Regiment: Blenheim, Ramillies, Oudenarde, Malplaquet, Dettingen, Martinique 1809, Niagara, Delhi 1857, Lucknow, Peiwar Kotal, Afghanistan 1878–80, Burma 1885–7, Defence of Ladysmith, South Africa 1899–1902.

Retreat from Mons, Marne 1914, Aisne 1914, Ypres 1914, 1915, 1917, Festubert 1915, Loos, Somme 1916, 1918, Arras 1917, 1918, Scarpe 1917, 1918, Cambrai 1917, 1918. Afghanistan 1919.

Normandy landing, Cassino II, Trasimene Line, Tuori, Capture of Forli, Rimini Line, Athens, Chindits 1943, 1944.

The Hook 1953, Korea 1952–3.

The Royal Norfolk Regiment: Bellisle, Havannah, Martinique 1794, Rolica, Vimiera, Corunna, Busaco, Salamanca, Vittoria, St Sebastian, Nive, Peninsula, Cabool 1842, Moodkee, Ferozeshah, Sobraon, Sevastopol, Kabul 1879, Afghanistan 1879–80, Paardeburg, South Africa 1900–2.

Mons, Le Cateau, Marne 1914, Ypres 1914, 1915, 1917, 1918, Somme 1916, 1918, Hindenburg Line, Landing at Suvla, Gaza, Shaiba, Kut al Amara 1915, 1917.

St Omer-La Bassee, Normandy landing, Brieux bridgehead, Venraij, Rhineland, North-west Europe 1940, 1944–5, Singapore Island, Kohima, Aradura, Burma 1944–5. Korea 1951–2.

The Royal Lincolnshire Regiment: Blenheim, Ramillies, Oudenarde, Malplaquet, Peninsula, Sobraon, Mooltan, Goojerat, Punjaub, Lucknow, Atbara, Khartoum, Paardeburg, South Africa 1900–2.

Mons, Marne 1914, Messines 1914, 1917, Ypres 1914, 1915, 1917, Neuve Chapelle, Loos, Somme 1916, 1918, Lys, Hindenburg Line, Suvla.

Dunkirk 1940, Normandy landing, Fontenay le Pesnil, Antwerp–Turnhout canal, Rhineland, North Africa 1943, Salerno, Gothic Line, Ngakyedauk Pass, Burma 1943–5.

The Devonshire Regiment: Dettingen, Salamanca, Pyrenees, Nivelle, Nive, Orthes, Toulouse, Peninsula, Afghanistan 1879–80, Tirah, Defence of Ladysmith, South Africa 1899–1902.

La Bassee 1914, Ypres 1915, 1917, Loos, Somme 1916, 1918, Bois des Buttes, Hindenburg Line, Vittorio Veneto, Doiran 1917, 1918, Palestine 1917–18, Mesopotamia 1916–18.

Normandy landing, Caen, Rhine, North-west Europe 1944–5, Landing in Sicily, Regalbuto, Malta 1940–2, Imphal, Myinmu bridgehead, Burma 1943–5.

The Suffolk Regiment: Dettingen, Minden, Seringapatam, India, South Africa 1851, 1852, 1853, New Zealand, Afghanistan 1878–80, South Africa 1900–2.

Le Cateau, Neuve Chapelle, Ypres 1915, 1917, 1918, Somme 1916, 1918, Arras 1917, 1918, Cambrai 1917, 1918, Hindenburg Line, Macedonia 1915–18, Landing at Suvla, Gaza.

Dunkirk 1940, Normandy landing, Odon, Falaise, Venraij, Brinkum, Singapore Island, North Arakan, Imphal, Burma 1943–5.

The Somerset Light Infantry: Gibraltar 1704–5, Dettingen, Martinique 1809, Ava, Ghuznee, Afghanistan 1839, Cabool 1842, Sevastopol, South Africa 1878–9, Burma 1885–7, Relief of Ladysmith, South Africa 1899–1902.

Marne 1914, 1918, Aisne 1914, Ypres 1915, 1917, 1918, Somme 1916, 1918, Albert 1916, 1918, Arras 1917, 1918, Cambrai 1917, 1918, Hindenburg Line, Palestine 1917–18, Tigris 1916, Afghanistan 1919.

Hill 112, Mont Pincon, Rhineland, North-west Europe 1944–45, Cassino II, Cosina canal crossing, Italy 1944–5, North Arakan, Ngakyedauk Pass.

The West Yorkshire Regiment: Namur 1695, Tournay, Corunna, Java, Waterloo, Bhurtpore, Sevastopol, New Zealand, Afghanistan 1879–80, Relief of Ladysmith, South Africa 1899–1902.

Armentieres 1914, Neuve Chapelle, Somme 1916, 1918, Ypres 1917, 1918, Cambrai 1917, 1918, Villers Bretonneaux, Lys, Tardenois, Piave, Suvla.

Keren, Defence of Alamein Line, Pegu 1942, Yenangyaung 1942, Maungdaw, Defence of Sinzweya, Imphal, Bishenpur, Meiktila, Sittang 1945.

The East Yorkshire Regiment: Blenheim, Ramillies, Oudenarde, Malplaquet, Louisburg, Quebec 1759, Martinique 1762, Havannah, St Lucia 1778, Martinique 1794, 1809, Guadaloupe 1810, Afghanistan 1879–80, South Africa 1900–2.

Aisne 1914, 1918, Armentieres 1914, Ypres 1915, 1917, 1918, Loos, Somme 1916, 1918, Arras, Cambrai 1917, 1918, Selle, Doiran 1917, Gallipoli 1915.

Dunkirk 1940, Normandy landing, Odon, Schaddenhof, North-west Europe 1940, 1944–5, Gazala, El Alamein, Mareth, Sicily 1943, Burma 1945.

The Bedfordshire and Hertfordshire Regiment: Namur 1695, Blenheim, Ramillies, Oudenarde, Malplaquet, Surinam, Chitral, South Africa 1900–2.

Mons, Marne 1914, Ypres 1914, 1915, 1917, Loos, Somme 1916, 1918, Arras 1917, 1918, Cambrai 1917, 1918, Sambre, Suvla, Gaza.

Dunkirk 1940, North-west Europe 1940, Tobruk sortie, Belhamed, Tunis, North Africa 1941–3, Cassino II, Trasimene Line, Italy 1944–5, Chindits 1944.

The Royal Leicestershire Regiment: Namur 1695, Louisburg, Martinique 1762, Havannah, Ghuznee 1839, Khelat, Afghanistan 1839, Sevastopol, Ali Masjid, Afghanistan 1878–9, Defence of Ladysmith, South Africa 1899–1902.

Aisne 1914, 1918, Neuve Chapelle, Somme 1916, 1918, Ypres 1917, Cambrai 1917, 1918, Lys, St Quentin Canal, France and Flanders 1914–18, Palestine 1918, Mesopotamia 1915–18.

Scheldt, North-west Europe 1944–5, Sidi Barrani, North Africa 1940–1, 43, Salerno, Gothic Line, Italy 1943-45, Crete, Malaya 1941-42, Chindits 1944.

Korea 1951–2.

The Royal Irish Regiment: Namur 1695, Blenheim, Ramillies, Oudenarde, Malplaquet, Afghanistan 1879–80, Tel el Kebir, Egypt 1882, Nile 1884–5, South Africa 1899–1902.

Mons, Le Cateau, Marne 1914, Ypres 1915, 1917, 1918, Somme 1916, 1918, Messines 1917, Hindenburg Line, Struma, Suvla, Gaza.

The Green Howards: Malplaquet, Belleisle, Alma, Inkerman, Sevastopol, Tirah, Relief of Kimberley, Paardeburg, South Africa 1899–1902.

Ypres 1914, 1915, 1917, Loos, Somme 1916, 1918, Arras 1917, 1918, Messines 1917, 1918, Valenciennes, Sambre, France and Flanders 1914–18, Vittorio Veneto, Suvla.

Afghanistan 1919.

Norway 1940, Normandy landing, Northwest Europe 1940, 44–5, Gazala, El Alamein, Mareth, Akarit, Sicily 1943, Minturno, Anzio.

The Lancashire Fusiliers: Dettingen, Minden, Egmont op Zee, Maida, Vimiera, Corunna, Vittoria, Pyrenees, Orthes, Toulouse, Peninsula, Alma, Inkerman, Sevastopol, Lucknow, Khartoum, Relief of Ladysmith, South Africa 1900-2.

Retreat from Mons, Aisne 1914, 1918, Ypres 1915, 1917, 1918, Somme 1916, 1918, Arras 1917, 1918, Passchendaele, Cambrai 1917, 1918, Hindenburg Line, Macedonia 1915–18, Landing at Helles.

Defence of Escaut, Caen, Medjez el Bab, Sangro, Cassino II, Argenta Gap, Malta 1941–2, Kohima, Chindits 1944, Burma 1943–5.

The Royal Scots Fusiliers: Blenheim, Ramillies, Oudenarde, Malplaquet, Dettingen, Belleisle, Martinique 1794, Bladensburg, Alma, Inkerman, Sevastopol, South Africa 1879, Burma 1885–7, Tirah, Relief of Ladysmith, South Africa 1899–1902.

Mons, Marne 1914, Ypres 1914, 1917, 1918, Somme 1916, 1918, Arras 1917, 1918, Lys, Hindenburg Line, Doiran 1917, 1918, Gallipoli 1915, Palestine 1917–18.

Ypres–Comines canal, Odon, Falaise, Scheldt, Rhine, Bremen, Landing in Sicily, Garigliano crossing, North Arakan, Pinwe.

The Cheshire Regiment: Louisburg, Martinique 1762, Havannah, Meeanee, Hyderabad, Scinde, South Africa 1900–2.

Mons, Ypres 1914, 1915, 1917, 1918, Somme 1916, 1918, Arras 1917, 1918, Messines 1917, 1918, Bapaume 1918, Doiran 1917, 1918, Suvla, Gaza, Kut al Amara 1917.

St Omer-La Bassee, Normandy landing, Capture of Tobruk, El Alamein, Mareth, Sicily 1943, Salerno, Rome, Gothic Line, Malta 1941–2.

The Royal Welch Fusiliers: Namur 1695, Blenheim, Ramillies, Oudenarde, Malpalquet, Dettingen, Minden, Corunna, Martinique 1809, Albuhera, Badajoz, Salamanca, Vittoria, Pyrenees, Nivelle, Orthes, Toulouse, Peninsula, Waterloo, Alma, Inkerman, Sevastopol, Lucknow, Ashantee 1873–4, Burma 1885–7, Relief of Ladysmith, South Africa 1899–1902, Pekin 1900.

Marne 1914, Aisne 1914, 1918, La Bassee 1914, Messines 1914, 1917, 1918, Armentieres 1914, Ypres 1914, 1917, 1918, Somme 1916, 1918, Hindenburg Line, Vittorio Veneto, Doiran 1917, 1918, Gallipoli 1915–16, Egypt 1915–17, Gaza, Baghdad.

St Omer-La Bassee, Caen, Lower Maas, Reichswald, Weeze, Rhine, Madagascar, Donbaik, North Arakan, Kohima.

The South Wales Borderers: Blenheim, Ramillies, Oudenarde, Malplaquet, Cape of Good Hope 1806, Talavera, Busaco, Fuentes d'Onor, Salamanca, Vittoria,Pyrenees, Nivelle, Orthes, Peninsula, Chillianwallah, Goojerat, Punjaub, South Africa 1877, 1978, 1979, Burma 1885–7, South Africa 1900–2.

Mons, Marne 1914, Ypres 1914, 1917, 1918, Gheluvelt, Somme 1916, 1918, Cambrai 1917, 1918, Doiran 1917, 1918, Landing at Helles, Baghdad, Tsingtao.

Norway 1940, Normandy landing, Sully, Caen, Le Havre, North-west Europe 1944–5, North Africa 1942, Mayu Tunnels, Pinwe, Burma 1944–5.

The King's Own Scottish Borderers: Namur 1695, Minden, Egmont op Zee, Martinique 1809, Afghanistan 1878–80, Chitral, Tirah, Paardeberg, South Africa 1900–2.

Mons, Aisne 1914, Ypres 1914, 1915, 1917, 1918, Loos, Somme 1916, 1918, Arras 1917, 1918, Soissonnais-Ourcq, Hindenburg Line, Gallipoli 1915–16, Gaza.

Dunkirk 1940, Odon, Caen, Arnhem 1944, Flushing, Rhine, Bremen,

Ngakyedauk Pass, Imphal, Irrawaddy. Kowang-San, Korea 1951–2.

The Cameronians: Blenheim, Ramillies, Oudenarde, Malplaquet, Mandora, Corunna, Martinique 1809, Guadaloupe 1810, South Africa 1846–7, Sevastopol, Lucknow, Abyssinia, South Africa 1877, 1878, 1879, Relief of Ladysmith, South Africa 1899–1902.

Mons, Marne 1914, 1918, Neuve Chapelle, Loos, Somme 1916, 1918, Ypres 1917, 1918, Hindenburg Line, Macedonia 1915–18, Gallipoli 1915, Palestine 1917–18.

Odon, Scheldt, Rhineland, Rhine, North-west Europe 1940, 1944–5, Sicily 1943, Anzio, Italy 1943–4, Chindits 1944, Burma 1942–4.

The Royal Inniskilling Fusiliers: Martinique 1762, Havannah, St Lucia 1778, 1796, Maida, Badajoz, Salamanca, Vittoria, Pyrenees, Nivelle, Orthes, Toulouse, Peninsula, Waterloo, South Africa 1835, 1846–7, Central India, Relief of Ladysmith, South Africa 1899–1902.

Le Cateau, Somme 1916, 1918, Ypres 1917, 1918, St Quentin, Hindenburg Line, France and Flanders 1914–18, Macedonia 1915–18, Landing at Helles, Gallipoli 1915–16, Palestine 1917–18.

North-west Europe 1940, Djebel Tanngoucha, North Africa 1942–3, Centuripe, Sicily 1943, Garigliano crossing, Cassino II, Italy 1943–5, Yenangyaung, Burma 1942–3.

The Gloucestershire Regiment: Ramillies, Louisburg, Guadaloupe 1759, Martinique 1762, Havannah, St Lucia 1778, Maida, Corunna, Talavera, Busaco, Barrosa, Albuhera, Salamanca, Vittoria, Pyrenees, Nivelle, Nive, Orthes, Toulouse, Peninsula, Waterloo, Chillianwallah, Goojerat, Punjaub, Alma, Inkerman, Sevastopol, Delhi 1857, Defence of Ladysmith, Relief of Kimberley, Paardeberg, South Africa 1899–1902.

Mons, Ypres 1914, 1915, 1917, Loos, Somme 1916, 1918, Lys, Selle, Vittorio Veneto, Doiran 1917, Sari Bair, Baghdad.

Defence of Escaut, Cassel, Mont Pincon, Falaise, North-west Europe 1940, 1944–5, Taukyan, Paungde, Pinwe, Myitson, Burma 1942, 1944–5.

Imjin, Korea 1950–1.

The Worcestershire Regiment: Ramillies, Belleisle, Mysore, Hindoostan, Rolica, Vimiera, Corunna, Talavera, Albuhera, Salamanca, Pyrenees, Nivelle, Nive, Orthes, Toulouse, Peninsula, Ferozeshah, Sobraon, Chillianwallah, Goojerat, Punjaub, South Africa 1900–2.

Mons, Ypres 1914, 1915, 1917, 1918, Gheluvelt, Neuve Chapelle, Somme 1916, 1918, Cambrai 1917, 1918, Lys, Italy 1917–18, Gallipoli 1915–16, Baghdad.

Mont Pincon, Seine 1944, Geilenkirchen, Goch, North-west Europe 1940, 1944–5, Keren, Gazala, Kohima, Mandalay, Burma 1944–5.

The East Lancashire Regiment: Gibraltar 1704–5, Cape of Good Hope 1806, Corunna, Java, Badajoz, Salamanca, Vittoria, St Sebastian, Nive, Peninsula, Waterloo, Bhurtpore, Alma, Inkerman, Sevastopol, Canton, Ahmed Khel, Afghanistan 1878–9, Chitral, South Africa 1900–2.

Retreat from Mons, Marne 1914, Aisne 1914, 1918, Neuve Chapelle, Ypres 1915, 1917, 1918.

Somme 1916, 1918, Arras 1917, 1918, Doiran 1917–18, Helles, Kut al Amara 1917.

Dunkirk 1940, Falaise, Lower Maas, Ourthe, Reichswald, Weeze, Aller, Madagascar, Pinwe, Burma 1944–5.

The East Surrey Regiment: Gibraltar 1704–5, Dettingen, Martinique 1794, Talavera, Guadaloupe 1810, Albuhera, Vittoria, Pyrenees, Nivelle, Nive, Orthes, Peninsula,

Cabool 1842, Moodkee, Ferozeshah, Aliwal, Sobraon, Sevastopol, Taku forts, New Zealand, Afghanistan 1878–9, Suakin 1885, Relief of Ladysmith, South Africa 1899–1902.

Mons, Marne 1914, La Bassee 1914, Ypres 1915, 1917, 1918, Loos, Somme 1916, 1918, Albert 1916, 1918, Cambrai 1917, 1918, Selle, Doiran 1918.

Dunkirk 1940, North-west Europe 1940, Oued Zarga, Longstop Hill 1943, North Africa 1942–3, Sicily 1943, Sangro, Cassino, Italy 1943–5, Malaya 1941–2.

The Duke of Cornwall's Light Infantry: Gibraltar 1704–5, Dettingen, St Lucia 1778, Dominica, Rolica, Vimiera, Corunna, Salamanca, Pyrenees, Nivelle, Nive, Orthes, Peninsula, Waterloo, Mooltan, Goojerat, Punjaub, Sevastopol, Lucknow, Tel el Kebir, Egypt 1882, Nile 1884–5, Paardeberg, South Africa 1899–1902.

Mons, Marne 1914, Ypres 1915, 1917, Somme 1916, 1918, Arras 1917, Passchendaele, Cambrai 1917, 1918, Sambre, Doiran 1917, 1918, Gaza.

Hill 112, Mont Pincon, Nederrijn, Geilenkirchen, Rhineland, North-west Europe 1940, 1944–5, Gazala, Medjez Plain, Cassino II, Incontro.

The Duke of Wellington's (West Riding) Regiment: Dettingen, Mysore, Seringapatam, Ally Ghur, Delhi 1803, Leswarree, Deig, Corunna, Nive, Peninsula, Waterloo, Alma, Inkerman, Sevastopol, Abyssinia, Relief of Kimberley, Paardeberg, South Africa 1900–2.

Mons, Marne 1914, 1918, Ypres 1914, 1915, 1917, Hill 60, Somme 1916, 1918, Arras 1917, 1918, Cambrai 1917, 1918, Lys, Piave, Landing at Suvla.

Afghanistan 1919.

Dunkirk 1940, St Valery-en-Caux, Fontenay le Pesnil, North-West Europe 1940, 1944–5, Djebel Bou Aoukaz 1943, Monte Ceco, Sittang 1942, Chindits 1944, Burma 1942–4.

The Border Regiment: Havannah, St Lucia 1778, Albuhera, Arroyo dos Molinos, Vittoria, Pyrenees, Nivelle, Nive, Orthes, Peninsula, Alma, Inkerman, Sevastopol, Lucknow, Relief of Ladysmith, South Africa 1899–1902.

Ypres 1914, 1915, 1917, 1918, Langemarck 1914, 1917, Somme 1916, 1918, Arras 1917, 1918, Cambrai 1917, 1918, Lys, France and Flanders 1914–18, Vittorio Veneto, Macedonia 1915–18, Gallipoli 1915–16.

Afghanistan 1919.

Dunkirk 1940, Arnhem 1944, North-west Europe 1940, 1944, Tobruk 1941, Landing in Sicily, Imphal, Myinmu bridgehead, Meiktila, Chindits 1944, Burma 1943–5.

The Royal Sussex Regiment: Gibraltar 1704–5, Louisburg, Quebec 1759, Martinique 1762, Havannah, St Lucia 1778, Maida, Egypt 1882, Abu Klea, Nile 1884–5, South Africa 1900–2.

Retreat from Mons, Marne 1914, 1918, Ypres 1914, 1917, 1918, Somme 1916, 1918, Pilckem, Hindenburg Line, Italy 1917–18, Gallipoli 1915, Palestine 1917–18, North-West Frontier India 1915, 1916–17.

Afghanistan 1919.

North-west Europe 1940, Abyssinia 1941, Omars, Alam el Halfa, El Alamein, Akarit, North Africa 1940–3, Cassino II, Italy 1944–5, Burma 1943–5.

The Royal Hampshire Regiment: Blenheim, Ramillies, Oudenarde, Malplaquet, Dettingen, Minden, Belleisle, Tournay, Barrosa, Peninsula, Taku forts, Pekin 1860, Charasiah, Kabul 1879, Afghanistan 1878–80, Burma 1885–7, Paardeberg, South Africa 1900–2.

Retreat from Mons, Ypres 1915, 1917, 1918, Somme 1916, 1918, Arras 1917, 1918, Cambrai 1917, 1918, Doiran 1917, 1918, Landing at Helles, Suvla, Gaza, Kut al Amara 1915, 1917.

Dunkirk 1940, Normandy landing, Caen, Rhine, Tebourba Gap, Hunt's Gap, Salerno, Cassino II, Gothic Line, Malta 1941–2.

The South Staffordshire Regiment: Guadaloupe 1759, Martinique 1762, Monte Video, Rolica, Vimiera, Corunna, Busaco, Badajoz, Salamanca, Vittoria, St Sebastian, Nive, Peninsula, Ava, Moodkee, Ferozeshah, Sobraon, Pegu, Alma, Inkerman, Sevastopol, Lucknow, Central India, South Africa 1878–9, Egypt 1882, Kirbekan, Nile 1884–5, South Africa 1900–2.

Mons, Marne 1914, Aisne 1914, 1918, Ypres 1914, 1917, Loos, Somme 1916, 1918, Cambrai 1917, 1918, St Quentin Canal, Vittorio Veneto, Suvla. Caen, Noyers, Falaise, Arnhem 1944, North-west Europe 1940, 1944, North Africa 1940, Landing in Sicily, Sicily 1943, Chindits 1944, Burma 1944.

The Dorset Regiment: Plassey, Martinique, Marabout, Albuhera, Vittoria, Pyrenees, Nivelle, Nive, Orthes, Peninsula, Ava, Maharajpore, Sevastopol, Tirah, Relief of Ladysmith, South Africa 1899–1902.

Mons, Marne 1914, Ypres 1915, 1917, Somme 1916, 1918, Hindenburg Line, Sambre, Suvla, Gaza, Shaiba, Ctesiphon.

St Omer-La Bassee, Normandy landing, Arnhem 1944, Aam, Geilenkirchen, Landing in Sicily, Malta 1940–2, Kohima, Mandalay.

The South Lancashire Regiment: Louisburg, Martinique 1762, Havannah, St Lucia 1778, Monte Video, Rolica, Vimiera, Corunna, Talavera, Badajoz, Salamanca, Vittoria, Pyrenees, Nivelle, Orthes, Toulouse, Peninsula, Niagara, Waterloo, Candahar 1842, Ghuznee 1842, Cabool 1842, Maharajpore, Sevastopol, Lucknow, New Zealand, Relief of Ladysmith, South Africa 1899–1902.

Mons, Aisne 1914, 1918, Messines 1914, 1917, 1918, Ypres 1914, 1915, 1917, 1918, Somme 1916, 1918, Lys, Doiran 1917, 1918, Sari Bair, Baghdad, Baluchistan 1918.

Afghanistan 1919.

Dunkirk 1940, Normandy landing, Bourgebus Ridge, Falaise, Rhineland, North-

west Europe 1940, 1944–5, Madagascar, North Arakan, Kohima, Nyaungu bridgehead.

The Welch Regiment: Martinique 1762, St Vincent 1797, Bourbon, Java, Detroit, Queenstown, Miami, Niagara, Waterloo, India, Ava, Candahar, Ghuznee, Cabool 1842, Alma, Inkerman, Sevastopol, Relief of Kimberley, Paardeberg, South Africa 1899–1902.

Aisne 1914, 1918, Ypres 1914, 1915, 1917, Gheluvelt, Somme 1916, 1918, Pilckem, Cambrai 1917, 1918, Macedonia 1915–18, Gallipoli 1915, Palestine 1917–18, Mesopotamia 1916–18.

Falaise, Lower Maas, Reichswald, Croce, Italy 1943–5, Canea, Kyaukmyaung Bridgehead, Sittang 1945, Burma 1944–5.

Korea 1951–2.

The Black Watch: Guadaloupe 1759, Martinique 1762, Havannah, North America 1763–4, Mysore, Mangalore, Seringapatam, Corunna, Busaco, Fuentes d'Onor, Pyrenees, Nivelle, Nive, Orthes, Peninsula, Waterloo, South Africa 1846–7, Alma, Sevastopol, Lucknow, Ashantee 1873–4, Tel el Kebir, Egypt 1882, 1884, Kirbekan, Nile 1884–5, Paardeberg, South Africa 1899–1902.

Marne 1914, 1918, Ypres 1914, 1917, 1918, Loos, Somme 1916, 1918, Arras 1917, 1918, Lys, Hindenburg Line, Doiran 1917, Megiddo, Kut al Amara 1917.

Falaise Road, Rhine, Tobruk 1941, El Alamein, Akarit, Tunis, Sicily 1943, Cassino II, Crete, Burma 1944.

The Hook 1952, Korea 1952–3.

The Oxfordshire and Buckinghamshire Light Infantry: Quebec 1759, Martinique 1762, Havannah, Mysore, Hindoostan, Martinique 1794, Vimiera, Corunna, Busaco, Fuentes d'Onor, Ciudad Rodrigo, Badajoz, Salamanca, Vittoria, Pyrenees, Nivelle, Nive, Orthes, Toulouse, Peninsula, Waterloo, South Africa 1851, 1852, 1853, Delhi 1857,

Relief of Ladysmith – the South Lancashires carry the last Boer trench on Pieter's Hill, 27 February 1900.

New Zealand, Relief of Kimberley, Paardeberg, South Africa 1900–2.

Mons, Ypres 1914, 1917, Langemarck 1914, 1917, Nonne Bosschen, Somme 1916, 1918, Cambrai 1917, 1918, Piave, Doiran 1917, 1918, Ctesiphon, Defence of Kut al Amara.

Cassel, Ypres–Comines canal, Normandy landing, Pegasus Bridge, Reichswald, Rhine, Enfidaville, Salerno, Anzio, Gemmano Ridge.

The Essex Regiment: Moro, Havannah, Badajoz, Salamanca, Peninsula, Bladensburg, Waterloo, Ava, Alma, Inkerman, Sevastopol, Taku forts, Nile 1884–5, Relief of Kimberley, Paardeberg, South Africa 1899–1902.

Le Cateau, Marne 1914, Ypres 1915, Loos, Somme 1916, 1918, Arras 1917, 1918, Cambrai 1917, 1918, Selle, Gallipoli 1915–16, Gaza.

Zetten, North-west Europe 1940, 1944–5, Palmyra, Tobruk 1941, Defence of Alamein Line, Enfidaville, Sangro, Villa Grande, Cassino I, Chindits 1944.

The Sherwood Foresters: Louisburg, Rolica, Vimiera, Talavera, Busaco, Fuentes d'Onor, Ciudad Rodrigo, Badajoz, Salamanca, Vittoria, Pyrenees, Nivelle, Orthes, Toulouse, Peninsula, Ava, South Africa 1846–7, Alma, Inkerman, Sevastopol, Central India, Abyssinia, Egypt 1882, Tirah, South Africa 1899–1902.

Aisne 1914, 1918, Neuve Chapelle, Loos, Somme 1916, 1918, Ypres 1917, 1918, Cambrai 1917, 1918, St Quentin canal, France and Flanders 1914–18, Italy 1917–18, Gallipoli 1915.

Norway 1940, Gazala, El Alamein, Tunis, Salerno, Anzio, Campoleone, Gothic Line, Coriano, Singapore Island.

The Loyal North Lancashire Regiment: Louisburg, Quebec 1759, Maida, Corunna, Tarifa, Vittoria, St Sebastian, Nive, Peninsula, Ava, Alma, Inkerman, Sevastopol, Ali Masjid, Afghanistan 1878–9, Defence of Kimberley, South Africa 1899–1902.

Mons, Aisne 1914, 1918, Ypres 1914, 1917, 1918, Somme 1916, 1918, Lys,

Hindenburg Line, Suvla, Gaza, Baghdad, Kilimanjaro.

Dunkirk 1940, Djebel Kesskiss, Gueriat el Atach Ridge, North Africa 1943, Anzio, Fiesole, Monte Grande, Italy 1944–5, Johore, Singapore Island.

The Northamptonshire Regiment: Louisburg, Quebec 1759, Martinique 1762, 1794, Havannah, Maida, Douro, Talavera, Albuhera, Badajoz, Salamanca, Vittoria, Pyrenees, Nivelle, Orthes, Toulouse, Peninsula, New Zealand, Sevastopol, South Africa 1879, Tirah, Modder river, South Africa 1899–1902.

Mons, Marne 1914, Aisne 1914, 1918, Ypres 1914, 1917, Neuve Chapelle, Loos, Somme 1916, 1918, Arras 1917, 1918, Epehy, Gaza.

North-west Europe 1940, 1945, North Africa 1942–3, Garigliano crossing, Anzio, Cassino II, Italy 1943–5, Yu, Imphal, Myinmu bridgehead, Burma 1943–5.

The Royal Berkshire Regiment: St Lucia 1778, Egmont op Zee, Copenhagen, Douro, Talavera, Albuhera, Queenstown, Vittoria, Pyrenees, Nivelle, Nive, Orthes, Peninsula, Alma, Inkerman, Sevastopol, Kandahar 1880, Afghanistan 1879–80, Egypt 1882, Tofrek, Suakin 1885, South Africa 1899–1902.

Mons, Ypres 1914, 1917, Neuve Chapelle, Loos, Somme 1916, 1918, Arras 1917, 1918, Cambrai 1917, Selle, Vittorio Veneto, Doiran 1917, 1918.

Dyle, Dunkirk 1940, Normandy Landing, Rhine, Sicily 1943, Damiano, Anzio, Kohima, Mandalay, Burma 1942–5.

The Queen's Own Royal West Kent Regiment: Vimiera, Corunna, Almaraz, Vittoria, Pyrenees, Nive, Orthes, Peninsula, Punniar, Moodkee, Ferozeshah, Aliwal, Sobraon, Alma, Inkerman, Sevastopol, Lucknow, New Zealand, Egypt 1882, Nile 1884–5, South Africa 1900–2.

Mons, Ypres 1914, 1915, 1917, 1918, Hill 60, Somme 1916, 1918, Vimy 1917, Italy 1917–18, Gallipoli 1915, Gaza, Defence of Kut al Amara, Sharqat.

Afghanistan 1919.

North-west Europe 1940, El Alamein, Medjez Plain, Centuripe, Sangro, Cassino, Trasimene Line, Argenta Gap, Malta 1940–2, Defence of Kohima.

The King's Own Yorkshire Light Infantry: Minden, Corunna, Fuentes d'Onor, Salamanca, Vittoria, Pyrenees, Nivelle, Orthes, Peninsula, Waterloo, Pegu, Ali Masjid, Afghanistan 1878–80, Burma 1885–7, Modder river, South Africa 1899–1902.

Le Cateau, Marne 1914, 1918, Messines 1914, 1917, 1918, Ypres 1914, 1915, 1917, 1918, Somme 1916, 1918, Cambrai 1917, 1918, Havrincourt, Sambre, Italy 1917–18, Macedonia 1915–17.

Norway 1940, Fontenay le Pesnil, North-west Europe 1944–5, Argoub Sellah, Sicily 1943, Salerno, Minturno, Anzio, Gemmano Ridge, Burma 1942.

The King's Shropshire Light Infantry: Nieuport, Tournay, St Lucia 1796, Talavera, Fuentes d'Onor, Salamanca, Vittoria, Pyrenees, Nivelle, Nive, Toulouse, Peninsula, Bladensburg, Aliwal, Sobraon, Goojerat, Punjaub, Lucknow, Afghanistan 1879–80, Egypt 1882, Suakin 1885, Paardeberg, South Africa 1899–1902.

Armentieres 1914, Ypres 1915, 1917, Frezenberg, Somme 1916, 1918, Arras 1917, 1918, Cambrai 1917, 1918, Bligny, Epehy, Doiran 1917, 1918, Jerusalem.

Dunkirk 1940, Normandy landing, Antwerp, Venraij, Hochwald, Bremen, North-west Europe 1940, 1944–5, Tunis, Anzio, Italy 1943–5.

Kowang-San, Korea 1951–2.

The Middlesex Regiment: Mysore, Seringapatam, Albuhera, Ciudad Rodrigo, Badajoz, Vittoria, Pyrenees, Nivelle, Nive, Peninsula, Alma, Inkerman, Sevastopol, New Zealand, South Africa 1879, Relief of Ladysmith, South Africa 1900–2.

Mons, Marne 1914, Ypres 1915, 1917, 1918, Albert 1916, 1918, Bazentin, Cambrai 1917, 1918 Hindenburg Line, Suvla, Jerusalem, Mesopotamia 1917–18.

Dunkirk 1940, Normandy landing, Caen, Mont Pincon, Rhine, El Alamein, Akarit, Sicily 1943, Anzio, Hong Kong.

Naktong bridgehead, Korea 1950–1.

The King's Royal Rifle Corps: Louisburg, Quebec 1759, Martinique 1762, Havannah, North America 1763–4, Rolica, Vimiera, Martinique 1809, Talavera, Busaco, Fuentes d'Onor, Albuhera, Ciudad Rodrigo, Badajoz, Salamanca, Vittoria, Pyrenees, Nivelle, Nive, Orthes, Toulouse, Peninsula, Mooltan, Goojerat, Punjaub, South Africa 1851, 1852, 1853, Delhi 1857, Taku forts, Pekin 1860, South Africa 1879, Ahmed Khel, Kandahar 1880, Afghanistan 1879–80, Tel el Kebir, Egypt 1882, Chitral, Defence of Ladysmith, Relief of Ladysmith, South Africa 1899–1902.

Mons, Marne 1914, Ypres 1914, 1915, 1917, 1918, Somme 1916, 1918, Arras 1917, 1918, Messines 1917, 1918, Epehy, Canal du Nord, Selle, Sambre.

Calais 1940, Rhineland, North-west Europe 1940, 1944–5, Egyptian Frontier 1940, Sidi Rezegh 1941, Alam el Halfa, El Alamein, North Africa 1940–3, Italy 1943–5, Greece 1941, 1944–5.

The Wiltshire Regiment: Louisburg, Nive, Peninsula, New Zealand, Ferozeshah, Sobraon, Sevastopol, Pekin 1860, South Africa 1879, 1900–2.

Mons, Messines 1914, 1917, 1918, Ypres 1914, 1917, Somme 1916, 1918, Arras 1917,

Bapaume 1918, Macedonia 1915–18, Gallipoli 1915–16, Palestine 1917–18, Baghdad.

Defence of Arras, Hill 112, Maltot, Mont Pincon, Seine 1944, Cleve, Garigliano crossing, Anzio, Rome, North Arakan.

The Manchester Regiment: Guadaloupe 1759, Egmont op Zee, Peninsula, Martinique 1809, Guadaloupe 1810, New Zealand, Alma, Inkerman, Sevastopol, Afghanistan 1879–80, Egypt 1882, Defence of Ladysmith, South Africa 1899–1902.

Mons, Givenchy 1914, Ypres 1915, 1917, 1918, Somme 1916, 1918, Hindenburg Line, Piave, Macedonia 1915–18, Gallipoli 1915, Megiddo, Baghdad.

Dyle, Defence of Arras, Caen, Scheldt, Lower Maas, Roer, Reichswald, Gothic Line, Malta 1940, Kohima.

The North Staffordshire Regiment: Guadaloupe 1759, Martinique 1794, St Lucia 1803, Surinam, Punjaub, Reshire, Bushire, Koosh-ab, Persia, Lucknow, Hafir, South Africa 1900–2.

Armentieres 1914, Somme 1916, 1918, Arras 1917, Messines 1917, 1918, Ypres 1917, 1918, St Quentin Canal, Selle, Sari Bair, Kut al Amara 1917, North-West Frontier India 1915.

Afghanistan 1919.

Dyle, Ypres–Comines canal, Caen, Brieux bridgehead, Medjez Plain, North Africa 1943, Anzio, Rome, Marradi, Burma 1943.

The York and Lancaster Regiment: Guadaloupe 1759, Martinique 1794, India 1796–1819, Nive, Peninsula, Arabia, New Zealand, Lucknow, Tel el Kebir, Egypt 1882, 1884, Relief of Ladysmith, South Africa 1899–1902.

Ypres 1915, 1917, 1918, Somme 1916, 1918, Messines 1917, 1918, Passchendaele, Cambrai 1917, 1918, Lys, Selle, Piave, Macedonia 1915–18, Gallipoli 1915.

Fontenay le Pesnil, Antwerp–Turnhout canal, Tobruk 1941, Mine de Sedjenane, Sicily 1943, Salerno, Minturno, Crete, North Arakan, Chindits 1944.

The Durham Light Infantry: Salamanca, Vittoria, Pyrenees, Nivelle, Orthes, Peninsula, Alma, Inkerman, Sevastopol, Reshire, Bushire, Koosh-ab, Persia, New Zealand, Relief of Ladysmith, South Africa 1899–1902.

Aisne 1914, 1918, Ypres 1915, 1917, 1918, Hooge 1915, Loos, Somme 1916, 1918, Arras 1917, 1918, Messines 1917, Lys, Hindenburg Line, Sambre.

Afghanistan 1919.

Dunkirk 1940, Tilly sur Seulles, Defence of Rauray, Gheel, Tobruk 1941, El Alamein, Mareth, Primosole Bridge, Salerno, Kohima.

Korea 1952–3.

The Highland Light Infantry: Gibraltar 1779–83, Carnatic, Hindoostan, Sholingur Mysore, Seringapatam, Cape of Good Hope 1806, Rolica, Vimiera, Corunna, Busaco, Fuentes d'Onor, Ciudad Rodrigo, Badajoz, Almaraz, Salamanca, Vittoria, Pyrenees, Nivelle, Nive, Orthes, Toulouse, Peninsula, Waterloo, South Africa 1851, 1852, 1853, Sevastopol, Central India, Tel el Kebir, Egypt 1882, Modder River, South Africa 1899–1902.

Mons, Ypres 1914, 1915, 1917, 1918, Loos, Somme 1916, 1918, Arras 1917, 1918, Hindenburg Line, Gallipoli 1915–18, Palestine 1917–18, Mesopotamia 1916–18.

Archangel 1919.

Odon, Scheldt, Walcheren causeway, Reichswald, Rhine, North-west Europe 1940, 1944–5, Keren, Cauldron, Landing in Sicily, Greece 1944–5.

The Seaforth Highlanders: Carnatic, Hindoostan, Mysore, Cape of Good Hope 1806, Maida, Java, South Africa 1835, Sevastopol, Koosh-ab, Persia, Lucknow, Central India, Peiwar Kotal, Charasiah, Kabul 1879,

Kandahar 1880, Afghanistan 1878–80, Tel el kebir, Egypt 1882, Chitral, Atbara, Khartoum, Paardeberg, South Africa 1899–1902.

Marne 1914, 1918, Ypres 1915, 1917, 1918, Loos, Somme 1916, 1918, Arras 1917, 1918, Vimy 1917, Cambrai 1917, 1918, Valenciennes, Palestine 1918, Baghdad.

St Valery en Caux, Caen, Rhineland, El Alamein, Akarit, Sicily 1943, Anzio, Madagascar, Imphal, Burma 1942–4.

The Gordon Highlanders: Mysore, Seringapatam, India, Egmont op Zee, Mandora, Corunna, Fuentes d'Onor, Almaraz, Vittoria, Pyrenees, Nive, Orthes, Peninsula, Waterloo, South Africa 1835, Delhi, Lucknow, Charasiah, Kabul 1879, Kandahar 1880, Afghanistan 1879–80, Tel el Kebir, Egypt 1882, 1884, Nile 1884–5, Chitral, Tirah, Defence of Ladysmith, Paardeberg, South Africa 1899–1902.

Mons, Le Cateau, Marne 1914, 1918, Ypres 1914, 1915, 1917, Loos, Somme 1916, 1918, Ancre 1916, Arras 1917, 1918, Cambrai 1917, 1918, Vittorio Veneto.

Odon, Reichswald, Goch, Rhine, North-west Europe 1940, 1944–5, El Alamein, Mareth, Sferro, Anzio.

The Queen's Own Cameron Highlanders: Egmont op Zee, Corunna, Busaco, Fuentes d'Onor, Salamanca, Pyrenees, Nivelle, Nive, Toulouse, Peninsula, Waterloo, Alma, Sevastopol, Lucknow, Tel el Kebir, Egypt 1882, Nile 1884–5, Atbara, Khartoum, South Africa 1900–2.

Marne 1914, 1918, Aisne 1914, Ypres 1914, 1915, 1917, 1918, Neuve Chapelle, Loos, Somme 1916, 1918, Delville Wood, Arras 1917, 1918, Sambre, Macedonia 1915–18.

St Omer-La Bassee, Reichswald, Rhine, Keren, Sidi Barrani, El Alamein, Akarit, Gothic Line, Kohima, Mandalay.

The Royal Ulster Rifles: India, Cape of Good Hope 1806, Bourbon, Talavera,

Busaco, Fuentes d'Onor, Ciudad Rodrigo, Badajoz, Salamanca, Vittoria, Nivelle, Orthes, Toulouse, Peninsula, Central India, South Africa 1899–1902.

Mons, Marne 1914, Ypres 1914, 1915, 1917, 1918, Neuve Chapelle, Somme 1916, 1918, Albert 1916, Courtrai, Struma, Suvla, Jerusalem.

Dyle, Dunkirk 1940, Normandy landing, Cambes, Caen, Troarn, Venlo Pocket, Rhine, Bremen, North-west Europe 1940, 1944–5.

Imjin, Korea 1950–1.

The Royal Irish Fusiliers: Monte Video, Talavera, Barrosa, Tarifa, Java, Vittoria, Nivelle, Niagara, Orthes, Toulouse, Peninsula, Ava, Sevastopol, Tel el Kebir, Egypt 1882, 1884, Relief of Ladysmith, South Africa 1899–1902.

Le Cateau, Marne 1914, Ypres 1915, 1917, 1918, Somme 1916, 1918, Arras 1917, Messines 1917, 1918, Lys, Macedonia 1915–17, Suvla, Palestine 1917–18.

St Omer-La Bassee, Bou Arada, Oued Zarga, Djebel Tanngoucha, Centuripe, Termoli, Sangro, Cassino II, Argenta Gap, Malta 1940.

The Connaught Rangers: Seringapatam, Talavera, Busaco, Fuentes d'Onor, Ciudad Rodrigo, Badajoz, Salamanca, Vittoria, Pyrenees, Nivelle, Orthes, Toulouse, Peninsula, Alma, Inkerman, Sevastopol, Central India, South Africa 1877, 1878, 1879, Relief of Ladysmith, South Africa 1899–1902.

Mons, Aisne 1914, Messines 1914, 1917, Ypres 1914, 1915, 1917, Guillemont, Cambrai 1918, Kosturino, Scimitar Hill, Megiddo, Kut al Amara 1917.

The Argyll and Sutherland Highlanders: Cape of Good Hope 1806, Rolica, Vimiera, Corunna, Pyrenees, Nivelle, Nive, Orthes, Toulouse, Peninsula, South Africa 1846–7, 1851, 1852, 1853, Alma, Balaklava,

Sevastopol, Lucknow, South Africa 1879, Modder river, Paardeberg, South Africa 1899–1902.

Mons, Le Cateau, Marne 1914, 1918, Ypres 1915, 1917, 1918, Loos, Somme 1916, 1918, Arras 1917, 1918, Cambrai 1917, 1918, Doiran 1917, 1918, Gaza.

Odon, Rhine, Sidi Barrani, El Alamein, Akarit, Longstop Hill 1943, Italy 1943–5, Crete, Grik Road, Malaya 1941–2.

Pakchon, Korea 1950–1.

The Leinster Regiment: Niagara, Central India, South Africa 1900.

Aisne 1914, Ypres 1915, 1917, 1918, Somme 1916, 1918, Guillemont, Vimy 1917, Messines 1917, St Quentin, Macedonia 1915–17, Gallipoli 1915, Jerusalem.

The Royal Munster Fusiliers: Plassey, Condore, Masulipatam, Badara, Buxar, Carnatic, Rohilcund 1774, 1794, Sholingur, Guzerat, Deig, Bhurtpore, Ghuznee 1839, Afghanistan 1839, Ferozeshah, Sobraon, Punjaub, Chillianwallah, Goojerat, Pegu, Delhi 1857, Lucknow, Burma 1885–87, South Africa 1899–1902.

Retreat from Mons, Ypres 1914, 1917, Aubers, Guillemont, St Quentin, Drocourt-Queant, Selle, Landing at Helles, Landing at Suvla, Jerusalem.

The Royal Dublin Fusiliers: Arcot, Plassey, Condore, Carnatic, Wandewash, Buxar, Amboor, Sholingur, Guzerat, Nundy Droog, Mysore, Seringapatam, Amboyna, Ternate, Banda, Maheidpore, Kirkee, Beni Boo Alli, Ava, Aden, Punjaub, Mooltan, Goojerat, Pegu, Lucknow, Relief of Ladysmith, South Africa 1899–1902.

Retreat from Mons, Marne 1914, Ypres 1915, 1917, 1918, Somme 1916, 1918, Cambrai 1917, 1918, Hindenburg Line, Selle, Macedonia 1915–17, Gallipoli 1915–16, Palestine 1917–18.

The Rifle Brigade: Copenhagen, Monte Video, Rolica, Vimiera, Corunna, Busaco, Barrosa, Fuentes d'Onor, Ciudad Rodrigo, Badajoz, Salamanca, Vittoria, Pyrenees, Nivelle, Orthes, Toulouse, Peninsula, Waterloo, South Africa 1846–7, 1852–3, Alma, Inkerman, Sevastopol, Lucknow, Ashantee, Ali Masjid, Afghanistan 1878–9, Burma 1885–87, Khartoum, Defence of Ladysmith, Relief of Ladysmith, South Africa 1899–1902.

Le Cateau, Marne 1914, Neuve Chapelle, Ypres 1915, 1917, Somme 1916, 1918, Arras 1917, 1918, Messines 1917, Cambrai 1917, 1918, Hindenburg Line, Macedonia 1915–18. Calais 1940, North-west Europe 1940, 1944–5, Beda Fomm, Sidi Rezegh 1941, Alam el Halfa, El Alamein. North Africa 1940–3, Cassino II, Capture of Perugia, Italy 1943–5.

The Parachute Regiment: Bruneval, Normandy landing, Breville, Arnhem 1944, Rhine, Southern France, Oudna, Tamera, Primosole Bridge, Athens.

2nd King Edward VII's Own Gurkha Rifles: Bhurtpore, Aliwal, Sobraon, Delhi 1857, Kabul 1879, Kandahar, Afghanistan 1878–80, Punjab frontier, Tirah.

La Bassee 1914, Festubert 1914, 1915, Givenchy 1914, Neuve Chapelle, Aubers, Loos, Tigris 1916, Kut al Amara 1917, Baghdad 1915, Persia 1918.

Afghanistan 1919.

El Alamein, Akarit, Tunis, Cassino I, Gothic Line, Jitra, Slim river, North Arakan, Irrawaddy, Tamandu.

6th Queen Elizabeth's Own Gurkha Rifles: Helles, Krithia, Suvla, Sari Bair, Gallipoli 1915, Suez Canal, Khan Baghdadi, Mesopotamia 1916–18, Persia 1918, North-West Frontier India 1915.

Afghanistan 1919.

Monte Chicco, Medecina, Italy 1944–5, Kyaukmyaung bridgehead, Mandalay, Fort Dufferin, Rangoon Road, Sittang 1945, Chindits 1944, Burma 1944–5.

7th Duke of Edinburgh's Own Gurkha Rifles: Egypt 1915, Meggido, Sharon, Palestine 1918, Kut al Amara 1915, 1917, Ctesiphon, Defence of Kut al Amara, Baghdad, Sharqat. Afghanistan 1919.

Cassino I, Poggio del Grillo, Tavoleto, Sittang 1942, 1945, Kyaukse 1942, Imphal, Bishenpur, Meiktila, Rangoon Road.

10th Princess Mary's Own Gurkha Rifles: Helles, Krithia, Suvla, Sari Bair, Gallipoli 1915, Suez Canal, Egypt 1915, Sharqat, Mesopotamia 1916–18.

Afghanistan 1919.

Coriano, Santarcangelo, Bologna, Imphal, Tuitam, Mandalay, Myinmu bridgehead, Meiktila, Rangoon Road.

The Special Air Service Regiment: North-west Europe 1944–5, Tobruk 1941, Benghazi Raid, North Africa 1940–3, Landing in Sicily, Termoli, Valli di Comacchio, Italy 1943–5, Adriatic.

THE ROYAL REGIMENT OF ARTILLERY HONOUR TITLES

The Royal Artillery (RA) used to be accredited with battle honours like other regiments, but in 1833 the motto *Ubique* was confirmed to the RA and the Royal Engineers (RE) in recognition of their ubiquitous services in all theatres of war and as an alternative to unnecessary awards of individual battle honours. In 1925 the War Office directed that distinctions originally attached to certain batteries should be acknowledged and honour titles were duly registered for batteries of the RA:

36 (Arcot) Bty, RA, for India, 1751.

9 (Plassey) Bty, RA, for India, 1757.

53 (Louisburg) Bty, RA, for Canada, 1758.

12 and 32 (Minden) Batteries, RA, for Germany, 1759.

18 (Quebec 1759) Bty, RA, for Wolfe's campaign to win Canada.

5, 19, 21, 22 and 23 (Gibraltar 1779–83) batteries, RA, for the Great Siege.

34 and 38 (Seringapatam) Batteries, RA, for India, 1799.

24 (Irish) Bty, RA, for service in the Americas and Flanders before the Royal Irish Artillery batteries were transferred to the Royal Artillery in 1801, after which the unit added to its war record.

F (Sphinx) Bty, Royal Horse Artillery (RHA), and 4, 7, 11 and 93 (Sphinx) batteries, RA, for Egypt, 1801.

10 (Assaye) Bty, RA, for India, 1803.

13 (Martinique 1809) and 74 (The Battleaxe Company), RA, for the West Indies, 1809.

52 (Niagara) Bty, RA, for Canada, 1813.

A Bty (The Chestnut Troop), RHA, for the Peninsular War.

I Bty (Bull's Troop), RHA, for the Peninsular War.

17 and 29 (Corunna) Batteries, RA, for Spain, 1808–9.

46 (Talavera) Bty, RA, for Spain, 1809.

97 Bty (Lawson's Company), RA, for Spain, 1808–13.

G (Mercer's Troop) and H Bty (Ramsay's Troop), RHA, and 16 (Sandham's Company), 30 Rogers's Company) and 43 (Lloyd's Company), RA, for Waterloo 1815.

O Bty (The Rocket Troop), RHA, for Leipzig, 1813, and Waterloo, 1815.

137 (Java) Bty, RA, for the Far East, 1811.

132 Bty (The Bengal Rocket Troop), RA, for Asia, 1816–61.

79 (Kirkee) Bty, RA, for India, 1817.

88 (Arracan) Bty, RA, for Burma, 1825.

57 (Bhurtpore) Bty, RA, for the Jat War, 1826.

T Bty (Shah Sujah's Troop), RHA, for Afghanistan, 1839.

51 (Kabul 1842) Bty, RA, for Arghanistan.

54 (Maharajpore) Bty, RA, for India, 1843.

N Bty (The Eagle Troop), RHA, for India, 1843.

8 (Alma) Bty, RA, for the Crimea, 1854.

49, 152 and 156 (Inkerman) batteries, RA, for the Crimea, 1854.

143 Bty (Tombs's Troop) for Delhi, 1857.

55 (The Residency) Bty, RA, for Lucknow, 1857.

76 (Maude's) Bty, RA, for the Indian Mutiny, 1857.

56 (Olphert's) Bty, RA, for Lucknow, 1857.

58 (Eyre's) Bty, RA, for the Indian Mutiny, 1857.

160 Bty (Middleton's Company), RA, for Lucknow and Cawnpore, 1857.

27 (Strange's) Bty, RA, for the Indian Mutiny, 1857.

P (Dragon) Bty, RHA, and 111, 127 and 129 (Dragon) batteries, RA, for China 1840–1.

94 (New Zealand) Bty, RA, for the Maori Wars, 1861–3.

145 (Maiwand) Bty, RA, for Afghanistan, 1880.

171 (The Broken Wheel) Bty, RA, for Egypt, 1882.

159 (Colenso) Bty, RA, for South Africa, 1899.

Q (Sanna's Post) Bty, RHA, for South Africa, 1900.

14 (Cole's Kop) Bty, RA, for South Africa, 1900.

92 (Le Cateau) Bty, RA, for France, 1914.

L (Nery) Bty, RHA, for France, 1914.

K (Hondegham) Bty, RHA, for Belgium 1940.

J (Sidi Rezegh) Bty, RHA, for Libya 1941.

42 (Alem Hamza) Bty, RA, for Libya 1941.

59 (Asten) Bty, RA, for Belgium 1944.

148 (Meiktila) Bty, RA, for Burma 1945.

170 (Imjin) Bty, RA, for Korea 1951.

GLOSSARY

armoured equipped with armoured cars or tanks; cavalry regiments that converted permanently from horse to armour between 1928 and 1942.

bag coloured cloth sewn to the top of a fur busby and falls to one side of it, originally on the top of a hussar's shako.

balmoral (or tam o' shanter) flat-topped bonnet, with a central tourie or pom-pom, worn by Scottish regiments in service dress from 1915.

battalion operational unit of an infantry regiment, composed of several companies, under the command of a lieutenant-colonel.

battery a permanent unit of an artillery regiment, from the collective noun for guns (usually six per battery). Approximately 100 gunners under the command of a major.

battle honour a public commemoration of a victory awarded to a regiment or battery by an army committee for display on its standard, colour, guidon, drums or badge.

bearskin a cap covered with the fur of bear, traditionally the Canadian Black bear. Worn by foot guards in full dress, fusilier officers prior to the First World War and grenadiers between 1768 and 1837.

bonnet a thick woollen cap worn in Scottish regiments from the eighteenth century.

braid tape used to strengthen hats and buttonholes in the eighteenth century.

breeches short trousers fastened just below the knee.

busby a fur or sealskin cap made to fusilier, hussars or rifles specification. Named after its original maker, W. Busby of the Strand.

cap headgear without a brim.

captain commissioned officer in charge of a company or troop.

cartouche cartridge (ball and powder) ammunition for firearms.

caubeen a voluminous beret-like bonnet traditional to Ireland, adopted by Irish regiments from the 1920s.

cavalry troops on horseback, from the Italian *cavalleria* which derived from the Latin *caballus* (horse).

chaco name given to the shako after 1844.

Chindits Gen Wingate's long-range penetration infantry, formed for the jungle campaign in Malaya, 1942.

coatee short jacket of the first half of the nineteenth century, with or without tails.

colonel field officer in overall command of a regiment.

colours revered silk 'flags' carried in infantry battalions, originally raised up in battle to show scattered soldiers where to regroup.

colour belt the broad 'sash' worn by subalterns with a small 'bucket' at its base for the pikestaff of a colour to be carried in.

commissariat supplier of stores and provisions for an army.

corps a body of soldiers of indeterminate strength; a support organisation (logistic, medical, admin, etc.) of varying strengths, the largest boasting several regiments.

coveralls common overalls or boiler suits worn when working on greasy vehicles.

cuirass body armour worn by cavalrymen in the seventeenth century and Household Cavalry troops in full dress from 1820 to the present day.

cypher interlaced initials, usually of a monarch, originally written as part of a secret code.

dicing a pattern of coloured squares normally worn as a band on Scottish caps.

doublet jacket with flaps or skirts, usually found in Scottish uniforms.

dragoons heavy cavalry named after a short musket of the sixteenth century called a *dragon* from the flame and smoke it belched out when fired. Early dragoons were infantry mounted on poor-quality horses for quick transportation to the enemy, where they would dismount to fire. Towards the end of the seventeenth century dragoons would be grouped with the cavalry in battle and thereafter quickly evolved as cavalry proper.

dragoon guards a title invented in 1746 to preserve the status of the regiments of horse that were relegated to dragoons for reasons of economy.

East India Company see Honourable East India Company.

ensign lowest commissioned infantry officer rank given the honour of carrying one of the battalion colours, which were originally called ensigns.

facings the coloured lining of a uniform coat revealed when the collar, cuffs, lapels and skirts were turned back in the eighteenth century. The word was applied to cuffs and collar of jackets from 1800.

fencibles regular regiments that were embodied for the course of a war.

field officer senior rank of commissioned officer.

flank company grenadier and light companies that used to take post on the flanks of a battalion in the eighteenth and nineteenth centuries.

foot an old term for infantry, which served on foot as opposed to horseback.

forage cap a cap worn in lieu of full-dress headgear, originally when foraging.

fusiliers originally (seventeenth-century) soldiers armed with a fuzil (matchless musket) and distinguished by grenadier caps.

glengarry a foldable woollen cap with ribbons hanging from the back.

gorget originally a piece of armour worn across the neck to protect against cuts to that area. Gorget patches on the collar are relics of attachments for the ribbons used to secure the gorget.

guidon regimental swallow-tailed 'flag' carried in dragoon regiments, from the French *Guyd Homme* – a flag flown from the lance of an inferior knight to show the way. Light cavalry regiments, which derive from dragoons, also carried a guidon but were ordered to lay them aside in 1834 so that they did not hamper their progress in the field. This rule was rescinded in 1956 and new guidons were presented to the hussar and lancer regiments.

hackle a stem of cut feathers worn as a short plume on fusilier berets, Highlanders' bonnets and Irish *caubeens*.

helmet heavy, protective, formal headgear with a top spike, worn in full dress by infantry and heavy cavalry regiments.

Highland a term applied to regiments and their dress native to the northern, mountainous part of Scotland.

Honourable East India Company a trading concern formed in 1600 that employed regiments of horse, foot and artillery to protect its interests in India. After the mutiny of 1857 the Honourable East India Company was run down and its troops transferred to the British Army.

horse a term used in the seventeenth and eighteenth century for cavalry.

Horse Guards British Army Headquarters in Whitehall that took its name from the mounted Guards which once occupied the buildings and traditionally stand guard there as the site of a former royal palace.

hose socks (or stockings) worn by pipers of several regiments and all soldiers of Highland regiments in parade uniforms.

hussars light cavalry, originally from Hungary, named after a form of dress introduced into the British Army during the Napoleonic Wars, when certain regiments of light dragoons were remodelled on the Hungarian cavalry.

infantry soldiers that serve on foot.

Jacobites supporters of James II and the Stuart cause after the 'Glorious Revolution' of 1688.

kilmarnock bonnet or cap worn by Scottish and Gurkha soldiers, named after their town of manufacture.

kilt pleated skirt of regimental tartan worn by pipers and soldiers of Highland regiments in parade dress.

lace braid, sometimes coloured or patterned to a regimental design.

lance cap a leather cap with a square 'mortar board' top worn by lancer regiments in full dress from 1816, when this Polish style of dress came into the army.

lancers medium cavalry armed with a lance. The first examples appeared in the army in 1816 with the conversion of three regiments of light dragoons.

lieutenant low-commissioned officer ranks, collectively known as subalterns.

light dragoons lightly equipped dragoons that were to be seen between 1756 and 1861.

Lowland regiments, people and a style native to the central lowlands and southern uplands of Scotland.

loyal toast the ritual in which officers drink to the health of the sovereign, originally to test their fealty to the crown.

major junior field officer, company commander in the infantry.

marching regiment a regiment of foot, infantry.

marines soldiers that serve on ship as well as land.

mechanise to equip with armoured cars or tanks.

militia civilians that were recruited locally to attend drill meetings and be ready to defend their territory in times of war.

overalls in the military sense, tight trousers worn by officers, regiments and corps that were originally mounted.

pagri see pugri.

Peninsula Spain and Portugal, and the war waged there between 1808 and 1814 with Napoleon's marshals.

pioneer a soldier employed to clear terrain obstacles for his regiment on the march.

plaid a tartan cloth worn on the shoulder in some forms of Scottish full dress.

plastron the broad lapels of a lancer's tunic buttoned back to reveal the facings.

private an ordinary soldier, the army's basic rank.

pugri (or puggaree) the cloth that is wound around a tropical helmet.

quaich a drinking cup with two handles, from the Gaelic *cuach*.

regiment a permanent army unit under the command of a colonel with its own badge, customs and distinctions.

rifle volunteers enthusiasts that willingly joined the 'rifle clubs' formed in 1859–60, forerunners of the Territorial Force of 1908 and the Territorial Army of 1921.

Royal Armoured Corps a training corps, formed

in 1939, for all armoured regiments apart from the Household Cavalry.

shako a peaked cylindrical cap worn in period styles between 1800 and 1878.

shell jacket a short garment without skirts or tails.

shoulder chains chain mail fastened to the top of the shoulders on cavalry tunics, a relic of the Victorian age, when it was worn to protect against sword cuts.

squadron a unit of a cavalry regiment, and some support corps, under the command of a major.

standard a silk 'flag' carried by heavy cavalry regiments and the Guards.

subaltern junior commissioned officers of the lieutenant ranks.

sutler women camp followers of the seventeenth and eighteenth centuries that supplied liquor and other comforts to soldiers in camp and on the march.

TA Territorial Army (1921) – battalions and regiments of part-time soldiers that serve in support of the Regular Army. Formed in 1908 as the Territorial Force.

tam o' shanter the flat-topped balmoral bonnet introduced in 1915 for Scottish soldiers to replace their impractical glengarries in trench warfare.

toast a drink to the health of a significant person.

trews a name given to tartan trousers worn in Scottish regiments.

troop a unit of a cavalry regiment commanded by a captain.

volunteers civilians that give of their spare time to serve in a regiment or corps on a part-time basis.

Wolfe Society an organisation formed at Westerham, Kent, in 1926 for regiments that were associated with Gen James Wolfe, who rose to command the army in Canada in 1759. The said regiments send a representative to the annual dinner in his honour.

yeomanry volunteer cavalry originally formed in 1794 from yeoman farmers and gentlemen horse-owners to counter the threat of French invasion to Britain. Troops were regimented and kept on through the nineteenth century as an aid to civil authorities. They were first sent to war in 1900.

BIBLIOGRAPHY

Anderson, Douglas N., *Scots in Uniform* (Holmes McDougall, 1972) and other works

Ascoli, David, *A Companion to the British Army 1660–1983* (Harrap, 1983)

Baker, Anthony, *Battle Honours of the British and Commonwealth Armies* (Ian Allen, 1986)

Barlow, L. and Smith, R.J. *Uniforms of the British Yeomanry Force 1794–1914* (Army Museums Ogilby Trust, 1980s)

Barnes, Maj R. Money, *A History of the Regiments and Uniforms of the British Army* (Seeley Service, 1950)

Barthorp, Michael, *Crimean Uniforms* (Historical Research Unit, 1974)

——, *British Infantry Uniforms* (Blandford Press, 1982)

Bowling, A.H., *British Hussar Regiments* (Almark Publishing, 1972)

——, *The Foot Guards Regiments* (Almark Publishing, 1972)

Brereton, J.M., *A Guide to the Regiments and Corps of the British Army* (Bodley Head, 1985)

Carman, W.Y., *British Military Uniforms from Contemporary Sources* (Hamlyn, 1968)

Chichester, H.M. and Burges-Short, G., *Records and Badges of the British Army, 1900* (Lionel Levanthal, 1986)

Dickinson, Lt-Col R.J., *Officers' Mess* (Midas Books, 1973)

Farwell, Byron, *Queen Victoria's Little Wars* (Allen Lane, 1973)

Fortesque, Hon. J.W., *History of the British Army* (McMillan & Co., 1910)

Hilton, Frank, *The Paras* (Book Club Associates, 1983)

Lawford, J.P. and Young, P. *Wellington's Masterpiece* (Allen & Unwin, 1973)

Lawson, C.C.P., *A History of the Uniforms of the British Army* (Kaye & Ward, 1969)

Macrory, Patrick, *Signal Catastrophe* (Hodder & Stoughton, 1966)

Mays, Spike, *The Band Rats* (Peter Davies, 1975)

Mileham, P.J.R., *The Yeomanry Regiments* (Spellmount, 1985)

Norman, C.B., *Battle Honours of the British Army* (David & Charles, 1911)

Pollock, Sam, *Mutiny for the Cause* (Leo Cooper, 1969)

Prebble, John, *Culloden* (Secker & Warburg, 1961)

——, *Mutiny* (Penguin, 1977)

Rogers, H.C.B., *The Mounted Troops of the British Army* (Seeley Service, 1959)

Steppler, Glenn A., *Britons, To Arms!* (Alan Sutton, 1992)

Sutherland, John, *Men of Waterloo* (Frederick Muller, 1966)

Swinson, Arthur, *A Register of the Regiments and Corps of the British Army* (Archive, 1972)

Turner, Gordon and Alwyn, *The History of British Army Bands* (Spellmount, 1996)

Walton, Lt-Col P.S., *Simkin's Soldiers* (Victorian Military Society, 1981)

Warner, Oliver, *With Wolfe to Quebec* (Collins, 1972)

Weller, Jac, *Wellington in the Peninsula* (Kaye & Ward, 1962)

Westlake, Ray, *The Volunteer Infantry 1880–1908* (Military Historical Society, 1992)

Wood, Stephen, *The Scottish Soldier* (Archive, 1987)

Regimental Histories

Daniell, David Scott, *Cap of Honour* (Harrap, 1953)

Fairrie, Lt-Col Angus, *A History of the Queen's Own Highlanders* (Regiment, 1983)

Hughes, Maj-Gen B.P., *Honour Titles of the Royal Artillery* (Dorset Press, 1976)

Linklater, Eric and Andro, *The Black Watch* (Barrie & Jenkins, 1977)

Manser, Roy, *The Household Cavalry Regiment* (Almark, 1975)

Oatts, Lt-Col L.B., *The Emperor's Chambermaids* (Ward Lock, 1973)

——, *I Serve* (Jarrold & Sons, 1966)

Various authors, *Famous Regiments* (20 vols, Hamish Hamilton, 1968)

Official Publications

Dress Regulations 1846 and *1900*
The Army List (HMSO, 1985, 2002, 2004)
Numerous regimental museum guides and journals 1970–2006

Periodicals

Crown Imperial (Society for the History, Traditions and Regalia of the Forces of the Crown 1984–5)

Regiment (Nexus/Grenadier Publishing 1994–2005)

Soldier (Magazine of the British Army 1945–2006)

Tradition (Journal of the International Society of Military Collectors 1965–74)

INDEX